Stuart, John F. Smyth

A Tour in the United States of America, Volume 2

ISBN: 978-1-948837-12-5

This classic reprint was produced from digital files in the Google Books digital collection, which may be found at http://www.books.google.com. The artwork used on the cover is from Wikimedia Commons and remains in the public domain. Omissions and/or errors in this book are due to either the physical condition of the original book or due to the scanning process by Google or its agents.

This edition of John Stuart's **A Tour in the United States of America, Volume 2** was originally published in 1784 (London).

Townsends
PO Box 415, Pierceton, IN 46562
www.Townsends.us

A
TOUR
IN THE
UNITED STATES
OF
AMERICA:

CONTAINING

An Account of the PRESENT SITUATION of that Country;

The POPULATION, AGRICULTURE, COMMERCE, CUSTOMS, and MANNERS of the Inhabitants;

ANECDOTES of several MEMBERS of the CONGRESS, and GENERAL OFFICERS in the American Army;

AND

Many other very singular and interesting Occurrences.

WITH

A Description of the INDIAN NATIONS, the general Face of the Country, Mountains, Forests, Rivers, and the most beautiful, grand, and picturesque Views throughout that vast Continent.

LIKEWISE

Improvements in HUSBANDRY that may be adopted with great Advantage in EUROPE.

By J. F. D. SMYTH, Esq.

VOL. II.

LONDON,

Printed for G. ROBINSON, Pater-noster-Row; J. ROBSON, New Bond-Street; and J. SEWELL, Cornhill.

MDCCLXXXIV.

A TOUR

IN THE

UNITED STATES

OF

AMERICA.

VOL. II.

———In struggling with misfortunes
Lies the true proof of virtue. SHAKSPEARE.

———Cold, hunger, prisons, ills without a cure,
All these men must, and guiltless, oft endure.

———Permitted laurels grace the lawless brow,
Th'unworthy rais'd, the worthy cast below.

Faith flies, and Piety in exile mourns,
And Justice, here oppress'd, to Heav'n returns. DRYDEN.

CONTENTS.

CHAP. XLIX.
Remarkable Places, Rivers, Bays, &c. Great Extent of the Rivers. Harbours. Beautiful Conntry and Coast. Choctaw Nation, or Flat-headed Indians. Their Disposition. The Manner they flatten their Heads. Number of Inhabitants in West Florida. Prodigious Fertility of the Soil. Distances of Places. Page 1

CHAP. L.
East Florida. Rivers. Apalache. St. John's-River. St. Augustine. Journey by Land. Description of the Rivers, Country, and Distances. Musquitto River. Indian Towns. - - - - 11

CHAP. LI.
Attempts to make Sugar on Musquitto-River failed. Culture of Sugar. Stone Quarry near St. Augustine. Singular Floors to the Houses. East Florida thinly settled. Loyalists take Refuge in it. Prices of Commodities and Stock. Rates of travelling. - 23

CHAP. LII.
Recover from Sickness. Leave East Florida. The Rivers Alatamaha, Great Ogetchee, and Savannah. The Town of Savannah. Indian War. Georgians made a poor Figure. Flourishing State of Georgia. Number of Inhabitants. Value of Land. Staple Commodities and Produce. Rates of travelling. Value of annual Exports and Imports. - - 40

CHAP. LIII.
Set out for Charles-Town. Afterwards proceed to Augusta, Ninety-Six, &c. Culture of Indigo. Culture

Vol. II.   a   *of*

CONTENTS.

of Rice. Culture of Cotton. Description of the Country. Of the Sea-Coast. Of the Back Country. Fertility of the Soil. Excellence of the Climate, &c. Page 51

CHAP. LIV.
Method of clearing the Land. Vast Herds of Cattle. Charles-Town. Port-Royal. George-Town. Wilmington in North-Carolina. Brunswick. Fort Johnson. American General Howe. Newbern. Bath-Town. Pamphlico Sound. Edinton. Albemarle Sound. — 77

CHAP. LV.
Description of the Country. Disagreeable and unhealthy. Vast Profit in making Tar and Turpentine. Process for making Pitch, Tar, and Turpentine. Exports of North-Carolina. South-Carolina and Virginia share great Part of the Trade of North-Carolina. The great Alligator. Dismal Swamp. The Great Dismal. Harbour for wild Beasts and runaway Negroes. 94

CHAP. LVI.
Leave Edinton. Arrive at Suffolk in Virginia. Description of Suffolk. Smithfield. Pagan's Creek. Cross James-River at Hog-Island. Arrive at Williamsburg. Part with Mr. Morris. College of William and Mary at Williamsburg. Foundation of it. Education of Indians. Return to their former savage and uncivilized State. — 103

CHAP. LVII.
Improvements in Farming. In the Culture of Wheat. In cutting it down. In getting it in and stacking it. In threshing it out of the Straw. In cleaning it from the Chaff. A Machine for that Purpose described. 110

CHAP. LVIII.
Improvements in cropping. Three Crops from one Field with only the Labour used in one. Virginia Method

CONTENTS.

of cultivating Tobacco. Inspecting it. Disused at the Commencement of the Revolt. Great Frauds and Impositions now practised in the Tobacco Trade. Different Species of Tobacco. Annual Exports of Virginia and Maryland. Annual Imports.   Page 123

CHAP. LIX.

Set out on another Journey. The Potomack, a Description of it. A most beautiful River. General Washington. An Account of him and Mrs. Washington. Chotank. Falmouth. Fredericksburg. An Innkeeper, named Weeden, an American General. Dr. Mercer, an American General. The Rappahannock. The Northern Creek of Virginia. Stanton. Green Briar River. Colonel Lewis. Indian War. The Great Kanhawah and Ohio. Severe Action. Indians defeated. A Stratagem in Bush-Fighting. The Earl of Dunmore penetrates into the Heart of the Indian Country, burns their Towns, and concludes a Peace. - 141

CHAP. LX.

Return to Colonel Lewis's. Fredericksburg. Dumfries. Colchester. Iron Works. Ocquaquan-River. General Washington. Piscattawa River. Port Tobacco. A most elegant Situation and Seat belonging to a Roman Catholic Priest. Establishments of the Jesuits in Maryland. Their Harams of beautiful Slaves. A profligate Priest. Estimation of landed Property. St. Mary's. Annapolis. Baltimore. Its flourishing Condition. Number of Inhabitants in Maryland. - 174

CHAP. LXI.

The Rebellion breaking out. Harassments on account of Loyalty. Political Opinions, Sentiments, and Impartiality of the Author. The Manner of forming the first Congress's Committees, &c. and the Persons who composed them. Against the private Inclinations of a great   *Majority*

CONTENTS.

Majority of the People. Politic Stroke or Measure. Severe Persecutions and extreme Hardships. Alexandria. - - Page 188

CHAP. LXII.

Alexandria. The Place where General Washington first began to countenance the general Revolt of the Colonies. A Loyalist tarred and feathered. Patuxent River. Benedict Town. Lower Marlborough. Upper Marlborough. Queen Anne. London Tavern. Annapolis. Severn River. A Hurricane. Baltimore. Patapsco-River. Elk Ridge. Examined by the Committee. My Servant tarred, feathered, and killed. Obliged to fly for Safety. Travel an hundred and ten Miles on Foot in two Days. Nottingham. Exhausted and overcome with Fatigue. In extreme Pain. Taken very ill. Dangerous Situations. Betrayed by a false Friend. Taken by the Rebels. Rescued. Most perilous Escape. - - - 204

CHAP. LXIII.

Set out for the Mississippi. In a miserable State of Health. Port-Royal. Character of the Inhabitants. Anecdote of an unfortunate young Gentleman. Arrive at Blandford. Royal Standard erected at Norfolk. Repair to it. Seized upon at Surry Court-House. Escape. Sleepy Hole on Nansemond-River. Arrive at Portsmouth. Wait on the Earl of Dunmore. Informed against as a Spy. Leave Portsmouth. Suffolk. Overtake my People, &c. at Maherren. Taken Prisoner. Escape. Set out again for Norfolk. Country alarmed. Take Refuge in the Great Dismal Swamp. A Description of it. Dreadful Conflagration. Astonishing Difficulties. Arrive again at Portsmouth. Suspected again for a Spy. Servant carried on Board the Governor's Ship by a Guard. Servant examined and acquitted. 224

CHAP.

CONTENTS.

CHAP. LXIV.

Embark on an Expedition to the Back Country. Proceed up the Potomack. Pass through Maryland. Frederick Town, a Description of it. Funk's Town. Taken Prisoner. Hagar's Town. Great Valley. Conningocheague. Extremely abused and maltreated. Robbed of our Money. Nature of the Expedition. A curious Manner of secreting Papers. Confined and in great Danger at Frederick Town. Escape. Fall through the Ice into the Potomack. Astonishing Dangers and Fatigue. Fly into the Mountains. Deep Snow. Break the Ice and wade deep Rivers. Wounded and lame. Robbed by a Man that I had placed Confidence in. Continue to push forward for Detroit and Illinois. Fort Cumberland. Romantic Situation. Cross the Allegany Mountains. Retaken by mere Accident on the Yohiogeny River. - - Page 243

CHAP. LXV.

Cause of Life being preserved. Instances of singular Maltreatment and Barbarity. Bound with Cords. Examined before the Committee at Frederick Town. A curious Description of the Committee and their Examination. Great Danger of being murdered. Confined in York Town Gaol, where a most worthy Loyalist Dr. Kersley was then a Prisoner. His Sufferings, and tragical Fate. Cross the Susquehannah on the Ice. An Account of Lancaster, York Town, and the Susquehannah. Arrival at Philadelphia. Carried before the Congress. Sent to Prison. Suffer unparalleled Barbarity. Health declining fast, and expect to be sacrificed. Wrote some Verses upon the Wall with Charcoal. - - - 270

CHAP. LXVI.

Insupportable Severity. Brought before the Congress. Promised better Treatment. Captain Campbell and General

CONTENTS.

General Prescot ill treated. Our Lives endangered by rigid Confinement. A Committee of the Congress sent to visit us. Their Illiberality and Abuse. Greater Severities than ever. Subsisted only on Bread and Water. Thrown into the Dungeon where we almost perished. Philadelphia expected to be attacked by the British Army. Congress fly to Baltimore. Twenty British Prisoners marched in Irons through Derby, Marcus Hook, Brandywine, Wilmington, Newport, Christeen-Bridge, and the Head of Elk. Shocking Instance of Brutality at Newport. Description of Philadelphia and the Delaware. Opulence, Trade, and Number of Inhabitants in Pennsylvania. - Page 286

CHAP. LXVII.

Description of the Guard. The Captain by Trade a Porter. Their Behaviour. Meet several Companies of Rebels. A curious Scene. Put on board of a Privateer, and thrown into the Hold in Irons. Insulted and maltreated by two American Colonels, by Trade, one a Hatter, the other a Lighterman. Arrive at Baltimore. Irons taken off. Kindly and generously treated by the Inhabitants. Congress disapprove of this Lenity, change the Guard, and order us to be treated with great Severity. Effect an Escape, one retaken. Set sail down the Chesapeak. Land on the Eastern Shore. Most alarming Situation. Find Friends. Meet with a most welcome Reception. - - - 310

CHAP. LXVIII.

Offered a Guard of two hundred Men. Decline it, and accept of two Guides. Receive the kindest Assistance from many of the principal Inhabitants. Arrive at Indian River. The Roebuck left that Station. The Falcon touched there, but would not take us on board. Cruel Disappointment. Ardour and Zeal of the Loyalists. Insurrection of the Loyalists. Persuade

both

CONTENTS.

both Sides to disperse. Friendship and Kindness of the Men, and great Goodness of the Women. Character of the American Ladies. Deep Snow. Discover some Ships. Set out in a Canoe. Driven out to Sea in a dark stormy Night. Dreadful Situation. Accidentally discover the Preston in a prodigious thick Fog. Received on board by Commodore Hotham and all the Officers of the Preston. A Hurricane destroys the Canoe, and blows the Ship out to Sea. Page 325

CHAP. LXIX.

Take a fine Prize. Singular Circumstance attending the Capture. Go on board the Daphne. Excellent Regulations on Bard. Affecting Story of a beautiful young Lady. Set sail for New York with the Prize Ship in Tow. Arrival at New York. Wait upon the Admiral and General. Meet with many Friends and Acquaintances. - - 349

CHAP. LXX.

Visit the British Posts and the Works thrown up by the Americans. Danbury Expedition. New England. Account of the Country, Inhabitants, &c. Their Inhospitality and Inquisitiveness. Connecticut River. Hartford. New Haven. Number of Inhabitants in Connecticut, Rhode Island, Massachussets Bay and New Hampshire. Newport. Providence. Boston. Salem. Portsmouth. - - 361

CHAP. LXXI.

Description of New York. Its delightful and advantageous Situation. Fort Washington. Long Island. Description of it. Hell Gates, a dreadful and dangerous Strait. Description thereof. Hampstead Plains. An Account of them. A very singular Insect. Dangerous Sand Banks. Loss of the Liverpool. Description of Staten Island. Account of the North River. Mohawks River, and Hudson's River. Albany. Trade of New York.

CONTENTS.

York. Fire. Dutch Inhabitants. Number of Souls in the Province. - - Page 372

CHAP. LXXII.

New Jersey. Description of it. Perth-Amboy. Burlington. Prince Town, &c. Produce shipped from New York and Philadelphia. Different Towns in New Jersey. Remarkable Cataract. This Province has suffered greatly during the War. 395

CHAP. LXXIII.

Climate extremely cold in Winter. The Winds and Weather peculiar to North America. Particular Description of the Mountains. Number of Inhabitants in New Jersey. The whole Number in all the United States of America. Great Proportion of Negroe Slaves. Astonishing and alarming Decrease in Population. Extreme Weakness of the American States, and their Want of Resources. Absolutely unable to defend themselves in any future War. - - 402

CHAP. LXXIV.

Brief Account of what befel several of the Persons formerly mentioned in the Course of this Work. The Fellow who robbed me in the Mountains. The poor friendless English Girl. The tyrannical barbarous Gaoler. The brutal Dutch Guard. Captain Cameron exchanged. Extraordinary Resolve of the American Congress and the Answer to it. Col. Connolly in Consequence thereof returned a Prisoner of War and exchanged. - - - 416

CHAP. LXXV.

Fatal Termination of the War. Inauspicious to both Countries. Consequences to America of Separation from Great Britain, and of Independence. Consequences of their Connections and Alliance with France. Oppression, Depopulation, &c. of America. Unfit Place of Residence. Reflections concerning the American Loyalists of every Description. 445

A TOUR
IN THE
UNITED STATES OF AMERICA.

CHAP. XLIX.

Remarkable Places, Rivers, Bays, &c. Great Extent of the Rivers. Harbours. Beautiful Country and Coast. Choctaw Nation, or Flat-headed Indians. Their Disposition. The Manner they flatten their Heads. Number of Inhabitants in West Florida. Prodigious Fertility of the Soil. Distances of Places.

TO return to West Florida on the eastern side of the Mississippi, after this long digression on the west, at the conclusion of the first volume, it may not be improper to mention most of the remarkable places, rivers, bays, &c. be-gining ginning at Apalachicola River, being the eastern boundary of the province.

The Apalachicola derives its source, in the province of South Carolina, near the heads of the rivers Alatamaha, Savannah, Santee, and Cherokee or Holston; it is formed by two large branches, the eastern is the Flint River, and the western is Cattahouachee River.

Each of these branches have several very large water-courses falling into them, and on their banks are the different towns of the upper, middle, and lower Creek nations, a particular description and even the recapitulation of the names of which would be only tiresome and disagreeable.

From the source of the Flint River, and Cattahouachee River, to the mouth of the Apalachicola is about six hundred miles in a direct line, and perhaps seven hundred and fifty including the meanders.

The Apalachicola enters the gulf of Mexico in twenty-nine deg. forty-three min. N. lat. and fifteen miles N. E. from Cape Escondido, or St. Blas.

There

There is some difficulty in finding this opening, because of the number of islands and lakes before and about it, and although it is a noble river, whose mouth forms a spacious harbour, yet it has not more than the depth of two and a half, or three fathoms of water at most, over the bar, but within it is very deep and large.

The tide flows higher up in this river than in any other on the coast, viz. about fifty miles.

The country here is a perfect level, and there is perceived a double current on this coast, one from the west, and another from the south, in the gulf of Mexico.

Proceeding west from hence, the next is the bay of St. Andrew; then the bay of St. Joseph, which is about thirteen miles long, and eight wide, and has very good anchorage in four, five or six fathoms water.

West of this is the bay of Santa Rosa, which is large and extensive.

The next is the road of Pensacola, which is one of the best in all the gulf of

Mexico, and veffels can lie in fafety therein againft every kind of wind.

The bottom is fandy, but mixed with fhells, and is excellent for anchorage: the bay is capable of containing a great number of fhips, and has fufficient depth of water, there being never lefs than twenty-one feet over the bar, in the middle of the channel.

The tides are irregular here, as well as upon all the reft of this coaft. All that has been remarked is, that in the fpace of twenty-four hours the tide ebbs out of the harbour from eighteen to nineteen hours, and is from five to fix hours flowing back again, and the greateft difference that hath been found between high and low water is about three feet, on certain days lefs, at other times without increafe or diminution, although the currents are changing daily, but with no regularity.

The town of Penfacola is fituated in a fandy fterile foil, and is a fmall difagreeable place.

But the finest bay in all Florida, or indeed in the gulf of Mexico, is that of Mobile, which forms a most noble and spacious harbour, six miles broad, running thirty miles north, and to the several mouths of the Alibama or Mobile River, and the Alibamous. It affords very good anchorage, and is capable of containing the whole British navy.

The river Mobile or Alibama is formed by five considerable rivers, which also take their rise among the Chickesaws, Upper Creeks, and Cherokee nations, running three hundred and fifty miles in a direct course, and with its meanders above six hundred.

This river consists of two large principal branches, each of which is divided into, or formed by many others. The Western branch is properly the Mobile; the East, which is the largest, is named the Alibama, or Alibamous.

The Mobile or western branch is formed by the rivers Sookhanatcha, the Tumbicbe, and the Tascaloosa, the two last of which take their rife in the Chickefaw nation.

West of the first is a ridge of mountains, running nearly north and south, parallel to the river.

And to westward still of these mountains is Dog River and Roebuck River, which fall into the Mobile, about fifty miles below the junction.

The Alibama is formed by the Cabo, the Pataga Nahchee, the Great Koofah, and the Okwhufke Rivers, which take their rife in the country of the Upper Creeks, and Over-hills Cherokees.

The conjunction of these large branches is above eighty or ninety miles above point Mobile.

The only confiderable rivers west of the Mobile is the Pafquagoula River, and Pearl River, both of which are navigable for a great diftance, and take their rife between the Choctaw and Chickefaw nations, being compofed of a number of beautiful branches, and delightful rivulets, running through the richeft lands,

lands, and moſt charming country in the world.

The Choctaws, or Flat-headed Indians, live on theſe laſt mentioned rivers, and have a vaſt number of fine towns and excellent plantations, being more inclined to agriculture than any other Indian nation on the continent. They are a ſtrong and powerful nation, for Indians, but not addicted to war, and are very peaceable and well diſpoſed.

However they are generally at variance with the Creek nations, betwixt whom and theſe there has long ſubſiſted an hereditary enmity.

They are more numerous than the Creeks, being able to bring five thouſand warriors into the field; but the Creeks are much the moſt warlike nation.

The Choctaws or Flat-heads are named ſo from having their foreheads flattened in their infancy, by a ſmall bag of ſand compreſſed on their foreheads while they are at the breaſt, when they are tied on a board with a hole cut through it for the back parts of their heads, and while the cranium is soft enough to be susceptible of the impression, which is continued constantly until the bones become of a firmer contexture, and retain the flatness, occasioned by this pressure, always afterwards.

This gives them a more disagreeable appearance, and hideous aspect than any other nation, and they suffer more of their hair to remain on their heads than any other Indians do, who generally keep it all pulled out by the roots, excepting a circular spot of about three inches diameter, exactly on the back part of the crown of the head, only the women, who commonly wear all their hair without pulling any of it out.

West Florida was in a very flourishing condition, for an infant country; the settlements increased so fast on the Mississippi, that had we not ceded the whole province to Spain, it is imagined the capital must have been removed from Pensacola, to a place named Monchack, on the banks of the Mississippi; and had this been done

before

before the war, the Spaniards would certainly have found greater difficulty in making a conqueſt of this fine province, if they had been able to have effected it at all, which is indeed extremely doubtful.

The higheſt of our ſettlements on the river Miſſiſſippi is the Natches.

The fertility of the ſoil upon this river is indeed aſtoniſhing, and appears incredible to one who has never been on the Miſſiſſippi. Mr. Edmond Gray removed there from St. John's River in Eaſt Florida in the year one thouſand ſeven hundred and ſeventy-four, with ſix hands (or ſlaves), and made a crop the ſame year of upwards of two thouſand buſhels of Indian corn, with hand hoes only, and alſo cleared the ground from the woods, beſides conſtructing temporary habitations (log houſes) to reſide in. Land was alſo at that time remarkably cheap to purchaſe.

Their commodities are Indian corn, proviſions, indigo, and lumber.

Their indigo bears a higher price than any other, excepting that of St. Domingo

or

or Hispaniola, from the superior richness and fertility of the soil on which it is produced, and they generally make about one hundred and fifty weight a share, that is, for each slave they work in the culture of it.

The country is healthy, especially about the Natches, with a most delightful happy climate, the summers temperate, and the winters mild.

There are judged to be above twelve hundred families in West Florida, the greatest part of which are settled on the Mississippi. And the most numerous nations of Indians on the continent are, in this part of America, of several of which I have already given some account.

From Pensacola to New Orleans is above one hundred miles, to Manchack one hundred and eighty, to Natches two hundred, to Yassous two hundred and twenty, and to St. Augustine about three hundred and twenty miles.

CHAP.

CHAP. I.

East Florida. Rivers. Apalache. St. John's River. St. Augustine. Journey by Land. Description of the Rivers, Country, and Distances. Musquitto River. Indian Towns.

DURING the whole of this voyage hitherto we had been so fortunate as to be favoured with the finest weather imaginable, and had scarcely been out of sight of land; sometimes indeed so very near it that one might have pitched a biscuit on shore, and sometimes remaining two or three days in one place, at least with our vessel only, for on such occasions we would frequently ramble a great distance from the spot where we landed.

Throughout this very delightful voyage I frequently took great pleasure in contemplating on the rich and bountiful hand of nature: for let me cast my eyes which way I pleased, I was equally attracted with a view of the most ravishing prospects.

The

The shore level, rising gradually into eminences clothed with the finest verdure, and most beautiful spontaneous productions promiscuously interspersed, as mulberry, cedar both red and white, cypress, cocoa, vanella, maho, tupelo, saffafrass, live-oak, and cabbage-trees, &c. the last towering with their round tops above the rest, as if conscious of its superiority, and sovereign dignity.

I also observed along this coast several plots of ground, which appeared to me to be like clumps or clusters of trees, and a kind of houses surrounded with pleasant gardens and corn.

Soon after, we arrived at St. Mark de Apalache, in East Florida, on the northern extremity of the bay of Apalaches, fourteen miles distant from the sea, on the north-east side of the river of Apalache, or St. Mark's.

This place is exceedingly healthful and pleasant, standing on the slope of a hill, and has been tolerably regular, being built of stone, excepting some few barackas.

There

There is also the appearance of the exterior parts of the town having been fortified in the Spanish mode, rather as a defence I suppose against the natives than Europeans; but the whole at present is in a state of utter ruin.

From the excellent and central situation of this fine port it might carry on a good trade in its own river, &c. and interior parts, as far as the Apalachean mountains, was it properly settled.

Indeed I understand it did so in the time of the Spaniards, and was then looked upon to carry on more commerce than all the other settlements in Florida put together.

There was once a pearl fishery in this bay, and there is said to be a silver mine some considerable distance up this river, at the foot of a mountain named Yamezee.

Apalache or Ogelagena river enters the bay of Apalache about forty miles to the eastward of Apalachioola River, and rises about one hundred and thirty miles from the sea, in the confines of Georgia.

It is not known to receive any river of note in all its courſe, until it comes near the bay, when one conſiderable river named Tagabona enters into it.

The Apalache is a very fine river, and its entrance forms a large bay, which has ſome ſhallows and rocks ſtretching out from the land, but in the middle there is five fathom water.

The courſe into the mouth of this river is north, and within is a good harbour.

This place lies north one quarter weſt from the Tortugas, and in the paſſage are found ſoundings, at a great depth, all the way.

A briſk trade was formerly carried on by ſmall craft between this place and the Havannah, by the Spaniards.

The old Spaniſh town of St. Mark de Apalache, from whence the bay derives its name, ſtands exactly in the ſame place that Garcilaſſo de la Vega fixes as the Port d' Auté.

The fort was built on a ſmall eminence, ſurrounded by marſhes, ſituated in the fork

fork of the two rivers; and at about two leagues diftance there is on this river a village of Apalachian Indians, called Santo Juan, as alfo fome others in the neighbourhood.

The country around is beautiful, being well fupplied with wood and water, and becomes more fertile the higher you advance into it.

From the mouth of this river we proceeded by land to St. Auguftine, by a road which is as follows.

Ocon is fifteen miles from St. Marks; and ten miles beyond it is Ayavalla (an old fort); twenty-four miles further is Machalla; and eleven miles from thence is St. Matheo; both thefe are fituated on branches of the Rio Vafifa, which is about eighty miles in length, and enters the gulf of Mexico fifteen miles fouth-eaft from St. Marks; twenty-five miles from St. Matheo is San Pedro, on the fouth fide of the river San Pedro, which is one hundred miles long, and enters the gulf of Mexico feventy miles from St. Marks;

eleven

eleven miles from San Pedro is Utoca; and in twelve miles more we came to Nuvoalla, fituated on the eaft fide of the Carolinian River, the courfe of which has not yet been juftly afcertained, but there is very good reafon to fuppofe that it runs a fouth courfe into the Rio Amafura; eight miles from Nuvoalla is Alochua, and in eight miles more we come to Jurla Noca.

All thefe places were formerly the ancient fettlements of the Atimucas Indians, who were driven from them, by the Englifh from Carolina in the year feventeen hundred and fix, and have fixed their fettlement on an ifland to the eaft of St. John's River, about fixty-five miles fouth-weft from St. Auguftine, and call their chief town Pueblo de Atimucas.

Twenty-fix miles from Jurla Noca we came to what had once been a Spanifh fettlement, on the banks of the river St. John, where a Mr. Spalding now has a ftore, or retail warehoufe of merchandize and European goods.

Through

Though the river St. John is here only two miles broad, yet it is eight miles over that and two islands to Fort Picolata, which is the last stage, and is thirty miles distant from St. Augustine.

By this road St. Augustine is one hundred and eighty-eight miles from St. Mark's.

The province of East Florida is bounded on the west by the Gulf of Mexico, and the river Apalachicola, which is formed by the conjunction of two rivers, the Catahouachee on the west, and the Flint River on the east; from the confluence a line drawn to the source of St. Mary's River, and that river, until it falls into the Atlantic Ocean, bound it on the north; and on the east and south it is bounded by the ocean, and the Gulf of Mexico, including all islands, &c. within six leagues of the coast.

From Cape Escondido, or St. Blais, at the mouth of the Apalachicola river, to the confluence of the Catahouchee and Flint Rivers north, is one hundred and twenty statute miles.

From this confluence to the fource of St. Mary's River is ninety miles, then to the mouth in a direct line one hundred and twenty-five miles; which makes the greateft breadth of this province, from eaft to weft, two hundred and fifteen miles.

Its greateft length from north to fouth, viz. from the confluence of the Catahouchee and Flint rivers, to the fouthern extremity of the Cape of Florida, is four hundred and fifty miles.

From St. Auguftine to the mouth of the Vafifa River, or from the mouth of St. John's River, in the Atlantic Ocean, to the neareft part of the Gulf of Mexico, is an hundred and twenty miles.

From St. Auguftine fouthward it is called the Cape, and is generally about eighty or eighty-five miles acrofs, from eaft to weft, viz. from the Atlantic Ocean to the Gulf of Mexico.

St. Auguftine, the capital, lies in twenty-nine degrees fifty minutes north latitude;

the

the town runs along the ſhore, at the foot of a pleaſant eminence adorned with trees.

Its form is oblong, divided by four regular ſtreets, croſſing each other at right angles.

Down by the ſide of the harbour, about three-fourths of a mile ſouth of the town, ſtood the church, and formerly a monaſtery, of St. Auguſtine.

The beſt built part of the town is on the north ſide, leading to the caſtle which is named St. John's Fort.

The Caſtle is a ſquare building of ſoft ſtone, fortified with whole baſtions, having a rampart twenty feet high, with a parapet nine feet thick, and it is caſe-mated.

The town is alſo ſtrengthened with baſtions, and encloſed with a ditch: the whole well furniſhed with cannon.

The harbour is formed by the north end of St. Anaſtaſia or Matanza's Iſland, and a long point of land, divided from the continent by the river St. Mark, which falls into the sea a little above the castle.

At the entrance of this harbour are the north and south breakers, forming two channels, whose bars have from eight to nine feet water over them at low water.

On the north and south, without the city, are two Indian towns.

There was formerly a little fort, situated at the entrance of a river into the river Matanzas (on which is the town of St. Augustine), about four miles south from the town, and at the end of a marsh.

There was another fort likewise, four miles north from St. Augustine, called Fort Musa.

The soil about St. Augustine is very disagreeable, sandy, and barren; but it is much better on the river St. John's, the nearest part of which, to this town, about twenty-seven miles due west.

Soon after our arrival here, we made an excursion as far as Musquito River, to Turnbull's, Taylor's, Biffet's, and Ofwald's plantations. The land is better there than at St. Auguftine, but inferior to that on the banks of St. John's River.

The mouth of the Musquito River lies in latitude twenty-eight degrees forty-eight minutes north. There is a direct communication through this river, by the Rio Amazura, into the Gulf of Mexico.

The Musquitoes are a tribe of Indians inhabiting both fides of this river.

There is another small Indian settlement named El Penon, on an island thirteen leagues to the north of Musquito River, situated at the entrance of the Matanzas River, through which there is a communication to St. Auguftine.

The bar of Matanzas has eight feet water on it, but afterwards, within the river, there is from ten to fifteen fathom. On the north fide of the entrance of
this

this river is high land, called the land of Rome.

St. Anaſtaſia or Matanzas Iſland, is twenty-ſeven miles in length, reaching from the bar of Matanzas to the entrance of the harbour of St. Auguſtine, which it helps to form.

CHAP. III.

Attempts to make Sugar on Musquito River failed. Culture of Sugar. Stone Quarry near St. Augustine. Singular Floors to the Houses. East Florida thinly settled. Loyalists take Refuge in it. Prices of Commodities and Stock. Rates of travelling.

SOME attempts have been made to cultivate the sugar cane on the Musquito River, but they have not succeeded, at least not sufficiently to render it an object; because the keen and penetrating north-west winds always nipt this tender plant, the sugar cane, and not only hindered it from coming to maturity, but also prevented its filling with the juice which produces the sugar, and likewise rendered that which was obtained, of an inferior quality.

However sugar might certainly be cultivated to great advantage nearer to Cape Florida, where none of these disadvantages, and impediments that obstruct its growth, would affect it.

As an account of the culture of this valuable commodity may be acceptable, I shall venture to insert it in this place, and nearly in the same terms of one I have already seen, which is certainly just and accurate.

' This commodity was not at all known to the Greeks and Romans, though it was made in China in very early times, from whence we had the first knowledge of it; but the Portuguese were the first that cultivated it in America, and brought it into request, as one of the materials of a very universal luxury in Europe.

' It is not settled whether the cane, from which the substance is extracted, be a native of America, or was brought thither by the Portuguese from India, and the coast of Africa; but however the matter may be, in the beginning they made the most, as they still do the best sugars which come to market in this part of the world.

The

The sugar cane grows to the height of between six and eight feet, full of joints about four or five inches asunder; the colour of the body of the cane is yellowish, and the top, where it shoots into leaves, of a vivid green: the coat is pretty hard, and within contains a spungy substance full of juice, the most lively, elegant, and least cloying sweet in nature, and which sucked raw has proved extremely nutritive and wholesome.

' They are cultivated in this manner. In the month of August, that is in the rainy part of the year, after the ground is cleared, and well hoed, they lay a piece of six or seven joints of the cane flat in a channel made for it, about half a foot deep; this they cover with the earth, and so plant the whole field in lines regularly disposed, and at proper distances.

' In a short time a young cane shoots out from every joint of the stock which was interred, and in twelve days grows to be a pretty tall and vigorous plant;
but

but it is not until after sixteen months, or thereabouts, that the canes are fit to answer the purposes of the planter, though they may remain a few months after, without any considerable prejudice to him.

'The longer they remain in the ground after they come to maturity, the less juice they afford, but this is something compensated by the superior richness of the juice.

'That no time may be lost they generally divide their cane ground into three parts.

'One is of standing canes, and to be cut that season; the second is of new planted canes; and the third is fallow, ready to receive a fresh supply.

'In some places they make second and third cuttings from the same root.

'The tops of the canes, and the leaves that grow upon the joints, make very good provender for their cattle, and the refuse of the cane, after grinding, serves for fuel; so that no part of this excellent plant is without its use.

'The

'The canes are cut with a billet, and carried in bundles to the mill, which is now generally a windmill; it turns three great cylinders, or rollers, plated with iron, set perpendicularly, and cogged so as to be all moved by the middle roller. Between these the canes are bruised to pieces, and the juice runs through a hole into a vat, which is placed under the rollers to receive it; from hence it is carried through a pipe into a great reservoir, in which, however, for fear of turning sour, it is not suffered to rest long, but is conveyed out of that by other pipes into the boiling house, where it is received by a large cauldron: here it remains until the scum, which constantly arises during the boiling, is all taken off; from this it is passed successively into five or six more boilers, gradually diminishing in their size, and treated in the same manner.

'In the last of these it becomes of a very thick clammy consistence, but more boiling is incapable of carrying it farther; to advance the operation they pour in a small quantity of lime-water; the immediate effect of this alien mixture is to raise the liquor into a very vehement fermentation, but to prevent it from running over, a bit of butter, no larger than a nut, is thrown in, upon which the fury of the fermentation immediately subsides; a vessel of two or three hundred gallons requiring no greater force to quiet it.

' It is now taken out and placed in a cooler, where it dries, granulates and becomes fit to be put into the pots, which is the last part of the operation.

' The pots are conical, or of a sugar loaf fashion, open at the point, which must be considered as their bottom; here a strainer is put acrofs.

' In these pots the sugar purges itself of its remaining impurity; the molasses, or treacly part, disentangles itself from the rest, precipitates, and runs out of the aperture at the bottom; it is now in the condition called Muscavedo sugar, of a yellowish brown colour, and thus it is generally

generally put into the hogſhead and ſhipped off.

But when they have a mind to refine it yet farther, and leave no remains at all of the molaſſes, they cover the pots, I have juſt mentioned, with a ſort of white clay, like that uſed for tobacco-pipes, diluted with water; this penetrates the ſugar, unites with the molaſſes, and with them runs off, leaving the ſugar of a whitiſh colour, but whiteſt at the top.

' This is called clayed ſugar; the operation is ſometimes repeated once or twice more, and the ſugar every time diminiſhing in quantity, gains conſiderably in value, but ſtill is called clayed ſugar.

' Farther than this they do not go in the plantations, becauſe a heavy duty, of ſix ſhillings per hundred weight, is laid upon all ſugars refined there; it is therefore unneceſſary to carry the account of the proceſs of refining it any farther.'

Of the molaſſes rum is made, in a manner that needs no deſcription, ſince

it

it differs in nothing from the manner of distilling any other spirit.

From the scummings of the sugar a meaner spirit is procured.

Rum finds its market throughout North America (where it is consumed by the white inhabitants, or employed in the Indian trade, or distributed from the continent to the fishery of Newfoundland, and the African commerce), besides what comes to Great Britain and Ireland.

However New England takes off a great quantity of molasses raw, and from thence is distilled there, a very inferior ill-tasted spirit, named New England or Yankee Rum, of a flavour and quality very much resembling that distilled in the French West-India islands.

They compute, that when things are well managed, the rum and molasses pay the charges of the plantation, and that the sugars are clear gain.

However by the particulars we have seen, and by others which we may easily imagine, the expences of a sugar-plantation muſt be very great, and the profits at the firſt view precarious; for the chargeable articles of the wind-mill, the boiling, cooling, and diſtilling-houſes, and the buying, and ſubſiſting a ſuitable number of ſlaves and cattle, will not ſuffer any man to begin a plantation here of any conſequence, not to mention the purchaſe of the land, under a capital of at leaſt five thouſand pounds.

Neither is the life of a planter a life of idleneſs and luxury; at all times he muſt keep a watchful eye over his overſeers, and even overſee himſelf occaſionally. But at the boiling ſeaſon, if he is properly attentive to his affairs, no way of life can be more laborious, and more dangerous to the health, from a conſtant attendance, day and night, in the extreme united heats of the climate and ſo many fierce furnaces; add to this the loſs by hurricanes, earthquakes, and bad ſeaſons, and then conſider, when the ſugars are in the caſk, that he quits the toils of a planter, to engage in
the

the hazards of a merchant, and ships his produce at his own risk.

The sum of all might make one believe, that it could never answer to engage in this business; but notwithstanding all this, greater estates are made in a shorter time from sugar-plantations, than from any other culture or produce in the world.

Large plantations are under the management or care of a chief overseer, who has commonly a salary of an hundred and fifty pounds a year, with overseers under him in proportion to the greatness of the plantation, one to about thirty Negroes, and at the rate of about forty pounds annually.

Such plantations too have a surgeon, at a fixed salary, employed to take care of the Negroes which belong to it.

But the course which is the least troublesome to the proprietor of the estate, is to let the land, with all the works, and the stock of cattle and slaves, to a tenant who gives security for the payment of the rent, and the keeping up repairs and the stock.

The

The eftate is generally eftimated to fuch a tenant at half the neat produce of the beft years. Such tenants, if frugal and induftrious men, foon make good eftates for themfelves.

The Negroes in thefe plantations are fubfifted at a very eafy rate. This is generally by alloting to each family of them a fmall portion of land, and allowing them two days in the week, Saturday and Sunday, to cultivate it.

Some are fubfifted in this manner, but others find their Negroes themfelves, with a certain portion of Indian corn, commonly a peck a week for each flave, and of fometimes a falt herring, or a fmall quantity of bacon, or falt pork a day. All the reft of the charge confifts in a cap, or coarfe hat, a fhirt, a pair of trowfers, ftockings, and fhoes, the whole not exceeding the value of forty fhillings a year.

The houfes here have a very fingular appearance within; being floored with a kind of reddifh ftucco, intermixed with fhells, shells, instead of plank, no where else to be met with in British America, and was performed by the Spaniards, when the province was in their possession.

In summer it is always washed very clean every day, which not only affords a grateful appearance to the eye, but also produces a pleasant coolness, that is not to be met with in rooms with flooring of plank.

In the island of Matanzas, or St. Anastasia, there is a quarry of soft stone, which becomes harder as it is exposed to the action of the external air.

Of this stone is composed all the masonry of the fort of St. John, which is indeed one of the strongest on the continent.

We proceeded from St. Augustine to the mouth of St. John's River, and staid the first night at the house of a Mr. Morris, a very kind hospitable planter, possessed of a tolerable house and plantation, and a considerable fortune.

Here

Here I was seized with a violent intermittent fever, which detained me thirteen days, during all which time I received the most humane and friendly treatment from Mr. Morris and his family, as well as from Mr. Groves and Mr. Lewis, who remained with and attended me until my recovery.

In this province the number of inhabitants rather decreased before the rebellion in North America, there being scarcely an hundred white families residing in the whole country out of St. Augustine, exclusive of the Negroes, and the estates of such proprietors as reside in Great Britain. In St. Augustine itself there are not many more, besides the garrison.

Settlements do not extend farther south than Musquito river, about sixty miles to the southward of St. Augustine.

From Augustine to the extremity of the cape, or Cape Florida, is three hundred miles; and although this part of the province consists of much the best lands, no settlements are extended farther south
from

from the capital than sixty miles, as I have just observed.

The nearest Indians, formidable in war, to St. Augustine are the Lower Creeks, who reside in the fork of Flint River, and a small tribe of them have this year gone down to the cape, perfectly good humoured, friendly, and well-disposed towards us.

Many families have removed from this province to West Florida, on account of the immense superiority of the soil in fertility, which prevents this province from increasing in population, and renders that of West Florida to advance in a surprising degree.

Besides the above, there was no assembly at that time, and the court of justice was said to be very oppressive, which also prevented the colony from increasing or improvement.

However since the revolt in America the face of things was changed in East Florida, greatly to its advantage, there being several thousand loyalists settled there for refuge, having fled, and being expelled,

expelled, from the revolted provinces, which enabled the Governor to have a Council, Affembly, &c. and advanced this province to a very flourifhing condition.)

The greateft inconvenience that attends the northern part of this province is dry feafons, and a general want of rain, as it lies under one of the tropics.

The fouthern part is more feafonable, feldom being without refrefhing fhowers for any length of time, both becaufe of the height of the land, and the hills therein which attract the clouds, as well as its being furrouuded with vaft and extenfive feas, from which vapours and moifture are perpetually exhaled.

Throughout the fettled and beft known parts of Eaft Florida the lands in general are pine barrens, with a fandy foil. About twenty or thirty miles back from the coaft they are clay with pines.

One thoufand acres of good land in a body is very feldom to be found.

Settlements are very thinly fcattered.

being five, ten, and twenty miles distant from each other.

The produce or growth of timber is principally pine; there are also live-oak, water-oak, saffafras, hiccory, gum, ash, maple, and tupalo, on the cape mahogany, and in the swamps abundance of cypress, besides cedar, and most other kinds of timber.

There is great plenty of good grass, and very fine marshes.

The highest price of improved lands is ten shillings per acre; the lowest three shillings, and even two. Corn sells now at two shillings and six pence per bushel, but it sometimes brings four shillings and six pence.

Horses are from four to five pounds each; a cow with calf two pounds; pork is purchased for twenty and twenty-five shillings per hundred weight neat.

The only produce of this province, worth mentioning for exportation, is indigo, which sells at five and six shillings per pound, according to the quality; one
hand,

hand, that is one flave, will make from one hundred to one hundred and fifty pounds weight of it, befides the general work on the plantation in the culture of corn and cotton for his fubfiftence and clothing.

Rates of travelling are as follow: dinner one fhilling, fupper one fhilling, breakfaft eight pence, fervants diet, fix pence each, if they are blacks, but for white fervants you pay the fame as for yourfelf, lodging four pence, ftabling for your horfes fix pence each, befides paying for their provender; Indian corn, or more generally rough rice, with which horfes are fed here, two pence per quart.

The common drink is rum and water, fometimes with fugar, and fometimes made into punch with fruit, at the rate of one fhilling per quart.

Every thing in the above rates is calculated in fterling, which indeed is the only currency both in Weft and Eaft Florida.

CHAP. LII.

Recover from Sickness. Leave East Florida. The Rivers Alatamaha, Great Ogetchee, and Savannah. The Town of Savannah. Indian War. Georgians made a poor Figure. Flourishing State of Georgia. Number of Inhabitants. Value of Land. Staple Commodities and Produce. Rates of Travelling. Value of annual Exports and Imports.

MY strength being sufficiently recovered to proceed on our journey, we left Mr. Morris's, and in thirty-six miles came to St. Mary's River, the northern boundary of the province.

We were ferried over this river in a skew, or flat boat, at Johnson's-ferry, and entered the province of Georgia.

This night we put up at the ferry on Great Sitilla River, which is twelve miles distant from St. Mary's, having forded a considerable water-course named Crooked or Dividing River.

All this country hitherto is in its infancy, with very few settlements, and the land

land but indifferent in quality, though there were several pretty pleasant situations, and some very good land.

On the day following we crossed Little Sitilla River, twelve miles distant from the other, also a rivulet named Tortoise River, and the great river Alatamaha at the distance of thirty-one miles from Little Sitilla.

Here we remained all night, at a place laid out for a town named Darien, on the northern banks of the river, where the inhabitants are chiefly Scots.

The Alatamaha is a large, extensive, and very fine river, with abundance of most excellent land on its banks.

It is at least as large as the Apalachicola, or the Roanoak, formerly mentioned, and derives its source near the head-springs of the rivers Apalachicola, and Euphaffee, the southern branch of the Hogohegee or Cherokee River.

It is formed by two large branches, the Ockmulghe on the south, and the Ockoonee on the north, each of which receives
several

several very confiderable rivers, paffing through a vaft body of extreme fine land. The great fork of the Alatamaha is about an hundred and twenty-five miles from the fea.

From the fource of the Okoonee to the mouth of the Alatamaha is not lefs than three hundred and thirty miles in a direct courfe, and above five hundred along with the meanders of the river.

Proceeding on our journey we left the Alatamaha, croffing a number of watercourfes, viz. Sapello River, fouth and north Newport Rivers, and another very large river named the Great Ogechee, juft below the place where a confiderable ftream enters into it, named Cowanoochee River, and at night arrived at Savannah, the capital of the province of Georgia, which is forty-three miles from Alatamaha.

The Great Ogechee River, which we croffed before we came to Savannah, is a large and excellent river, with a great quantity of fine land upon it, but not fo rich

United States of America. 43

rich in quality as the lands on the Alatamaha, nor is this river so large as it.

This river runs almost parallel to the Alatamaha, near the head of which it also derives its source, and falls into the ocean at great Warsaw sound, after a direct course of three hundred miles, or with its meanders at least five hundred.

The town of Savannah is situated on the southern banks of the river of that name, which also runs nearly parallel to the Great Ogechee and Alatamaha Rivers, near the head of which the Savannah likewise derives its source, and runs into the ocean at Tybee, after a course in direct lines of three hundred miles, and near six hundred including its meanders.

It is nearly about the magnitude of the Alatamaha, although I do not imagine it contains quite so much water as that river.

The banks of the river on which the Savannah is built are high and commanding, and the opposite side being low, renders the situation of the town the more pleasant.

It

It lies about ten miles from the sea, and contains perhaps one thousand, or twelve hundred inhabitants, white and black.

This river is navigable to Augusta, above two hundred and ten miles farther up in the country, a large town, but spread over a great and unproportionable extent of ground.

The town of Augusta is so commodiously situated for the Indian trade, that, from the first establishment of the colony, it has been in a very flourishing condition, and maintained very early six hundred Whites in that branch of commerce alone.

The Indian nations, whose trade centers here, are some of the most numerous and powerful tribes in America.

The trade of skins with these people is the largest we have; it includes that of East Florida, part of West Florida, all Georgia, North and South Carolina, and the greatest part of Virginia.

We are supplied with some furs also from them, but they are of an inferior sort. All species of animals that bear the fur, by a wise Providence, have it more thick, and

and of a softer and finer kind as you go to the northward; the greater the cold, the better they are clad.

I made excursions from Savannah to the towns of Puryſburg, Ebenezer, and every place of any note around, an account of which would be little better than a mere repetition of what has already been deſcribed.

The land around the town of Savannah is ſandy and poor, and the timber chiefly pines.

However this province was certainly in a very flouriſhing condition, but the richeſt lands in it lie on the river Alatamaha, which was becoming a very thriving ſettlement, and increaſed very faſt.

The lands throughout this province, as far as I have ſeen, are richer than that of Eaſt Florida; and it is beyond any compariſon better ſettled, being ſaid to contain, according to the computation publiſhed by the firſt American Congreſs, one hundred eleven thouſand and ſeventy-five inhabitants; which account I think exaggerated, nor

nor do I imagine, from the beft information of the principal perfon in the province, that it really contains more than one hundred thoufand fouls, white and black, of which number not more than one-fifth are white.

This province is bounded on the north by the river Savannah, which divides it from South Carolina; and by a line drawn from the head fpring of Georgia Creek, a branch of Little River which runs into the Savannah on the fouth fide about thirty miles above Augufta, due weft, until it enterfects the Miffiffippi; by the river Miffiffippi on the weft; on the fouth by Weft and Eaft Florida, as already defcribed; and on the eaft by the Atlantic ocean, including all iflands, &c.

It lies between thirty-one and thirty-three degrees north latitude, and between eighty-one and ninety-one degrees weft longitude.

In the fettlement of Georgia it was originally intended for a kind of military frontier government, as a barrier againft the

the Spaniards when they poffeffed the Floridas, for this purpofe it had every countenance and affiftance from government.)

But this laudable defign failing, the fettlement was placed exactly on the fame footing as South Carolina, in which condition it has greatly improved, and thereby arrived at its prefent flourifhing ftate.

However in this light of defence it lately cut but a very indifferent figure.

In the year one thoufand feven hundred and feventy-four, the Indians commenced hoftilities throughout a great part of the continent, particularly in Virginia, South-Carolina, and Georgia.

In Virginia, where they were by far the moft formidable, the Governor, the Earl of Dunmore, went out againft them in perfon, a fevere action was fought with them on the banks of the great Kanhawah and Ohio, wherein the Indians were defeated, and his Lordfhip alfo at the head of a confiderable force penetrated into the heart of their country, burnt their towns,

made

made them sue for and conclude a peace, and give hostages for the continuance of it.

In South Carolina there was an engagement likewise, and the Whites were victorious.

In this province, two hundred Georgian militia were sent out against them. Hearing the Indians were approaching, a chosen detachment, consisting of thirty in number, was advanced some distance in front of the main body.

This party, discovering some of the enemy, made a halt, to consult whether to attack them on horseback or on foot.

It was carried to make the attack on horseback, in order, as the event proved, to enable them the better to run away.

The Indians, who were only seventeen in number, perceiving them halt, marched boldly forward and fired upon them; these doughty heroes instantly wheeled to the right about and fled to a man with the greatest precipitation without firing a single shot, and the whole two hundred
followed

followed their example, in the utmost confusion and dismay.

The Indians being elated, upon this success, committed many depredations, until all their ammunition was expended.

The Georgians, greatly terrified, sent to Great Britain for troops. These harassments, and many divisions amongst themselves, prevented their sending delegates to the first American Congress at Philadelphia.

However they soon found means to bring these their Indian enemies to their own terms, by immediately shutting up every avenue of trade with them, from whence alone the Indians derived their only supplies of ammunition, which indeed is their sole resource for procuring food, subsistence, and cloathing, as well as for war: the Georgians also began to raise more forces.

The Indians upon this made every concession that could be desired, delivered up all who had been most guilty of the depredations and murders, and thereby obtained peace and a renewal of trade.

They are now quite reconciled again, and perfectly friendly.

Georgia is indeed a fine country, where it is well cultivated; there is certainly a vast quantity of poor barren land in the province, but there is also a great deal very good and valuable.

The best lands in excellent culture sell for high prices, bringing from three, to twelve pounds sterling an acre; so much has the value of landed property increased, by the culture of indigo and rice, under a mild and free government.

The rates of travelling are much the same as those mentioned in East Florida, and the currency here is also sterling.

The trade of Georgia, at the commencement of the general revolt in America, although in its infancy, was rapidly increasing. The exports then amounted to more than seventy-four thousand pounds, and the imports to forty-nine thousand pounds sterling annually.

CHAP.

CHAP. LIII.

Set out for Charles Town. Afterwards proceed to Augusta, Ninety-Six, &c. Culture of Indigo. Culture of Rice. Culture of Cotton. Description of the Country. Of the Sea Coast. Of the Back Country. Fertility of the Soil. Excellence of the Climate, &c.

MR. Groves left us at Savannah, and set out for his own house in the interior, or rather the back part of Georgia, being on the Great Ogechee River, a considerable distance farther back than Augusta.

But Mr. Lewis and I were equally fortunate in meeting with agreeable company, for Mr. Morris of St. John's River, at whose house I had received such kind and hospital treatment when I was sick in East Florida, having some business in Maryland which, while I was at his house, he proposed transacting there next year, having changed his mind, resolved to commence the journey immediately, and had pushed

pushed hard to overtake us, as we should accompany each other almost the whole way.

He came to me at Savannah, and acquainted me with his intentions, proposing for us to make the journey together, which I most gladly acceded to, as Mr. Lewis and I were to part at Charles Town, from whence he intended to take the route home to Augusta in Virginia; and Mr. Morris accordingly staid with us some days, making excursions to every place worthy of notice around Savannah, before we proceeded on our journey.

Having remained in and near Savannah about ten days, we crossed the river into South Carolina, and set out for Charles Town, where we arrived after four easy days ride, having turned aside from the main road to the right, and staid all night at Beaufort, or, as it is sometimes called, Port Royal, from the harbour which is the best in the province, and having crossed several inconsiderable rivers in this journey, the principal of which were the

Coosa-

Coofahatche River, the Saltketchers or Cambahe River, and the Eddifto, or Ponpon River, remarkable for rich widows, frolic, and feafting.

The diftance from Savannah to Charles Town is one hundred and thirty miles, through a country the greateft part of the way as beautiful, and perhaps richer, than is to be met with in any other part of the world.

The great produce of this country is indigo and rice.

The former is a fource of wealth, greater and more eftimable than gold and filver mines, and the latter adds plenty to riches, and beauty in its culture.

Silk was formerly made here, but it is now difcontinued and has given place to the prefent more profitable ftaple.

The Eddifto or Ponpon has been remarked by every one for the number of opulent widow ladies who refide on the banks of that river, and for the perpetual round of entertainments and diffipation purfued by the inhabitants of that gay fettlement.

The cause of so many widows being there is easily discovered; that part of the country, though rich and fertile, is extremely unhealthy; this, added to the great intemperance of the men, and the excesses of every kind they are perpetually involved in, generate acute bilious disorders which quickly carry them off.

The lives of the women are only preserved by their manner of life being more temperate, and their being less addicted to excesses, which secures them from the violent diseases that prove fatal to the men.

Immediately after our arrival in Charles Town, Mr. Morris being unexpectedly called on business to Augusta and Ninety-Six, I also accompanied him on this journey, being desirous of seeing as much of the country as possible.

To recapitulate the particulars of this journey would appear so much like a repetition of what has been already described, that I shall pass it over, with only these general observations, that it was three weeks before we returned to Charles Town, every day of which we were engaged in travelling either more or less.

We went through Dorchester, crossed Ponpon or Eddisto, went up the Salt-ketchers to Fort More, from thence to Augusta, then to New Bourdeaux, and across the country to Ninety-Six; returning by Orangeburg on the north fork of Eddisto, then crossing the country to Santee River, and came into Charles Town through Monk's Corner, St. Thomas's, &c. having travelled in this journey at least seven hundred miles.

When we set out on this tour to Augusta from Charles Town, we took our final leave of Mr. Lewis, as he proposed to depart from hence, by the upper road through Salisbury, &c. for his own house in Augusta county in Virginia, before our return; and accordingly when we came back we were informed that he had left Charles Town about ten or twelve days before.

As a description of the culture of indigo, the source from whence this province has derived its superior wealth, may be acceptable to the generality of readers, I shall take this opportunity of inserting a very accurate one, (which has already been published, that I know to be just and exact.

' Indigo is a dye, made from a plant of the same name, which probably was so called from India, where it was first cultivated, and from whence for a considerable time we had the whole of what we consumed in Europe.

This plant is somewhat like the fern when grown, and when young is hardly distinguishable from lucern grass, its leaves in general are pennated, and terminated by a single lobe; the flowers consist of five leaves, and are of the papilionaceous kind, the uppermost petal being longer and rounder than the rest, and lightly furrowed on the side, the lower ones are short, and end in a point; in the middle of the flower is formed the style, which

after-

afterwards becomes a pod containing the seeds.

They cultivate three forts of indigo in Carolina, which demand the same variety of foils.

Firſt the French or Hiſpaniola indigo, which ſtriking a long tap root will only flouriſh in a deep rich foil, and therefore, though an excellent fort, is not ſo much cultivated in the maritime parts of the province, which are generally fandy, but it is produced in great perfection, an hundred miles backwards; it is neglected too on another account, for it hardly bears a winter ſo ſharp as that of Carolina.

The fecond fort, which is the falſe Guatimala or true Bahama, bears the winter better, is a more tall and vigorous plant, is raiſed in greater quantities from the fame compaſs of ground, is content with the worſt foil in the country, and is therefore more cultivated than the firſt fort, though inferior in the quality of its dye.

The

The third sort is the wild indigo, which is indigenous here; this, as it is a native of the country, answers the purposes of the planter best of all, with regard to the hardiness of the plant, the easiness of the culture, and the quantity of the produce: of the quality there is some dispute, not yet settled amongst the planters themselves; nor can they as yet distinctly tell when they are to attribute the faults of their indigo, to the nature of the plant, to the seasons, which have much influence upon it, or to some defect in the manufacture.

The time of planting the indigo is generally after the first rains succeeding the vernal equinox: the seed is sown in small straight trenches, about eighteen or twenty inches asunder; when it is at its height it is generally eighteen inches tall.

It is fit for cutting, if all things answer well, in the beginning of July.

Towards the end of August a second cutting is obtained, and if they have a
mild

mild autumn there is a third cutting at Michaelmas.

The indigo land muſt be weeded every day, the plants cleanſed from worms, and the plantation attended with the greateſt care and diligence; about twenty-five negroes may manage a plantation of fifty acres, and complete the manufacture of the drug, beſides providing their own neceſſary ſubſiſtence, and that of the planter's family.

Each acre yields, if the land be very good, ſixty or ſeventy pounds weight of indigo, at a medium the produce is fifty pounds.

This, however, is reckoned by many ſkilful planters but a very indifferent crop.

When the plant is beginning to bloſſom it is fit for cutting, and when cut great care ought to be taken to bring it to the ſteeper without preſſing or ſhaking it, as great part of the beauty of the indigo depends upon the fine farina which adheres to the leaves of this plant.

The

The apparatus for making indigo is pretty confiderable, though not very expenfive, for befides a pump, the whole confifts only of vats and tubs, of cyprefs wood, common and cheap in this country.

The indigo (when cut is firft laid in a vat,) about twelve or fourteen feet long and four deep, to the height of about fourteen inches, to macerate and digeft: then this veffel, which is called the *fleeper*, is filled with water; the whole having laid from about twelve to fixteen hours, according to the weather, begins to ferment, fwell, rife, and grow fenfibly warm; at this time fpars of wood are run acrofs, to mark the higheft point of its afcent; when it falls below this mark, they judge that the fermentation has attained its due pitch, and begins to abate; this directs the managers to open a cock, and let off the water into another vat which is called the *beater*, the grofs matter that remains in the firft vat is carried off to manure the ground, for which purpofe it is excellent, and new cuttings
are

are put in, as long as the harveſt of this weed continues.

When the water, ſtrongly impregnated with the particles of indigo, has run into the ſecond vat or beater, they attend with a ſort of bottomleſs buckets with long handles to work and agitate it, which they do inceſſantly, until it heats, froths, ferments, and riſes above the rim of the veſſel that contains it, to allay this violent fermentation oil is thrown in as the froth riſes, which inſtantly ſinks it.

When this beating has continued for twenty, thirty, or thirty-five minutes, according to the ſtate of the weather, for in cool weather it requires the longeſt continued beating, a ſmall muddy grain begins to be formed, the ſalts and other particles of the plant, united and diſſolved before with the water, are now re-united together, and begin to granulate.

To diſcover theſe particles the better and to find when the liquor is ſufficiently beaten, they take up ſome of it from time to time on a plate, or in a glaſs;
when

when it appears in a hopeful condition, they let loose some lime water from an adjacent vessel, gently stirring the whole, which wonderfully facilitates the operation; the indigo granulates more fully, the liquor assumes a purplish colour, and the whole is troubled and muddy; it is now suffered to settle; then the clearer part is permitted to run off into another succession of vessels, from whence the water is conveyed away as fast as it clears on the top, until nothing remains but a thick mud, which is put into bags of coarse linen. These are hung up and left for some time until the moisture is entirely drained off.

To finish the drying, this mud is turned out of the bags, and worked upon boards of some porous timber, with a wooden spatula; it is frequently exposed to the morning and evening sun, but for a short time only: and then it is put into boxes or frames, which is called the curing, exposed again to the sun in the same cautious manner, until with great labour and attention the operation

tion is finished, and that valuable drug or die called indigo fitted for the market.

The greatest skill and care is required in every part of the process, or there may be great danger of ruining the whole; the water must not be suffered to remain too short or too long a time, either in the steeper or beater; the beating itself must be nicely managed, so as not to exceed or fall short; and in the curing the exact medium between too much or two little drying is not easily attained.

Nothing but experience can make the overseers skilful in these matters.

There are two methods of trying the goodness of indigo; by fire and by water.

If it swims it is good, if it sinks it is naught, the heavier the worse; so if it wholly dissolves in water it is good.

Another way of proving it, is by the fire ordeal; if it entirely burns away it is good, the adulterations remain untouched.'

There is perhaps no branch of manufacture in which so large profits may

be

be made upon so moderate a fund as that of indigo, and there is no country (excpeting on the banks of the Miffiffippi) in which this manufacture can be carried on to such advantage as Carolina, where the climate is healthy, provisions plentiful and cheap, and every thing necessary for that business had with the greatest ease.

To do justice to the Carolinians they have not neglected these advantages; and if they had not revolted from Great Britain, and had continued to improve their natural advantages in the culture of this most valuable commodity, and diligently attended to the quality of their goods, they would necessarily have come to supply the consumption of the principal part of the world therewith, and consequently have rendered their country the richest, as it is one of the pleasantest and most fertile parts of North America.

Rice anciently formed by itself the staple of this province; this wholesome grain makes a great part of the food of
all

all ranks of people in the southern parts of the world; in the northern it is not so much in requeft.

Whilft the rigour of the Britifh act of navigation obliged them to send all their rice directly to England, to be re-shipped for the markets of Spain and Portugal, the charges incident to this regulation lay so heavy upon the trade, that the cultivation of rice, especially in time of war, when these charges were greatly aggravated by the rise of the freight and insurance, hardly answered the charges of the planter.

But after the legiflature had relaxed the law in this respect, and permitted the South Carolinians to send their rice directly to any place to the southward of Cape Finifterre, this prudent indulgence reftored the rice trade; and although they have gone largely, and with great spirit into the profitable article of indigo, it has not diverted their attention from the cultivation of rice.

Juſt before the rebellion in America they raiſed near three times the quantity of what they made formerly, and this branch alone of their commerce was then, at the loweſt eſtimation, worth two hundred thouſand pounds ſterling annually, viz. at the commencement of the revolt juſt mentioned.

The culture of rice is as follows.

Rice is a hard grain, with a coarſe thick huſk ſomewhat reſembling Engliſh barley, only whiter and much harder.

It is ſowed as ſoon as it conveniently can be after the vernal equinox, from which period until the middle, and even the laſt of May, is the uſual time of putting it in the ground.

It grows beſt in low marſhy land, and ſhould be ſowed in furrows twelve inches aſunder; it requires to be flooded, and thrives beſt, if ſix inches under water; the water is occaſionally drained off, and turned on again to overflow it, for three or four times.

When ripe the ſtraw becomes yellow, and it is either reaped with a ſickle, or cut down with a ſcythe and cradle, ſome time in the month of September; after which it is raked and bound, or got up looſe, and threſhed or trodden out, and winnowed in the ſame manner as wheat or barley.

Huſking it requires a different and particular operation, in a mill made for that purpoſe.

This mill is conſtructed of two large flat wooden cylinders, formed like ſmall mill-ſtones, with channels or furrows cut therein, diverging in an oblique direction from the centre to the circumference, made of an heavy and exceedingly hard timber called lightwood, which is the knots of the pitch pine.

This is turned with the hand like the common hand mills, for they have not as yet arrived at ſuch a ſtate of improvement and perfection in this buſineſs as to make uſe of horſe mills, which might certainly

certainly be rendered much more advantageous and useful.

After the rice is thus cleared of the husks, it is again winnowed, when it is fit for exportation.

After this process the value of this grain upon the spot is about ten shillings sterling per hundred weight.

A bushel of rice will weigh about sixty-five or sixty-six pounds, and an acre of middling land will produce twenty-five bushels.

It is calculated that each slave may make about seventy-five bushels of rice, or about twenty-five pounds sterling, at a medium annually.

Cotton is also a most useful production of this country, and of all the southern provinces.

It is cultivated in this manner.

About eight of the seeds, which somewhat resemble those of the sun-flower, are planted together in small hills, about two feet asunder; for this purpose rich gravelly soil is much the most proper,

aud

and that number of feeds are put in the ground becaufe fo many of them are faulty that it is very feldom more than two or three of all the eight or nine vegetate.

In about ten days it is feen above the ground, and then it refembles the leaf of the kidney-bean. As the fummer advances it muft be weeded, worked, and the earth thrown towards the roots of the plants.

As it grows it fhoots forth into eight, ten, twenty or more different branches, and when ripe is about twelve or eighteen inches high above the ground: the pods are then about the fize of a black walnut, of a dark colour, round, and pointed at the extremity. When perfectly ripe this pod burfts itfelf, with an audible crack, and the cotton expands itfelf out of four or five different cells, each of which contains a feed, furrounded by a quantity of fine cotton of a fnowy whitenefs.

It then has the appearance, at a diftance, of large and elegant white rofes, of the moſt beautiful and perfect whiteneſs, and at this time it is gathered, which is about the fall of the leaf, that is the latter end of October.

Little negroes and uſeleſs hands are employed every night in picking the ſeeds from the cotton, which is a very tedious and tireſome operation.

Cotton in this ſtate upon the ſpot is worth three pence ſterling per pound including the ſeeds, and when they are picked from it, it ſells for a ſhilling ſterling per pound.

An acre of land in the culture of cotton contains about ſeven thouſand five hundred hills, and at a medium would produce perhaps five hundred pounds weight.

One hand or ſlave might cultivate five acres, which would thus produce about thirty-two pounds ſterling, by ſelling it in the ſeed, as it would be impoſſible for ſuch a quantity to be picked by any number of hands a planter could ſpare.

There

There is a more expeditious method of picking cotton by a machine called a gin, which however breaks many of the seeds amongſt the cotton, and renders it of leſs value than what is picked by hand.

Beſides the above two ſtaple commodities, indigo and rice, South Carolina affords a very conſiderable quantity of lumber, proviſion, &c. in common with the reſt of the provinces, for annual exportation.

In South Carolina the ſoil in general is richer, and more fertile than in Georgia.

Thunder and lightning is likewiſe frequent, and dreadfully tremendous.

This province is alſo ſubject to hurricanes, but they are very rare, and not ſo violent as thoſe of the Weſt Indies.

Part of the month of March, all April, May, and the greateſt part of June are here inexpreſſibly temperate and agreeable; but in July, Auguſt and September the heat is exceedingly intenſe; and though the winters are very ſharp, eſpecially when

when the north-west wind prevails, yet they are seldom severe enough to freeze any considerable water, affecting only the mornings and evenings; the frosts have never sufficient strength to resist the noon-day sun; so that many tender plants, that do not stand the winter in Virginia, flourish in South Carolina, for they have oranges in great plenty, in and near Charles Town, and excellent in their kinds, both sweet and sour. Olives are also produced, though they are rather neglected by the planter, than denied by the climate.

The vegetation of every kind of plant is here almost incredibly quick, for there is something so kindly in the air and soil, that where the latter has the most barren and unpromising appearance, if neglected for a while it throws out an immense quantity of those various plants, and beautiful flowering shrubs, for which this country is so famous, and of which such fine drawings have been made in the Natural History of Carolina.

The

The whole country is in a manner one univerfal foreft, where the planters have not cleared it.

The trees are almoft the fame in every refpect with thofe produced in Virginia, and by the different fpecies and growth of thefe, the quality and excellence of the foil is eafily difcovered; for thofe grounds which bear the oak, the poplar, the walnut, the faffafras and the hickory, are extremely fertile; they are of a dark fand, intermixed with loam, and as all their lands abound with nitre, it is a long time before it is exhaufted, for here they never ufe any manure.

The pine barren is the worft of all; this is an almoft perfectly white fand, yet it bears the pine tree, and fome other ufeful plants naturally, yielding good profit in pitch, tar, and turpentine: when this fpecies of land is cleared, for two or three years together it produces very tolerable crops of Indian corn and peafe, and when it lies low and is flooded it even anfwers well for rice; for this grain,

as

as I have already obferved, muft be under water more than half the time of its culture.

But what is the beft of all for this province, this worft kind of land is favourable to a fpecies of the moft valuable of all its products one of the kinds of indigo.

There is another fort of ground, which lies low and wet, upon fome of their rivers, this is called *fwamp*, which in fome places is in a manner ufelefs, in others it is far the richeft of all their grounds; it is a black fat earth, and bears their great ftaple rice, which muft have in general a very rich foil, in the greateft plenty and perfection.

The country near the fea, and at the mouth of the navigable rivers, is much the worft; for moft of the land there is of the fpecies of the pale light fandy coloured ground, and what is otherwife in thefe parts is little better than an unhealthy and unprofitable falt marfh.

But

But the country as you advance in it improves continually, and at an hundred miles diſtance from Charles Town, where it begins to grow hilly, the ſoil is of a prodigious fertility, fitted for every purpoſe of human life.

The air is pure and wholeſome, and the ſummer heats much more temperate than in the flat country, for both the Carolinas are all an even plain, for eighty and ſometimes an hundred or more miles from the ſea; no hill, no rock, ſcarce even a pebble to be met with; ſo that the beſt of the maritime country, from this ſameneſs, muſt want ſomething of that fine effect, which its beautiful products would have by a more variegated and advantageous diſpoſition; but nothing can be imagined more pleaſant to the eye than the back country, and its fruitfulneſs is almoſt incredible.

Wheat grows extremely well there, and yields a prodigious increaſe. In the other

other parts of South Carolina they raise but little, where it is apt to mildew, and spend itself in straw; and these evils the planter takes very little care to redress, as they turn their whole attention to the culture of indigo and rice, which is more profitable, and in which they are unrivalled, being supplied with what wheat and flour they want, in exchange for this grain, from New York and Pensylvania.

CHAP.

CHAP. LIV.

Method of clearing the Land. Vaſt Herds of Cattle. Charles Town. Port Royal. George Town. Wilmington in North Carolina. Brunſwick. Fort Johnſon. American General Howe. Newbern. Bath Town. Pamphlico Sound. Edinton. Albemarle Sound.

THE land in South Carolina is very eaſily cleared every where, as there is little or no underwood.

Their foreſts, which is indeed the whole country, conſiſt moſtly of large and lofty trees at a conſiderable diſtance aſunder ſo that they can clear in South Carolina more land in a week than in ſome of the foreſts of Europe they can do in a month.

Their method is to cut them down at about a foot from the ground, and then ſaw or ſplit the trees into boards, or convert them into ſtaves, heading, or other ſpecies of lumber, according to the nature of the wood, or the demands of the market.

If

If they are too far from navigation, they heap them together, and leave them to rot. The roots soon decay, and before that they find no inconvenience from them where land is so plenty.

The aboriginal animals of this country are in general the same with those of Virginia, but there is yet a greater variety of beautiful fowls and birds, among which the humming bird claims the pre-eminence in extreme beauty and delicacy.

All the animals of Europe are here in plenty; black cattle are multiplied prodigiously.

About seventy years ago, it was a thing extraordinary for one planter to have above three or four cows; now some have a thousand; some in North Carolina, especially in the back parts, a great many more; but to have two or three thousand is very common.

These ramble all day at pleasure in the woods, but their calves being separated from them, and kept in fenced pastures, the cows return every evening to them; they are then milked,

milked, detained all night, again milked in the morning, and then let loose.

The hogs range in the same manner, and return like the cows, but not so regularly, by having shelter and some victuals provided for them at the plantation; these are vastly numerous, and many quite wild that never come near the house.

Many horned cattle and horses too run wild in the woods, as I have related in the former volume, though at the first settlement of this country there was not one of these animals in it.

They drive a great many cattle, as well as hogs, down to the sea-ports, to be slaughtered there, and salted for the West Indies; but the beef is neither so good, nor does it keep near so long, as what is sent to the same market from Ireland.

They also export a considerable number of live cattle to Pensylvania and the West Indies.

Sheep are not so plenty as the black cattle or hogs, neither is their flesh good, and their wool is very ordinary.

The

The people of South Carolina, while under the mild and eafy government of Great Britain, lived in the fame plentiful and luxuriant manner with the Virginians defcribed in the former volume.

Poverty was then almoft an entire ftranger in this province, and the planters were the moft hofpitable people that could be met with, to all ftrangers, and efpecially to fuch as by accident or misfortune were rendered incapable of providing for themfelves.

But now the appearance of this fine province is totally changed fince the general and unhappy revolt,

There is no longer the face of plenty to be feen, nor are the doors of hofpitality now open to the ftranger, whofe life, as well as property, is not even by any means fecure.

Charles Town is fo generally known, and has been fo frequently defcribed already, that any thing concerning it can be little elfe than a repetition of what has often been mentioned by others; but as

fome

some account of it will be expected, I shall only just observe, that it lies in latitude thirty-two degrees forty minutes north, and longitude eighty degrees forty minutes west, and is the only town in the province, or indeed in all the southern provinces, worthy of notice.

It is the metropolis of South Carolina, and for size, beauty, and trade, may be considered as one of the first cities in British America.

Charles Town is situated on a point of land at the confluence of two navigable rivers, named Astley, and Cooper Rivers, one of which is navigable for ships twenty miles above the town, and for smaller vessels near forty.

The situation is admirably chosen, for almost every purpose, and it has been long considered among the first in Americr for strength, commerce, and beauty.

The harbour is good in every respect, but that of a bar, which hinders vessels of more than two hundred tons burden from entering.

The town is regularly, and at this time very ftrongly fortified, both by nature and art; the ftreets are well formed, the houfes are large and well built, fome of them are of brick, and others of wood, but moft of them handfome and elegant, and rent is extremely high.

The ftreets are wide and ftraight, interfecting each other at right angles, thefe running eaft and weft extend about a mile from one river to the other.

It contains about a thoufand houfes, and is the feat of the Governor, and the place of meeting of the affembly.

The principal courts of juftice are alfo held here ftill; a few years ago there were courts of judicature no where elfe in the province; but fuch are now held alfo at the capital of each of the fix precincts, which determine all trifling matters, and inferior caufes.

The neighbourhood of Charles Town is beautiful beyond defcription.

There is a road particularly fo, that extends the diftance of fix or eight miles, which surpasses every thing of the kind in the world.

Several handsome equipages are kept here. The planters and merchants are rich, and well-bred; the people are showy, and expensive in their dress and way of living; so that every thing conspires to make this the liveliest, the pleasantest, and the politest place, as it is one of the richest too, in all America.

The large fortunes that have been acquired in this city, from the accession and circulation of its trade, must necessarily have had great influence on the manners of the inhabitants; for of all the towns in North America it is the one in which the conveniences of luxury are most to be met with.

Considerable additions, and new works, have been added to the fortifications of Charles Town at very great labour and expence, both by the Americans and British, since the general revolt; a cut or canal has been formed from river to river, across the peninsula, without the town, which now renders it an island.

As South Carolina met with infinitely more attention from government than the other provinces, the commerce of this country alone employed an hundred and forty ships; and its exports to Great Britain of native commodities, on an average of three years, amounted to more than three hundred and ninety-five thousand pounds sterling annual value, and its imports to three hundred and sixty-five thousand pounds a year.

The trade between South Carolina and the West Indies was very large; that with the Indians was likewise in a very flourishing condition, and they carried British goods on pack-horses five or six hundred miles into the country west of Charles Town.

Charles Town was computed to contain about fifteen or sixteen thousand inhabitants, before it was evacuated by the British; but now it contains scarcely half that number.

The best harbour in this province is to the southward, near the borders of Georgia, named Port Royal. This

This might give a capacious and safe reception to the largeſt fleets of the greateſt bulk and burden, yet the town, which is called Beaufort, (where we juſt called and remained at one night, on our journey to Charles Town from Savannah,) built upon an iſland of the ſame name with the harbour, is not as yet confiderable, being only an infignificant ſtraggling village.

We remained in Charles Town only a week, after our return from Ninety-ſix, and ſet out on our journey northward.

On the ſecond day at night we arrived at George Town, on the weſt ſide of Winyah Bay, which is the mouth of the river Peedee deſcribed in the former volume, after croſſing an inconſiderable water-courſe at a ferry, named Sawee, and the large and very fine river Santee, which is the mouth of the rivers Congaree, Wateree, and Catawba, an account of which has alſo been given already.

George Town is the capital of a precinct of the ſame name, has a good harbour for small vessels, and carries on a considerable trade.

It is about twice as large as Beaufort, and may contain about an hundred houses.

The distance from Charles' Town to this place is about sixty-five miles.

We staid in George Town only two days, and then set out on our journey, which now lay very near the sea-shore.

On the third evening we came to Wilmington, for a considerable time the capital of North Carolina, having dined that day at a little town named Brunswick, situated on the west side of Cape Fear River or Bay, and sixten miles distant from Wilmington.

Wilmington is situated on the east side of Cape Fear River, which is the entrance into the Atlantic of the Deep River, Little River, and Haw River, formerly described, and is also composed of two principal branches, one named the North-west River, or North-west branch of Cape Fear, which is much the largest, the other is called the North-east River, or the north-east branch of Cape Fear, the confluence of which is at Wilmington, and the entrance of this river into the Atlantic is at Cape Fear, a remarkable promontory on the American coaſt, a little diſtance from Fort Johnſon which is about nine miles below Brunſwick.

Wilmington has no appearance of ever having been the capital of a province, being nothing better than a village, containing near about two hundred houſes, a few of which however are pretty good and handſome.

There is a very excellent harbour here for ſmall veſſels, but a bar at the mouth prevents large ones from getting in.

It is about one hundred miles from George Town in South Carolina, and one hundred and ſixty-five from Charles Town.

The land around this place is miſerably poor, being nothing but a ſand-bank covered with pines; but Wilmington notwithſtanding carries on a conſiderable trade, eſpecially to the Weſt Indies, and to the northern colonies.

The little town of Brunfwick ftands in a exceedingly pleafant fituation, but is very inconfiderable; nor does it contain more than fifty or fixty houfes.

Fort Johnfon, which was intended to defend the mouth of this harbour, is a place of no ftrength, and it is too ridiculous to give it the name of a Fort. However there is annually an eftablifhed fum granted for fupporting the appearance of a garrifon in it, and alfo under pretence of keeping it in repair.

Here Mr. Robert Howe commanded; a man of no fmall confequence in his own eftimation, who has fince arrived at the rank of major general in the American army.

Mr. Howe, otherwife not an unworthy man, was always fo very fond of oftentation, that he almoft ftarved his poor wife and family at home, in order that he himfelf might be able to cut a figure every year at the races in Virginia and Maryland.

About eighteen miles from Wilmington is More's Creek Bridge, where the unfortunate North Carolina loyalifts were defeated. The

The settlements upon this river and its branches are greatly depopulated, or decreased in the number of inhabitants, since the general revolt, in a more considerable degree perhaps than any other part of America.

After two days stay in Wilmington, we pursued our journey to Newbern, where we arrived at the end of three more days, being about ninety-five or an hundred miles from Wilmington.

Newbern, which is now the capital of North Carolina, is situated at the confluence of the rivers News and Trent.

It is a pretty little town, somewhat larger than Wilmington, and contains several exceeding good and even elegant houses.

The low grounds on the News and Trent Rivers are here very wide, and uncommonly low; being subject to be flooded, there are sometimes inundations of several miles in extent, which render this part of the country very unwholesome.

Newbern is certainly more central than any other town in North Carolina, and

and on that account it is that it is now fixed on to be the metropolis of the province.

We remained only one day in Newbern, and then set out for Bath Town, where we arrived on the following evening, being about thirty-two miles from Newbern.

Bath Town is a pretty little place, situated at the extremity of a small bay that comes out of the north side of Pamphlico River, which is the mouth of Tar River, and runs into Pamphlico Sound, about twenty-five miles below this place.

This river has already been described in the first volume.

Pamphlico Sound is a prodigious body of water, lying between Cape Hatteras, and the main land or continent, communicating with the ocean by several inlets, all of which have dangerous bars with shallow water upon them; and the bay or sound itself is equally hazardous, being full of shoals, and dreadful sand-banks.

Although

Although this found contains such an immense body of water, it receives no rivers of any note, but News River, and Tar River, which are by no means confiderable.

We fet out from Bath Town on the afternoon of the next day, and on the following evening came to Duckenfield, on the fouth ... of Albemarle found, oppofite to Edenton, which is forty-five miles from Bath Town.

The ferry being at this place feven or eight miles wide, we were obliged to ftay here all night, and the next day alfo, the wind blowing too hard for the ferry-boats to crofs.

Duckenfield is a moft delightful and charming fituation, but the land is poor, as indeed it is every where that way, and the accommodations here are miferable, as they likewife are all along this road the whole way, excepting in the towns, and in them your horfes muft fuffer.

Neither could we enjoy the beauties of the perfpective, and delightfulnefs of the
fituation

situation of this place, on account of the anxiety of our minds, and the vexation of being detained at it, even in sight of Edenton, the place where we were so desirous of reaching.

However on the second day the wind abated, and we were carried over this wide and beautiful sound to Edentown, where we arrived soon enough for dinner.

Albemarle Sound is the mouth of the Roanoak River, a very particular description of which has already been given in the former volume; it also receives the waters of the Maherren, Nottoway, Black Water and Chowan Rivers, and contains an immense body of water.

It communicates with the sea by several inlets, but by reason of bars at the mouth of each of them only small vessels and ships of light burden can come into it.

This is a vast impediment to the trade of Edenton, and is also the great misfortune of all North Carolina.

The town of Edenton stands on the north side of Albemarle Sound, is about the

the size of Newbern, perhaps something larger, and for a considerable time was also the capital of the province.

It is by far the most pleasant and beautiful town in North Carolina, and drives on a very considerable commerce, although the harbour is but indifferent, besides the disadvantages of the bars at the inlets to Albemarle Sound which prevent ships of any considerable burden from approaching it.

CHAP.

CHAP. LV.

Description of the Country. Disagreeable and unhealthy. Vast Profit in making Tar and Turpentine. Process for making Pitch, Tar, and Turpentine. Exports of North Carolina. South Carolina and Virginia share great Part of the Trade of North Carolina. The great Alligator. Dismal Swamp. The Great Dismal. Harbour for wild Beasts and runaway Negroes.

DURING all this long journey of about three hundred and ninety or four hundred miles, I have scarce seen any good land since I left George Town in South Carolina.

It is all universally an immense sand-bank covered with pines, which however generally grow very tall and lofty.

It is likewise totally a wide extended dead flat, covered in a thousand places with stagnated water, which without doubt must be extremely unhealthful; this the sallow cadaverous complexion and countenances of the inhabitants sufficiently evinces. How-

However, what is very extraordinary is, that this land that appears, and actually is, totally barren and altogether useless and unfit for any kind of culture, yields more profit to the occupiers, from the smallest capital imaginable, than can well be conceived was it not so well authenticated, and is not to be paralleled in any country in the universe.

This prodigious profit is derived from making tar, which is one of the most estimable staples of North Carolina.

In making this commodity, they have not occasion for more than two, three, or four slaves, and they can clear by each share or labourer from one hundred pounds, to two hundred pounds sterling, and upwards, annually.

The processes of making, turpentine, tar, and pitch are as follow.

Being all the produce of one tree, viz. the pine, the turpentine is drawn simply from incisions, or rather notches cut in the tree: they are made from as great a height as a man can reach with an hatchet.
These

These incisions meet at the bottom of the tree in a point, where they pour their contents into a vessel placed there to receive them.

There is nothing farther in this process.

Tar requires a more considerable apparatus, and greater trouble.

They prepare a circular floor of clay, declining a little towards the center; from this is laid a pipe of wood, the upper part of which is even with the floor, and reaches ten feet without the circumference; under the end the earth is dug away, and barrels placed to receive the tar as it runs.

Upon the floor is built up a large pile, in form of a circular pyramid, of pine-wood split in pieces, and surrounded, or rather covered over with a wall, coat, or body of earth, leaving only a small aperture at the top where the fire is first kindled.

When the fire begins to burn, they cover this opening likewise; to confine the fire from flaming out, and to leave only sufficient heat to force the tar downwards to the floor. They temper the heat as they

they pleafe, by running a ftick into the wall or thick coat of clay, and giving it air.

Barrels are placed at the end of the pipe of wood to receive the tar, and are carried away as they are filled, empty ones being put in their places.

Pitch is made by boiling tar in large iron kettles fet in furnaces, or burning it in round clay holes made in the earth.

Great quantities of pitch, tar, and turpentine are made in this province, and of thefe confifts a great part of their exports by fea.

In the fouthern parts of North Carolina they make confiderable quantities of rice and indigo, the chief part of which is fhipped from South Carolina.

In the northern parts of this province they make a great deal of tobacco, which is chiefly tranfported by land-carriage into Virginia, and fhipped from thence.

In the back frontiers of North Carolina they raife a great many cattle and hogs, and make very confiderable quantities of butter and flour, almoſt all of which alſo is carried into Virginia to market, beſides the greateſt part of the ſkins and furs which they annually collect.

On the ſea-coaſt and near it, they make large quantities of Indian corn, peas, pitch, tar, and turpentine, all of which only is ſhipped from the ports of this province.

By this it may be readily perceived how difficult a taſk it would be to aſcertain the real annual produce of North Carolina, conſidering the great value of the products of this province which are carried every year both to South Carolina and Virginia, bearing the name of, and adding to the exports of theſe provinces.

However the apparent exports of North Carolina are computed at more than ſixty-eight thouſand pounds ſterling annually, and her imports at eighteen thouſand at leaſt.

This I do not conceive to be more than one-third of the produce of the province; nor one-fourth of the value of the goods brought into it, the reſt of which come through

through the channels of Virginia, and South Carolina, by the means of land-carriage.

So that the annual value of the merchantible products of North-Carolina may be about two hundred and ten thousand pounds sterling, and her consumption of European or foreign goods about seventy thousand pounds.

In this view, deducting the proportion of the North Carolina commodities from the exports of Virginia and South Carolina, this province will plainly appear to be of more consequence and estimation than she has hitherto been held in.

No province nor colony on the continent was in a more flourishing condition than North Carolina before the general revolt, but since that fatal period, and at this present time, I believe there is none more truly miserable and wretched.

The difference between the currency of North Carolina and sterling is thirty-three and a third per cent, in favour of the latter.

The rates and expence of travelling are

not materially different from those already mentioned in the more southern provinces, but accommodations are almost every where, especially on and near the sea-coast, intolerably bad, and nothing can be more dreary, melancholy and uncomfortable than the almost perpetual solitary dreary pines, sandy barrens, and dismal swamps, that are met with throughout the whole of that part of the country.

But there is a swamp in this province which is indeed dismal far beyond description, and can only be exceeded by another, on the borders next to Virginia, actually distinguished by the name of the *Great Dismal Swamp*, in dreadful and horrid preheminence.

This one first mentioned is also called the *Great Alligator dismal Swamp*, and lies between those two vast expanses of water, or rather seas, named Pamphlico and Albemarle Sounds.

This astonishing and horrible place is about forty miles in length, and about fifteen or twenty in breadth, with a large lake

lake in the middle several miles in diameter. It is reported to be named from a monstrous Alligator or Crocodile of a most prodigious magnitude that once was seen here, many of which of the common size still infest it.

As the account I had of this *Dismal Swamp* is only from the report of those who have been in and around it, and who resided in its vicinity, I shall defer any farther description of it until I come to mention the *Great Dismal* itself, which I examined personally and passed through; as I understand they bear so strong a similitude, that a representation of the one will give a good idea of the other.

At present I shall only just observe that these places are in a great degree inaccessible, and harbour prodigious multitudes of every kind of wild beasts peculiar to America, as well as run-away Negroes, who in these horrible swamps are perfectly safe, and with the greatest facility elude the most diligent search of their pursuers.

Run-

Run-away Negroes have resided in these places for twelve, twenty, or thirty years and upwards, subsisting themselves in the swamp upon corn, hogs, and fowls, that they raised on some of the spots not perpetually under water, nor subject to be flooded, as forty-nine parts out of fifty of it are; and on such spots they have erected habitations, and cleared small fields around them; yet these have always been perfectly impenetrable to any of the inhabitants of the country around, even to those nearest to and best acquainted with the swamps.

We ourselves travelled upon the edge of this *Great Alligator Dismal Swamp* the greater part of the way from Bath Town to Duckenfield,

CHAP. LVI.

Leave Edenton. Arrive at Suffolk in Virginia. Description of Suffolk. Smithfield. Pagan's Creek. Cross James River at Hog Island. Arrive at Williamsburg. Part with Mr. Morris. College of William and Mary at Williamsburg. Foundation of it. Education of Indians. Return to their former savage and uncivilized State.

WE remained in Edenton only a few days, and then pursued our journey northward, through a country covered with sand and pines, a continued dead flat, infested with swamps, and the land every where miserably poor and barren.

On the second day after we left Edenton in North Carolina we arrived at a town named Suffolk, in Virginia, having also travelled around on the edge of the *Great Dismal* the principal part of this journey.

Suffolk is situated on a small navigable water-course named Nansimond River, a branch

branch of the James River, which it enters at Crany Island on the west side of Hampton Roads, opposite to New Port-Noose.

It is sixty miles from Edenton, and about twenty-two miles within the boundary line of Virginia.

Suffolk contains about an hundred houses, and carries on a pretty brisk trade, having a very considerable share of the commerce of the northern counties of North Carolina.

It is ninety miles from Halifax, and thirty from Norfolk, the road to which from hence is carried round, and through part of the *Great Dismal.*

Suffolk stands on a soil so very sandy, that in every step in the street the sand comes above your ancles, which renders it extremely disagreeable; to remedy this inconvenience in some small degree, near their doors they have emptied barrels of tar or pitch, which spreads wide, the sand incorporating with it, and forming

a hard

a hard solid consistence, some kind of an apology for pavement, and thereby renders walking much more tolerable.

The houses in Suffolk are low, being generally not more than one story high, which is indeed the ground story only; the river Nansemond is navigable at and above the town, but there is a wooden bridge over it here, and only small vessels can come up even to Suffolk.

The trade of this place consists chiefly of turpentine, tar, pitch, tobacco, and pork which is killed, salted, and barrelled up here, also lumber, Indian corn, and some wheat.

We tarried only one day in Suffolk, and on the following afternoon rode through a little town called Smithfield, situated upon a small branch of James River named Pagan's Creek.

This town is scarcely half as large as Suffolk, and carries on but a very inconsiderable trade, which is chiefly in tobacco, here being an inspection for that commodity, and public warehouses likewise, wife, named Pagans. Smithfield is about eighteen or twenty miles from Suffolk.

It is very unwholesome on account of extensive marshes just in its vicinity, and Pagan's Creek is navigable to the town. This creek is crossed in a ferry boat, which is both disagreeable and dangerous.

We went about twelve miles beyond Smithfield that night, and next morning arrived at James River.

The weather being fine, and the water remarkably smooth and calm, we had a very agreeable passage over at a place called Hog Island Ferry, and arrived at Williamsburg to dinner.

As the college of William and Mary at Williamsburg, being the only institution of the kind in the southern part of America, has not as yet been adverted to, I shall embrace this opportunity of just giving a sketch of its foundation, and present establishment, before I leave the colony of Virginia, and close this chapter.

This college was founded by the reverend Mr. James Blair, a Scots clergyman,

by

by voluntary fubfcription, towards which King William and Queen Mary, whofe names it bears, gave two thoufand pounds fterling in money, and twenty thoufand acres of land, with authority to purchafe and hold lands to the annual value of two thoufand pounds, and likewife granted it a duty of one penny per pound on all tobacco exported from Virginia to the other plantations. Mr. Blair was the firft prefident, and continued in that fituation near fifty years.

There is a prefident, fix profeffors, and other officers, who are nominated by the governors and vifitors.

The honourable Mr. Boyle made a very large donation to this college for the education of Indian children; but this part of the inftitution has not by any means fucceeded.

Some experiments have evinced that thofe Indians who have been educated at this college, and thereby brought to civilized and polifhed manners, have always embraced the firft opportunity of return-

returning to their former wild habits, and uninformed ſtate, into which they immediately plunged, forgetting and totally loſing every trace of their former civilization, and of all they had been taught. Yet notwithſtanding this, their geniuſſes are found to be bright, and they receive any branch of education with great facility.

Here I ſhall terminate this tour, which has included the greateſt part of the places of note throughout the ſouthern part of the Britiſh Settlements in North America, after having travelled at leaſt four thouſand eight hundred miles, and undergone a multitude of dangers and extreme fatigue; accompanied, and attended almoſt the whole way, much to my convenience and ſatisfaction, by my faithful back-wood's man, whom at firſt I conſidered as little better than a ſavage, but from whom I found more aſſiſtance than I could poſſibly have received from the moſt complete profeſſed ſervant in Europe. For theſe American back-wood's men can perform

form a little not only almoft in every handicraft, or neceffary mechanical trade, but they poffefs a fund of refources, more ferviceable on fuch occafions than money; for in many places money could not procure them, nor fupply the wants which are furnifhed by their ready and indeed fingular contrivances.

I parted with Mr. Morris about twenty-five miles from Williamfburg who purfued his journey northward after exacting a folemn promife from me to keep up a correfpondence with him that was only terminated by the unhappy rebellion, which indeed fubverted every thing.

Having fettled in Virginia foon after this, and being particularly attached to planting, agriculture, and rural amufements, I continued to employ this faithful back-wood's man as an overfeer, in which capacity he acquitted himfelf as well, and equally to my advantage and fatisfaction, as he had done during our journey.

CHAP.

CHAP. LVII.

Improvements in Farming. In the Culture of Wheat In cutting it down. In getting it in and stacking it. In threshing it out of the Straw. In cleaning it from the Chaff. A Machine for that Purpose described.

HAVING changed my place of residence from Virginia to Maryland, I entered largely on farming, as well as making tobacco; and on the second year sowed no less than three hundred and fifty-three acres of land in wheat, all in fields adjoining each other, besides fifty acres in buck-wheat and oats, twelve acres in potatoes, thirty-six acres in tobacco, and two hundred acres in Indian corn.

In cultivating this very large crop I only employed fifteen labourers (slaves), which were by no means a sufficient number; but I depended on hiring people in harvest to get in my wheat, as the crops of Indian corn and tobacco would en-

gage

gage every hour of the time of my own people.

That year it had happened, that every confiderable planter in the country had likewife fown large quantities of wheat, I mean large in refpect to what they had ever done before, but in no proportion like me, although many of them had more hands. Thefe planters having engaged all the fpare labourers that were to be hired during harveft, left me without any refources for getting in mine, excepting my own people, whofe hands were already too full of the other crops.

It was this extreme diftrefs for want of hands that firft induced me to invent and hazard innovations, which experience has proved to be confiderable improvements, in the ufual methods of agriculture; and as the object thereof was wheat, which makes fo great a part of the produce of Great Britain, I have ventured to relate, and give fome defcription of thefe improvements here, as they may likewife be adopted for any other grain cultivated in

this

this climate; and shall be extremely happy indeed, if either the public, or any one individual should derive the least benefit or advantage therefrom; but it is from experience alone that its utility can be ascertained.

I myself had the strongest impediments to combat with.

The planters in America are wedded to their old methods used by their fathers and grandfathers, and entertain the most violent prejudices in their favour. This induced them to ridicule me for innovations and improvements, which in fact necessity compelled me to discover and adopt, to prevent the utter ruin, and entire loss of my whole crop; yet these very persons, who were the most violent against these new methods, after they saw their utility and success, and examined the principles on which they were founded, were not only ready enough to adopt the same methods themselves, but also did me the honour of consulting with me, and paid as great attention to my sentiments and opinions

nions on the subjects of agriculture, as if I had been the most skilful, experienced, and old established planter.

In the first place, as it would have been impossible to have cut down my grain with common reapers and reap-hooks or sickles, I was under the necessity of having nine of my hands taught to use the scythe and cradle, with which I had an hundred acres of wheat cut down before I began to get any of it up and secured from the weather.

In the next place, I found that binding would have taken up more time than cutting it down, and so far from securing the wheat from rain, which in this country is very sudden and heavy, that the sheaves so wetted were more damaged, more difficult to be re-dried being obliged to be opened again, than the wheat that lay on the ground unbound without being gathered or raked in heaps; I therefore concluded to lay aside this operation entirely, and have it drawn in in carts unbound; in accomplishing which I found very little loss, difficulty, or inconvenience, but thereby saved faved the labour of three days out of four, to what I fhould have done in binding.

In the third place, as all the tobacco-houfes and barns on my plantation would not have contained one-quarter of the crop of wheat, I had it ftacked out of doors, on an eminence furrounding a large barn, and contiguous to the landing on the river where it would be fhipped; and fo far from its being more difficult to be ftacked unbound, I found that circumftance a confiderable advantage; only when the ftack became high enough for the ufe of a pitchfork in throwing up the wheat, by the ready and expeditious ufe of two cords, that alfo was eafily accomplifhed without any lofs of time.

In the next place, to prevent lofs and wafte in the fields, both from unfkilful cutting down and carting, I had wooden rakes made eleven feet in length, with very long teeth, and with handles fixed therein pointing towards each other at the extremity, with a ftrap of leather from one to the other, like the fhafts of a two-wheeled chaife.

chaise. (To each of these a man yoked himself, and dragged it across the lands, when full, just raising it over the heap of wheat thus raked together, until the whole field was gone over in this manner; (by this means none was lost, and I obtained three large stacks more) containing above an hundred and fifty bushels of wheat in each.

When the wheat, after it was cut down, was caught in the rain, it received no damage thereby, as it was spread thin on the ground, not being raked together; because the sun, which is seldom over-cast, and is very powerful in this country, immediately dried it again, before it could receive any prejudice.

And the wheat being stacked loose rendered the ricks or stacks firmer more even regular and secure, being thereby destitute of those hollow places, and vacancies, which frequently cause the stacks made with sheaves to sink on one side, and sometimes overset, besides occasioning leaks therein, which admit rain, and by that means often damage the whole.

In the fifth place, as it would have been impossible for my people to have been able to threſh out this prodigious quatity of wheat in any reaſonable time, with flails even had they been employed conſtantly at that work, I was therefore obliged to invent ſome method to expedite this operation, and at the ſame time ſave labour.

For this purpoſe I had a circular floor made, one hundred and fifty yards in circumference, and of the width of twelve feet, with a very gentle declivity to the circumference every way. On each ſide of this a fence was made all round the edges of the floor, with ſtakes and wattles, in which were four gates oppoſite to each other, and this floor was made in the moſt commodious part of my wheat-yard, around the large barn in the center.

On this floor I laid down as much wheat in the ſtraw as would yield five hundred buſhels, and having a large ſtock of horſes and cattle, turned them into this circular floor, driving them round ſeparately, the horſes from the cattle, upon

the

the wheat, pretty briskly, until they trod out the grain from the straw, occasionally turning them off into a pen or inclosure, until the uppermost part of the straw, from which the grain was separated, was taken off.

The wheat being first laid on the floor sloping, with the heads upwards, the cattle and horses were always driven one way, that is, in the direction in which the wheat lay, and the straw was also raked off in the same direction, without turning, until such time as the horses feet touched the ground in some places, which is after the last raking off of the straw, then what remains upon the floor is turned over, and the horses and cattle driven round in the opposite direction, for the last time; after which the straw is all taken off, and the wheat mixed with the chaff, which remains on the floor, pushed up together in large heaps, with square boards three feet in length and fifteen inches broad, through the center of which a long stick is fastened for a handle.

The whole of this operation thus far, of separating the wheat from the straw, is performed in one day, to the quantity of five hundred bushels, with only three or at most four hands (labourers.)

But afterwards I found it a task equally tedious, difficult, and troublesome, to separate the grain from the chaff, which I also found to engage the labour of more hands than I could spare for that purpose.

This again obliged me to have recourse to invention, and,

In the last place, I had riddles made of this construction, viz. four feet long, three feet and a half wide, and sixteen inches deep, with the splits very narrow and nearly an inch asunder each way; this riddle had two long handles like a barrow, and was suspended by cords and a pulley fastened to the extremity of an elastic pole, or long springy spar of wood, such as is made use of by turners for turning their work in their lathe. The barn in the center of the treading-ring-floor had four large doors, one in every direction, over each of which one

one of these spars was fixed, and at whatever door the wind came in, this riddle was fastened thereto, and suspended about three feet from the floor.

A child, by holding the handles, could easily work it, by only moving it backwards and forwards; for the elasticity of the spar, to which it was suspended, gave it a play from the least motion; and one person could fill it from the heap of wheat mixed with chaff.

By means of this contrivance two weak hands, or a man and a boy, could easily perform more work at this operation, than could be done by ten strong men with riddles in the usual way in the same space of time.

It was then run through Dutch fans, of which I kept two, to clean it perfectly, and was immediately fit for delivery.

The whole of this second operation, of separating and cleaning five hundred bushels of grain from the chaff, and rendering it fit for market, was also performed in one day only.

So that in four days, with favourable weather, I could by this method and machinery get out a thousand bushels of wheat from the straw, separate it from the chaff, clean it, and deliver it, ready for market, with the labour only of five slaves, exclusive of those who assisted to lay down the beds of wheat on the circular treading floor, which was generally done so early in the morning, as to begin to tread a little after sun-rise.

It was very fortunate for me that I fell upon these inventions and improvements, for thereby I saved all my crops, the most part if not the whole of which I should otherwise certainly have lost.

My wheat also was cleaner, and superior in every respect to any in the country around, and it was rendered so by the following means.

In the first place I had procured Sicilian or forward white wheat for seed, which is of the heavy white flinty species, and ripens about a fortnight sooner than the common English or red wheat, than which it is

also

alſo heavier, the flour too is whiter, and makes the moſt eſtimable ſuperfine flour in the world; this wheat, on that account bearing a ſuperior price to any other. By being more forward than any other wheat, it likewiſe eſcapes the ruſt or ſmut, ſo prejudicial to this crop, and to which, in this country, common wheat is ſo very ſubject.

To prevent my ſeed being mixed with darnel, cheat, or falſe grain, which had begun to infeſt my plantation and fields of wheat, I ſteeped all my ſeed in a brine of ſalt and water ſtrong enough to bear an egg, for the ſpace of ten or twelve hours, and after ſkimming off all that ſwam on the ſurface, I had the ſeed, when taken out of the brine, immediately mixed with fine ſifted ſtrong ſhell lime, ſowed, and plowed in, always within thirty-ſix hours, and generally in twenty-four hours, after it had been firſt put into the brine.

By this means all my fields conſiſted entirely of fine healthful clean wheat, without a ſingle head of darnel or cheat to be diſcovered by the cloſeſt examination;
while

while every crop in the vicinity, and indeed throughout the whole country, was infested and filled with cheat and falſe grain.

I made many more experiments, both in the time and method of ſowing this grain, as well as in ſeveral other reſpects, which cannot here be particulariſed.

CHAP. LVIII.

Improvement in cropping. Three Crops from one Field with only the Labour used in one. Virginia Method of cultivating Tobacco. Inspecting it. Disused at the Commencement of the Revolt. Great Frauds and Impositions now practised in the Tobacco Trade. Different Species of Tobacco. Annual Exports of Virginia and Maryland. Annual Imports.

I Likewise discovered a method of obtaining three crops from one piece of ground, by the labour only used in the culture of one crop.

This was performed in the following manner.

Just before the last ploughing of the Indian corn (called *laying-it-by,*) I had the full quantity of buck or French wheat and English or Sicilian wheat mixed and sown together amongst the Indian corn, a proper and full proportion of seed of each; this last ploughing of the Indian corn, which I had generally delayed about ten days later than common, served to plough and cover it in, in, and what the plough did not sufficiently cover was performed with the hand-hoes made use of for chopping round the stalks of the corn in *laying-it-by*.

Thus the seed of two more crops was put in the ground, without any kind of additional expence, excepting the sowing.

The former four ploughings, which were necessarily used in the culture of the crop of Indian corn, rendered the same service as fallowing the land, and brought it into excellent condition, being thereby perfectly well broke, mellow, and fit to receive the seed wheat. This last operation was done about the middle or latter end of July.

The intense heat of the sun in this country, which is really very prejudicial to wheat, was allayed by the Indian corn, then from five to seven feet high, which afforded a grateful cooling shade, and a beneficial moisture to the seed just put in the ground, by which advantages it flourished greatly, and quickly became strong and vigorous; for it received a sufficient

ficient share of the sun-shine to promote its vegetation, and forward its maturity. Neither was this at all prejudicial to the Indian corn, but rather advantageous; for this being a season of the year when the weather is remarkably dry for a considerable length of time, the Indian corn is apt to be scorched and parched up by the extreme heat of the sun on the roots of the plant, which this young vegetation of the wheat effectually prevents, and also affords a slight degree of moisture to the roots of the Indian corn; nor does this deprive it of the smallest share of its nourishment, the roots of the Indian corn being nearly a foot in the earth below the roots of the wheat.

Some time in October, just before the frosts set in, the buck-wheat is ripe, and is cut down with a scythe, amongst the Indian corn, the stalks of which are not touched.

It is suffered to remain two or three days in the field, for the straw to dry and cure sufficiently, it being a very succulent juicy plant, and afterwards is gathered together and

and beaten out with rods, or tobacco-sticks, for flails would bruise the grain, which is soft large and triangular very much resembling beech nuts.

After this the wheat continues to vegetate, and to spread considerably, becoming like a mat all over the ground.

After the Indian corn is gathered, the stalks are left standing, which afford an excellent and very necessary shelter for the young wheat against the sharp and cutting north-west winds in winter, which are cold, keen, and penetrating, beyond any thing ever felt in England.

In the spring, when the chief part of the cold weather is gone, these stalks are cut down, gathered together, and carried out of the field, otherwise they would not only be prejudicial to the vegetation and growth of the wheat, but would also particularly incommode the cutting it down with the scythe and cradle which cuts the straw quite close to the ground.

The wheat is got in at the usual time, generally between the twentieth of June and the twelfth of July.

However this method of cropping should only be adopted in ftrong rich land, which all mine was, for it will not anfwer fo well in weak and poor foil, as fuch has generally difficulty enough to produce one tolerable crop.

I was alfo accuftomed to fow a quantity of faulty wheat, fuch as was unfit for fale or ufe, in my tobacco grounds, when I gave them the laft ploughing, or *laid them by*, which proved extremely ufeful and beneficial, not only in affording a moft excellent rich fucculent pafture for milch-cows, and colts, during the fall and winter, but likewife, being ploughed in in the fpring, acted as manure, and improved the land.

As the method of cultivating tobacco in Virginia cannot be much, if at all known here, and as a defcription of it may be agreeable, I fhall embrace this opportunity of giving juft a fketch of the manner of producing that narcotic plant which has become a commodity fo beneficial to commerce.

Several

Several rich, moist, but not too wet spots of ground are chosen out, in the fall, each containing about a quarter of an acre, or more, according to the magnitude of your crop, and the number of plants it may require.

These spots, which are generally in the woods, are cleared, and covered with brush or timber, for five or six feet thick and upwards, that is suffered to remain upon it until the time when the tobacco seed must be sowed, which is within twelve days after Christmas.

The evening is commonly chosen to set these places on fire, and when every thing thereon is consumed to ashes the ground is dug up, mixed with the ashes and broken very fine; the tobacco-seed, which is exceedingly small, being mixed with ashes also, is then sown, and just raked in lightly; the whole is immediately covered with brush for shelter to keep it warm, and a slight fence thrown around it.

In this condition it remains until the frosts are all gone, when the brush is taken off,

off, and the young plants are expofed to the nutritive and genial warmth of the fun, which quickly invigorates them in an aftonifhing degree, and foon renders them ftrong and large enough to be removed for planting, efpecially if they be not fown too thick.

Every tobacco planter, affiduous to fecure a fufficient quantity of plants, generally has feveral of thefe plant-beds in different fituations, fo that if one fhould fail another may fucceed ; and an experienced planter commonly takes care to have ten times as many plants as he can make ufe of.

In thefe beds along with the tobacco they generally fow kale, colewort, and cabbage-feeds, &c. at the fame time.

There are feven different kinds of tobacco, particularly adapted to the different qualities of the foil on which they are cultivated, and each varying from the other. They are named Hudfon, Frederick, Thick joint, Shoe-ftring, Thickfet, Sweet-fcented, and Oroonoko.

Vol. II. But

But although thefe are the principal, yet there are a great many different fpecies befides, with names peculiar to the fituations, fettlements, and neighbourhoods, wherein they are produced, which it would be too tedious here to fpecify and particularife.

The foil for tobacco muft be rich and ftrong.

The ground is prepared in this manner; viz. after being well broke up, and by repeated working, either with the plough or handhoes, rendered foft, light, and mellow, the whole field is made into hills, each to take up the fpace of three feet and flattened on the top.

—In the firft rains, which are here called feafons, after the vernal equinox, the tobacco plants are carefully drawn while the ground is foft, carried to the field where they are to be planted, and one dropped upon every hill which is done by the negro-children; the moft fkilful flaves then begin planting them, by making a hole with their finger in each hill, inferting the plant

with

with the tap-root carefully placed ftraight down, and preffing the earth clofe on each fide of it. This is continued as long as the ground is wet enough to enable the plants to take root, or there be plants fufficiently grown to draw and fet; and it requires feveral different feafons, or periods of rain, to enable them to complete planting their crop, which operation is frequently not finifhed until July.

After the plants have taken root, and begin to grow, the ground is carefully weeded, and worked either with hand-hoes or the plough, according as it will admit. After the plants have confiderably increafed in bulk, and begin to fhoot up, the tops are pinched off, and only ten, twelve, or fixteen leaves left, according to the quality of the tobacco and the foil.

The worms alfo are carefully picked off and deftroyed, of which there are two fpecies that prey upon tobacco.

One is the ground-worm, which cuts it off juft beneath the furface of the earth, this muft be carefully looked for, and trodden to death. It is of a dark-brown colour, and short.

The other is the horn-worm, some inches in length, as thick as your little finger, of a vivid green colour, with a number of pointed excreſſences, or feelers, from his head like horns: theſe devour the leaf, and are always upon the plant.

As it would be endleſs labour to keep their hands conſtantly in ſearch of them, it would be almoſt impoſſible to prevent their eating up more than half the crop had it not been diſcovered that turkeys are particularly dexterous at finding them, eat them up voraciouſly, aud prefer them to every other food. For this purpoſe every planter keeps a flock of turkeys, which he has driven into the tobacco grounds every day by a little negroe that can do nothing elſe; theſe keep his tobacco more clear from horn worms, than all the hands he has got could do, were they employed ſolely for that end.

When the tops are nipped off, a few plants are left untouched for ſeed. On the

the plants that have been topped young fprouts are apt to fpring out, which are termed fuckers, and are carefully and conftantly broken off left they fhould draw too much of the nourifhment and fubftance from the leaves of the plant. This operation is alfo performed from time to time, and is called *fuckering to- bacco*.

For fome time before it is ripe, or ready for cutting, the ground is perfectly co- vered with the leaves which have in- creafed to a prodigious fize; and then the plants are generally about three feet high.

When it is ripe, a clammy moifture or perfpiration comes forth upon the leaves which appear as it were ready to be- come fpotted, and they are then of a great weight and fubftance.

When the tobacco is cut it is done when the fun is powerful, but not in the morning nor evening: the plant if large is fplit down the middle three or four inches, and cut off two or three inches below the extremity of the fplit: it is then

then turned directly bottom upwards, for the sun to kill it more speedily, to enable the slaves to carry it out of the field, else the leaves would break off in transporting it to the scaffolds.

The plants are cut only as they become ripe, for a whole field never ripens together. There is generally a second cutting likewise, for the stalk vegetates, and shoots forth again; and in good land with favourable seasons there is sometimes a third cutting also cured; notwithstanding acts of the legislature to prevent cutting tobacco even a second time.

When the tobacco plants are cut and brought to the scaffolds, which are generally erected all round the tobacco houses, they are placed with the split across a small oak stick an inch and better in diameter and four feet and a half long, so close as each plant just to touch the other without bruising or pressing; these sticks are then placed on the scaffold, with the tobacco thus suspended in the middle to dry or cure, and are called *tobacco sticks*,

As

As the plants advance in curing the sticks are removed from the scaffolds out of doors into the tobacco house, on other scaffolds erected therein in succesive regular gradation from the bottom to the top of the roof, being placed higher as the tobacco approaches to a perfect cure, until the house is all filled, and the tobacco quite cured; and this cure is frequently promoted by making fires on the floor below.

When the tobacco house is quite full, and there is still more tobacco to bring in, all that is within the house is struck or taken down, and carefully placed in bulks, or regular rows one upon another, and the whole covered with trash tobacco, or straw, to preserve it in a proper condition, that is moist, which prevents its wasting and crumbling to pieces.

But to enable them to strike the cured tobacco they must wait for what is there called a season, that is rainy or moist weather, when the plants will then bear handling, for in dry weather the leaves would all crumble

crumble to pieces in the attempt. By this means a tobacco houſe may be filled two, three, or four times in one year.

Every night the negroes are ſent to the tobacco houſe to ſtrip, that is to pull off the leaves from the ſtalk, and tie them up in hands or bundles; this is alſo their daily occupation in rainy weather. In ſtripping they are careful to throw away all the ground leaves, and faulty tobacco, binding up none but what is merchantable. The hands or bundles thus tied up are alſo laid in what is called a bulk, and covered with the refuſe tobacco or ſtraw, to preſerve their moiſture.

After this the tobacco is carefully packed in hogſheads, and preſſed down with a large beam laid over it, on the ends of which prodigious weights are ſuſpended, the other end being inſerted with a mortice in a tree, cloſe to which the hogſhead is placed; this vaſt preſſure is continued for ſome days, and then the caſk is filled up again with tobacco until it will contain
no

no more; after which it is headed up, and carried to the public warehouses for inspection.

At these warehouses two skilful planters constantly attend, and receive a salary from the public for that purpose. They are sworn to inspect, with honesty, care, and impartiality, all the tobacco that comes to the warehouse, (and none is allowed to be shipped without being regularly inspected.)

The cask is taken off, and the tobacco is opened by means of large long iron wedges, and great labour, in such places as the inspectors direct; after this strict and attentive examination, if they find it good and merchantable, it is replaced in the cask, weighed at the public scales, the weight of the tobacco, and of the cask also, cut in the wood on the cask, stowed away in the public warehouses, and a note given to the proprietor, which he disposes of to the merchant, and neither sees nor has any trouble with his tobacco more.

The

The weight of each hogfhead muft be nine hundred and fifty pounds neat, exclufive of the cafk, for lefs a note will not be given under the name of a Crop hogfhead; however the general weight is from a thoufand to twelve or thirteen hundred pounds neat.

But if the tobacco is found to be totally bad, and refufed as unmerchantable, the whole is publickly burnt, in a place fet apart for that purpofe.

However, if it be judged that there is fome merchantable tobacco in the hogfhead, the owner muft unpack the whole publicly on the fpot, for he is not permitted to take any of it away again, and muft felect and feparate feparate the good from the bad; the laft is immediately committed to the flames, and for the firft he receives a Transfer note, fpecifying the weight, quality, &c.

This great and very laudable care was taken by the public to prevent frauds, which however was not always effectual; for even with all thefe precautions many acts of iniquity and impofition were committed.

But how many more are to be expected now in that line, when each obftacle and impediment to frauds and impofition is removed, and the door is opened wide to every fpecies of iniquity, deceit, and wicked artifice?

Immediately on the commencement of the rebellion thefe infpectors of tobacco were all fet afide, and every planter fhipped or fold all the trafh he could make and pack up.

Thus it has continued; and in this hopeful ftate remains the whole tobacco trade of the United States of America at prefent.

This grand ftaple of both Virginia and Maryland was cultivated in both thefe provinces, previous to the rebellion, to a very great extent.

Virginia exported at leaft an hundred thoufand hogfheads of tobacco, annually, of about one thoufand pounds each; of which

which between ten and fifteen thousand might be the produce of North Carolina.

Maryland exported between forty and fifty thousand hogsheads also every year.

From this province, as well as from the greater part of Virginia, besides Indian corn, provisions, skins, lumber, hemp, and some iron, there were very large quantities of wheat and flour exported. Of wheat from Virginia not less than five hundred thousand bushels, and from Maryland at least six hundred thousand bushels annually; besides perhaps fifteen thousand barrels of flour from each province, were shipped for Europe and the West Indies.

The total amount of the exports of both these provinces before the revolt might amount to nine hundred thousand pounds sterling annually, and their imports at least to a million sterling every year.

CHAP.

CHAP. LIX.

Set out on another Journey. The Potomack, a Description of it. A most beautiful River. General Washington. An Account of him and Mrs. Washington. Chotank. Falmouth. Fredericksburg. An Innkeeper, named Weeden, an American General. Dr. Mercer, an American General. The Rappahannock. The northern Creek of Virginia. Stanton. Green Briar River. Colonel Lewis. Indian War. The Great Kanhawah and Ohio. Severe Action. Indians defeated. A Stratagem in Bush-Fighting. The Earl of Dunmore penetrates into the Heart of the Indian Country, burns their Towns and concludes a Peace.

I Undertook another very considerable journey, in consequence of a most pressing invitation from two gentlemen, sons to Colonel Andrew Lewis, of Green Briar River, in Virginia. This journey was to the Green Briar and the Great Kanhawah Rivers, through the new countries of Fincastle and West Augusta.

One

One of these gentlemen having married a considerable planter's daughter in my neighbourhood, we had contracted an intimacy, and I agreed to accompany him on his return to the back country.

As several very singular occurrences happened during this journey worthy of notice, I have chosen it out, in preference to many others which I have made, judging the relation might not prove unacceptable.

We crossed the Potowmack at Hoes Ferry from Maryland into Virginia, where the river is something more than three miles wide.

Here we were not a little diverted at a reply made by the owner of this ferry to a person enquiring after the health of one of his nearest relations.

This gentleman, as well as most of his family being remarkably attached to the use of hard words and a turgid bombulous style, which they considered as insignia of dignity and superior consequence, had made it his study to convey all his ideas and thoughts, even in common conversation, in the language of pompofity and affected oftentation, in fuch a degree as to render himfelf altogether unintelligible to the common people, who at beft are fufficiently ignorant in any country; and of this peculiarity all the family were not a little proud.

As the anfwer he made to this perfon concerning his father's health was fo completely clothed in the drefs of formal circumlocution, I fhall repeat it here in his own words, as a curiofity in its way.

"Sir, (faid he,) the intenfe frigidity of
"the circumambient atmofphere had fo
"congealed the pellucid aqueous fluid of
"the enormous river Potomack, that with
"the moft eminent and fuperlative re-
"luctance, I was conftrained to procrafti-
"nate my premeditated egreffion to the
"Palatinate Province of Maryland for the
"medical, chemical, and Galenical co-
"adjuvancy and co-operation of a dif-
"tinguifhed fanative fon of Efculapius,
"until the peccant deleterious matter of
"the Athritis had pervaded the cranium,
into

" into which it had afcended and pene-
" trated, from the inferior pedeftrial ma-
" jor digit of my paternal relative in con-
" fanguinity, whereby his morbofity was
" magnified fo exorbitantly as to exhibit an
" abfolute extinguifhment of vivification."

This fingular and bombaftic genius is a near relation of the American General Wafhington, and it would certainly afford high entertainment to hear this gentleman's account of his relation's feats of prowefs, and the unexpected fuccefs of the Americans.

This river is the boundary between Virginia and Maryland from its mouth to its fource, in which laft mentioned province the river is included as far as high water mark on the Virginia fhore, confequently all the iflands therein are in Maryland.

The Potomack is certainly the moft noble, excellent, and beautiful river I ever faw, indeed it can be excelled by no other river in the univerfe.

Its entrance into the Chefapeak is near an hundred miles from the Atlantic. It is

navi-

navigable for the largeſt ſhips as far as Alexandria, and even to George Town, which is cloſe to the falls and eight miles above Alexandria, about two hundred miles along with the courſe of the river from its mouth, and three hundred miles from the ſea.

The breadth is generally from two miles to ſix miles and upwards; at the mouth, from Smith's Point it is twenty-five miles over to the other ſide at Point Lookout.

The ſituations and gentlemen's ſeats on this river are beyond compariſon or deſcription beautiful.)

Every advantage, every elegance, every charm, that bountiful nature can beſtow, is heaped with liberality and even profuſion on the delightful banks of this moſt noble and ſuperlatively grand river. All the deſirable variety of land and water, woods and lawns, hills and dales, tremendous cliffs and lovely vallies, wild romantic precipices and ſweet meandring ſtreams adorned with rich and delightful meadows, in short (all the elegance, beauty, and grandeur that can be conceived in perspective,) are here united, to feast the sight and soul of those who are capable of enjoying the luxurious and sumptuous banquet.

To describe the most delightful and charming situations and villas on this majestic river would far exceed the bounds of a volume; merely to enumerate a few of the most striking, is all I can here undertake, beginning at Alexandria, a little below the falls.

On the Virginia side Mr. Alexander's, General Washington's, Colonel Martin's, Colonel Fairfax's, Mr. Lawson's near the mouth of Oquaquan, Colonel Mason's, Mr. Lee's near the mouth of Quantico, Mr. Brent's, Mr. Mercer's, Mr. Fitzhugh's, Mr. Alexander's of Boydshole and all Chotank, Colonel Frank Thornton's on Marchodock, Mr. Thacker Washington's, Mrs. Blair's, Mr. M'Carty's, Colonel Phil. Lee's of Nominy, all the cliffs of Nominy, Yocomico, Wicocomcio, &c. are

are among the multitude of extremely fine situations, all so very beautiful that none can claim the pre-eminence.

In Maryland, Mr. Addison's, Mrs. Addison's, as well as George Town and Bladenburg, Mr. Rosier's, Mr. Diggs's, General Smallwood's, Mr. Dent's, Mr. Harrison's, Mr. Brent's, a Roman Catholic priest Father Hunter's, General Dent's, Mr. Phil. Fendall's, Mr. Lee's, Mr. Compton's, Mr. Sly's, the Roman Catholic priest Mr. Lewis's, Mr. Clark's, Mr. Wolstenholme's, Mr. Smyth's, &c. &c. cannot be exceeded in elegance and beauty of situation, although there are hundreds of places besides on this extensive river that do equal them.

After we had passed this noble river we entered one of the most agreeable, as well as respectable settlements in Virginia, named Chotank. In this place Mr. George Washington was born, who has become somewhat distinguished for being at the head of an inactive timid army which never performed a gallant exploit,

yet

yet have succeeded in their pursuits far beyond even their most sanguine expectations or hopes.

General Washington is descended from a family of good repute, in the middle rank of life, now residing in this settlement of Chotank, every individual planter throughout this numerous and extensive settlement being actually related to him by blood.

He received a common, but by no means liberal education, and made the principal part of his fortune by marriage, although he has no children to inherit it.

Mrs. Washington is of a family named Dandridge, some of whom formerly were officers in the royal navy, and was the widow of Colonel Custos, who possessed an immense fortune for Virginia, and having two children by her left her his sole executrix as well as guardian to his children.

By this marriage Mr. Washington obtained possession of the whole of Custos's large estates. Being remarkable for œconomy, industry, and good management,

he

he foon acquired a fortune for himfelf nearly equal to that of Cuftos.

And, in the former war having been an officer in the Virginia regiment, the command of which at length devolved on him, being fenfible, cool, and very popular, the command of the American army was offered to him for two reafons; firft, becaufe he was the only public man then known, either calculated to command, or proper to be entrufted therewith; and the next reafon was, becaufe thereby they fecured the attachment of the whole colony of Virginia, the moft extenfive, the richeft, and the moft powerful of all the provinces.

Mr. Wafhington has uniformly cherifhed and fteadfaftly purfued an apparently mild, fteady, but afpiring line of conduct, and views of the higheft ambition, under the moft fpecious and effectual of all cloaks, that of moderation, which he has invariably appeared to profefs. This has been evinced by a multitude of inftances, but particularly by his

accept-

accepting the continuance of the chief command of the American army, after the Congress had suddenly declared for Independence, of which measure he always before affected to disapprove and on that account pretended to be inclined to resign the command, an intention of all others the most distant from his mind.

His total want of generous sentiments, and even of common humanity, has appeared notoriously in many instances, and in none more than his sacrifice of the meritorious, but unfortunate Major André.

As a General he is equally liable to censure, which is well known even to every *intelligent Frenchman* who has been in America, as well as to every person whatsoever who has had any opportunity of observing his military operations: nor during his life has he ever performed a single action that could entitle him to the least share of merit or praise, much less of glory.

But as a politician he has certainly distinguished himself; having by his political

tical manœuvres and his cautious plausible management raised himself to a degree of eminence in his own country unrivalled, and of considerable stability.

However in his private character he has always been respectable, and highly esteemed; and has supported a name fair and worthy.

As we rode along the heights of Chotank, and some distance beyond it, we could plainly see the south-west or Blue Mountains, which were at least eighty or an hundred miles from that place.

After passing through a small town named Falmouth, at the falls of the river Rappahannock, we crossed that river in a ferry-boat, and arrived at Fredericksburg, putting up at an inn or public house kept by one Weedon, who is now a general officer in the American army, and was then very active and zealous in blowing the flames of sedition.

Fredericksburg is situated on the banks of the river Rappahannock, about a mile and a half below the falls. It is a very hand-

handsome town, considerably larger than Suffolk, but inferior to Williamsburg; part of the town is built on a considerable ascent, which is extremely pleasant.

Opposite to Fredericksburg, on a fine commanding eminence, there is a beautiful seat the property of a Mr. Fitzhugh, and just above Falmouth there is a very valuable forge, and iron-works, belonging to a Mr. Hunter.

The Rappahannock is navigable to the falls, about a mile and a half above Fredericksburg, at which place the little town of Falmouth has been erected. This certainly is a fine river, but not to be compared to the Potomack, nor is it so large as the James; however it is navigable between eighty and an hundred miles, and is generally from half a mile to five miles in breadth. There are also a multitude of fine situations on the banks of this river; but after one has seen the Potomack, and the grand majestic perspectives thereon, all others are totally eclipsed.

The

This river, from the fource in the Blue Ridge, where it is called Rapid-Anne River, to its entrance into the Bay of Chefapeak, which is about twenty-one miles to the fouthward of the Potomack, is the boundary between that part of Virginia belonging to the king, which is on the fouth fide, and the northern neck, whereof lord Fairfax is proprietor, which lies between this river and the Potomack, comprehending a large and moft valuable territory eftimated at the annual value of fifteen thoufand pounds fterling to his lordfhip.

The length of the Rappahannock, from its fource to the Bay of Chefapeak, is about a hundred and fifty or two hundred miles in direct lines, this river alfo running in a remarkable ftraight courfe.

But the Potomack is at leaft three hundred and fifty, or perhaps four hundred miles in extent in direct lines; and including its multitude of bendings, for which it is particularly diftinguifhed, it cannot be lefs than five hundred miles, of

which

which about two hundred are navigable for the largeſt ſhips.

In Frederickſburg I called upon a worthy and intimate friend Dr. Hugh Mercer, a phyſician of great merit and eminence, and, as a man poſſeſſed of almoſt every virtue and accompliſhment. He was a native of Scotland, was bred to phyſic and ſurgery, but having a talent for military affairs, left the line of healing for that of war, in which, he ſoon diſtinguiſhed himſelf, and acquired the provincial rank of Lieutenant-Colonel during the former war, wherein he had ſerved with great credit and character, had been dangerouſly wounded, and ſurmounted many great perils and difficulties. Dr. Mercer was afterwards a Brigadier-General in the American army; to accept of which appointment I have reaſon to believe he was greatly influenced by General Waſhington, with whom he had been long in habits of intimacy and bonds of friendſhip; for Dr. Mercer was generally,

of

of a juft and moderate way of thinking, poffeffed liberal fentiments and a generofity of principle very uncommon among thofe with whom he embarked.

This worthy but miftaken and unfortunate perfon was killed at Prince Town in the Jerfeys, where he was then commanding in the American army as one of their Brigadier-Generals. The lofs to them was great, and truly lamented by his friend General Wafhington.

In this town alfo lived another Mr. Mercer named James, whofe profeffion was the law, and who afterwards became a member of the Congrefs; but his family was from Ireland, and no way related to the other.

We left Frederickfburg on the fecond day, and purfued our journey weftward; paffing by Orange Court-houfe, going up on the weft fide of Rapid-Anne River, croffing the Rippanna River, and the South-weft or Blue Mountains, and fording the South River and a number of other branches of the river Shannandore, we
arrived

arrived at the town of Stanton in Augusta county, on the third day after we left Fredericksburg.

Stanton is a pretty large town, considering it lies beyond the mountains, and carries on a brisk inland trade, a great share of which appeared to be in the hands of two merchants named George and Samson Matthews, natives of Ireland; which almost all the inhabitants in this part of the country also seem to be. Mess. Matthews were very intelligent persons, shewed us many civilities which rendered two days that we remained in Stanton very agreeable, and greatly to our satisfaction they also accompanied us to the Green Briar and the Kanhawah.

Stanton is situated in that remarkably rich and fertile valley between the South mountain or Blue Ridge and the North mountain or the Great Ridge, within a few miles of the foot of the Great North Ridge.

It is not built on any water-course, the nearest to it being at two miles distance and is a branch of the South river or Shannandore,

nandore, the head spring of which is not far from this town.

Our company being thus increased, we left Stanton on the third day, and began to travel through a country extremely rough, rocky, and mountainous, which is named Augusta County, being very large and extensive, and Stanton is the capital.

After crossing the Great North Mountain, passing through the Calf Pasture, and the Cow Pasture, we came to Jackson's mountain; the road over which being intolerably bad, we found greater difficulty in crossing this mountain than any we had come over hitherto. However having at length accomplished it, we crossed Jackson's River, a branch of the Fluvannah River or the upper branch of the James River, and afterwards crossing some more mountains, we fell in upon the Green Briar River, at Howard's Creek, and arrived at Colonel Lewis's just four days after we left Stanton.

This

This journey was extremely fatiguing, and by no means agreeable, although we met with inhabitants all the way, and better accommodations than could be expected in that remote part of the country.

The Green Briar River is not so large as the New River, at the junction of which is formed the Great Kanhawah; but however it is a very considerable stream of water, extremely pleasant, with abundance of most excellent land upon its banks.

All the way as we advanced we heard many alarming, although vague reports about the Indian war; but when we arrived at Colonel Lewis's we found the whole settlement in confusion.

Colonel Lewis had raised all the militia of the back country, nearest to him, and had marched down the Great Kanhawah, in consequence of orders he had received from the Earl of Dunmore, then Governor of Virginia, who had also marched out in person against the Indians by the way of Pittsburg.

Captain

Captain John Lewis, who had been lately married, being taken ill, was unable to proceed after his father and the troops under his command, notwithstanding his extreme defire of following them as he had a company there; but his brother Thomas, the two Mathews's, and I, having croffed the river, pushed forward with all the expedition we could make to come up with them. However they had reached the mouth of the Great Kanhawah a confiderable time before we arrived at their camp) for with all the difpatch we could poffibly make ufe of, it was four fevere days journey, notwithftanding we travelled at the rate of forty miles a day.

Here I was not a little furprifed as well as pleafed to meet with two old acquaintances, viz. Major Fields, whofe houfe I had been at, and by whom we had been very hofpitably entertained on the Miffiffippi, who as well as myfelf had come to this place accidentally; the other was Major Lewis, my former fellow-traveller fo long, with whom I had parted at Charles Town,

Town, and whose habitation was in Augusta County through which we had passed.

I was exceedingly happy to see him, having always greatly esteemed and respected him. Here we again became inseparable companions, for his sentiments, inclinations, and manners were more congenial to mine than any other person's in the camp.

Major Lewis was also the life and soul of the troops. They esteemed, respected and loved him; for he was really active and enterprising, good-natured, generous, and brave.

There was a company for each of Colonel Lewis's sons, and but one of these gentlemen being present, I, who on this expedition was only a volunteer, had the honour of being appointed to command the absent officer's men, if a set of white savages, without regularity, order, or discipline, can said to be under command.

However as this was intended as a compliment paid to me, I very cheerfully accepted it, for it was neither trouble nor expence

expence to me, and I had and expected no emolument or advantage therefrom.

When we entered the camp we found it a scene of confusion and filth, with only a very slender appearance of military order and discipline; however we were scarce arrived therein before an action ensued, entirely by chance, more considerable and obstinate than any that has been fought with the Indians for many years past, in which, although the Indians were unfortunate, yet they gained and merited a high degree of military honour, merit, and applause.

This camp was situated near the banks of the Great Kanhawah, and was injudiciously chosen on several accounts; particularly because the spring, from whence a great part of the water used by the troops was procured, was certainly too far distant: nor was that spring covered with a piquet, nor secured by any other method of defence.

It is true there was water much nearer, and indeed almost close to the camp, but it was neither so good in itself as the water of this spring, nor even fit for use, being besides, by a deficiency in regulations and want of discipline, always kept foul and dirty.

With both his flanks and his front covered by the vast rivers Ohio and Great Kanhawah, Colonel Lewis considered himself as perfectly secure; but especially as he had lately received intelligence that the Earl of Dunmore was advanced as far into the Indian country as the river Hockhocking with eight or nine hundred men, which by all accounts were under much better discipline and subordination than ours, being then on his march to penetrate into the heart of the Shawnese nation, and to destroy their towns.

If any thing could excuse a commanding officer's ideal security, it would be such a situation as this; but there can never be any defence, apology, or extenuation for the least slackness of discipline, or remissness of any kind in the military line; for a good officer, commanding an army, a regiment, or a detachment, ought always to make use of every precaution and vigilance

lance as if he was conſtantly in the face of, and in danger of being attacked by, a ſuperior enemy; for the leaſt relaxation may be of fatal conſequence, and never can admit even of a palliation.

We ourſelves, viz. Major Lewis, Captain Lewis and I, had for two days reconnoitered the country for ten miles around, without diſcovering the leaſt appearance of an enemy; but on the third morning after our arrival, the whole camp was not a little alarmed at a conſiderable firing, juſt by the ſpring already mentioned, which continued to increaſe, and at length became very heavy.

This circumſtance was ſingular enough, and was thus occaſioned.

The Shawneſe, joined by the Delawares, the Mingos, and ſome other warriors of different nations, to the number of near nine hundred, had advanced from the Shawneſe town, which is ſixty miles up the Siotto River, had marched no leſs than ſeventy-five miles in two days, had croſſed the large river Ohio, which is by far more confiderable than the Danube, without either fhips, boats, canoes, or pontoons, and without implements or time for making any, upon *rafts*, which they formed inftantly from the trees growing on the banks by means only of their tomahawks.

All this they performed with the utmoft fecrecy, in the face of one fuperior enemy in their front, and nearly in the face of another equal to them in their rear; and approached within one mile indeed little more than half a mile of our camp without being difcovered. All this they did without the affiftance of cannon or cavalry.

This action commenced entirely by accident, as I have already obferved, which was a fortunate circumftance for us, as they intended to furprife us in our camp; and had they been able to have done fo, it muft certainly have proved fatal, confidering our great deficiency in point of difcipline and precaution, notwithftanding our fuperiority in numbers, for there might be

more

more than twelve hundred men under Colonel Lewis's command.

Early that morning, viz. on the tenth of October, some of our men having met a few Indians who had also come to that spring (formerly mentioned) for water, immediately fired upon them, and they returned it. Each side was reinforced, until the action became very severe and almost general, and was maintained with great obstinacy by both armies during the principal part of the day; but their manner of fighting was totally different from any thing of the kind in Europe, and it was that alone enabled both sides to continue the engagement for such a length of time, without one or both being entirely cut off.

Every man ran to a tree for cover, from behind which he fired upon the enemy, whenever he could discover any of them in a vulnerable situation; this care in firing was however more the practice of the Indians, who seldom threw away any of their shot promiscuously, and did all in their power to fire with effect. Our men also

also took the same precautions to cover themselves from the musquetry of the enemy, but were by no means as frugal of powder and ball, which they wasted without much regard to aim.

In this manner of fighting, want of subordination is of less prejudice than in any other, and officers are of less service and consequence; as here appeared to be no mœnuvres, no turning of flanks, no charging with bayonets, for nothing was seen or heard but a perpetual popping from all quarters; and one side could not attempt to turn the flank of the other, because they could immediately extend it as far as that of the first.

In this situation, with little advantage on either side, Major Field, Major Lewis, and I (having been close together all day), discovered a ravine, or large hollow way, in the rear of the enemy, which was full of trees and thick underwood, and seemed to be unsecured.

It immediately occurred to us that if we could be able to march a small detachment

ment by a circuitous route to seize on that ravine, and under cover of it attack them suddenly in the rear, it must decide the fate of the day in our favour.

Upon this Major Lewis and I went and desired Colonel Lewis, (who, for what reason I am ignorant, had not left the camp all day,) to furnish us with this detachment; and it was with some difficulty we obtained it, as he appeared apprehensive of the camp being left without a sufficient guard.

For this purpose we lost no time in marching to get in the rear of the enemy, intending to make a circuit of some miles to accomplish it undiscovered, and therefore we had to pass a ravine, in the rear of our own camp, upon the left.

We ordered a serjeant and two men to pass this hollow place first, and to examine it as they passed: they soon went over, and beckoned to us that all was safe; when Major Lewis advancing boldly forward was shot dead by five Indians, who lay there in ambush to prevent our sending any detachments that way, and suffered the first party to pass unmolested, judging rightly that they would be of inferior consequence and estimation to those that followed after. But we instantly fell upon them, and pursued them so closely, that not a man of them escaped to alarm the enemy, which would have frustrated the whole design. After leaving a corporal and some men with Major Lewis's body, I marched on with all expedition, and gained the ravine without noise or being discovered, from whence I immediately commenced a sudden and very heavy fire upon the enemy's left flank and rear, who were all open and quite exposed to this attack.

Their loss was considerable, and they instantly gave way, but with a good countenance, firing as they retreated from tree to tree, and not without carrying off all their wounded, and a great part of their dead also.

Had it been possible to have made our troops charge them at the instant of their breaking, the rout would have been general and complete; but without a much
greater

greater share of discipline it is impossible to make them leave off that habit of bush-fighting, or keeping themselves covered by trees; for without that, I am convinced that by the charge of the bayonet half the number of British troops would have routed them in an instant, and killed three times the number that was done in this action during the greater part of the whole day.

The Indians also not only effected their retreat with their wounded, &c. but also crossed the Ohio again upon their rafts that night, about eight miles from the field of action, by which they were effectually secured from any future attacks from us.

In this engagement the number of killed and wounded on each side was nearly as follows, viz. forty-six of our troops killed, and about eighty or eighty-five wounded; and of the Indians there might be thirty or upwards killed, and at least as many or more wounded; however the real number of the wounded of the

the enemy could never be properly ascertained.

The principal officer among the slain on our side, besides Lieutenant Colonels Fleming and Morrow, Captains M'Clanahan, Blueford, Charles Cameron, and Wilson, as well as three or four others who died of their wounds, was Major Charles Lewis, a sensible, worthy, and enterprising man, and a brave gallant officer. His loss was deservedly, and most truly lamented; for he was extremely popular and much esteemed.

Numbers of stratagems were made use of in the action of this day, peculiar to this mode of fighting.) But in these the whites shewed more dexterity and skill than the Indians, which is indeed very unusual.

I shall relate only one of these stratagems, as thereby an idea may be formed of the others, and of the nature of them.

A white man, who had taken shelter behind a log to cover him from the fire of the Indians, perceiving an Indian watching for an opportunity to fire at him, raised

his

his hat on a stick a little above the log behind which he lay for cover; the Indian, taking it for his head, and imagining that he was looking up, fired, and sent a ball through the hat; the white man, to support the deception, pretended to be wounded, and began to kick and struggle. Upon this the Indian jumped from behind his tree to give him the *coup de grace* with his tomahawk, which is their mode of exultation and triumph; but as soon as he approached within a few steps of him, the white man raised up his firelock, took aim and killed him, making the Indian act the part of a dying man in reality, which he himself had only done in appearance.

It was not this action with Colonel Lewis that completely humbled the Indians. It was upon their return to their towns to find the Earl of Dunmore with an army in the heart of their country; who had laid their towns in ashes, and destroyed all their provisions.

It was this that induced them to sue for peace in the most submissive and supplicating

plicating terms to his Lordship, whom they found as generous a conqueror, as they had experienced him a resolute, enterprising and formidable enemy.

After this his Lordship gained such an influence and ascendancy over them that he may be said to have conquered their hearts, as well as to have subdued their country.

As this war with the Indians had never met with my private approbation, it being solely from motives of curiosity and by accident that I happened to be present and engaged in it, having accompanied Captain Lewis without any such expectation, or the least idea of such an event, and the conduct of the Indians in this action had not only increased my respect and good opinion which was always very favourable towards them, but it actually made me admire and venerate them, I concluded in my own mind to leave the camp, and return with all possible expedition, as soon as there was any prospect of doing so in safety.

How-

However by some unaccountable precaution Colonel Lewis took it in his head to be all at once extremely vigilant left we should be attacked by the enemy in our camp, of which he had actually become extremely apprehensive; and with these ideas in his mind, which he had in some measure communicated to many more, they were not a little alarmed, some days after the engagement, by a great noise of hollowing and whooping like Indians approaching the camp.

But all their fears and uneasiness were dispelled when the person who made this mighty clamour came nearer and arrived in the camp, as he proved to be one Girthy, a messenger from Lord Dunmore to Colonel Lewis, who first confirmed the report of the retreat and dismay of the Indians.

By his arrival and intelligence we were fully satisfied that the whole country southeastward of us was clear of the enemy, and in perfect security, quietness, and peace.

CHAP.

CHAP. LX.

Return to Colonel Lewis's. Fredricksburg. Dumfries. Colchester. Iron Works. Ocquoquan River. General Washington. Piscattawa. Port Tobacco. A most elegant Situation and Seat belonging to a Roman Catholic Priest. Establishments of the Jesuits in Maryland. Their Harams of beautiful Slaves. A profligate Priest. Estimation of landed Property. St. Mary's. Annapolis. Baltimore. Its flourishing Condition. Number of Inhabitants in Maryland.

MY reflections on the unfortunate situation of the poor Indians, and the death of my intimate and much-respected friend Major Lewis, had cast such a damp on my spirits, that I could not enjoy any satisfaction in that place; and as my own private affairs likewise called me home, I made the best of my way up the Great Kanhawah for the Green Briar settlement, being furnished with the most favourable and flattering letters for Captain John Lewis, which in reality was only paying a compliment

pliment to his company, whose good behaviour on the day of action had certainly been distinguished, but from the very short time I was with them could reflect little or no credit or honour on me.

When I arrived at Colonel Lewis's, I found his son still extremely indisposed, and in such a state of imbecility and disease that I advised him to endeavour to go to the warm springs in Augusta county for the restoration and benefit of his health; which he readily consented to do.

Having remained only one night here I pushed forward to Stanton, and from thence made the best of my way to Fredrickburg, returning the same way that I went out.

At Fredrickburg happening in company with an acquaintance that proposed to travel round by Dumfries and Colchester in Virginia, and Piscattawa and Port Tobacco in Maryland, I agreed to accompany him.

After crossing the Rapphannock at Falmouth, Potomack Creek, and Acquia Creek,

Creek, both of which fall into the river Potomack, we arrived at Dumfries, a little town situated on a pretty water-course named Quantico Creek.

Here we met with excellent accommodations at an inn, one of the best perhaps in America, kept by a Mr.———, a Scotsman, where we dined, and afterwards travelled as far as another little town named Colchester, upon the river Ocquaquan, which also, as well as Quantico Creek, falls into the Potomack.

If the accommodations were good at Dumfries, they were proportionably bad at Colchester at a house kept by one Coates, whom we found to be equally disagreeable with the entertainment we met with.

Colchester, although it be larger than Dumfries, has not half as much trade, and is an ill-built nasty little town, situated on the north side of the river Ocquaquan, within three miles of the Potomack, of which the eminences above it command a very fine view.

There

There are some iron-works, furnaces, and forges, worked by cuts from the Ocquaquan, just above Colchester, on the south side of the river, carried on by a very ingenious person named Ballantine, which are of great public utility.

The trade of Dumfries and Colchester consists chiefly of tobacco and wheat; and there is a very fine back country to support it, and a considerable number of ships were loaded here annually.

The face of all that part of Virginia, named the Northern Neck, which is between the rivers Rappahannock and Potomack, is quite different from the rest of that country which is generally level being almost a dead flat from the ocean to the mountains; but the Northern Neck on the contrary is extremely broken and hilly, the land too is generally stiff, but very rich, strong, and fertile and the situations and perspectives are delightful and in the highest degree elegant, grand, and commanding.

The rich variety of land and water, hills and dales, woods and fields, that are to be seen from every eminence bordering on the Potomack, is beyond description beautiful, and is not to be paralleled perhaps in the world.

We left Colchester in the forenoon, and went to General Washington's at Mount Vernon, on the banks of the Potomack, where we dined, and afterwards crossed the river about a mile below his house, to Maryland; and reached Piscattaway, a small town situated upon a creek of the same name, to supper.

Piscattaway is low and unhealthy, but has a tolerable share of trade, which consists of tobacco entirely.

On the day following I returned home to my own house, having dined at another small town named Port Tobacco, sixteen miles from Piscattaway, which is built upon a creek of the same name, that falls into the Potomack, as well as Piscattaway Creek.

Port Tobacco is not larger than Piscattaway, neither of them containing more than forty or fifty houses; but it carries on a much more confiderable trade, which confifts of fome wheat, but chiefly tobacco.

Near the town of Port Tobacco, upon a commanding eminence overlooking the Potomack, is a feat belonging to the late fociety of the Jefuits, in occupation of a Roman Catholic prieft named Hunter, in a fituation the moft majeftic, grand, and elegant in the whole world. The houfe itfelf is exceedingly handfome, executed in fine tafte, and of a very beautiful model; but imagination cannot form the idea of a perfpective more noble, rich, and delightful, than this charming villa in reality is.

And as the beft defcription I could give of it would come fo far fhort, as even to difgrace the place itfelf, I fhall not hazard the attempt.

I accordingly terminated this journey, after travelling at leaft nine hundred and fifty miles, and returned to my own houfe, quite overcome with wearinefs and fatigue.

The province of Maryland, which was first granted as an asylum for Roman Catholics, still contains a great majority of them, although the church of England is the established church, to which they pay an equal proportion as the protestants. There are in all probability three Roman Catholics for one protestant throughout this province; and in the counties of St. Mary's, Charles, Calvert, and Prince George's, there are at least six parts out of seven of the inhabitants that profess that religion.

Previous to the dissolution of the society, the Jesuits had a powerful establishment in Maryland, and were possessed of an immense property in that province, consisting chiefly of land and slaves.

Three of their principal seats or establishments are in Charles's and St. Mary's counties; one already mentioned just by Port Tobacco, the most beautiful place and most elegant situation in the world, in the possession of the reverend father Hunter, who was the principal or head of the society in this province; the next is at the mouth of Briton's Bay, on the river Potomack, possessed by father Lewis; and the third is at the mouth of Mary's River, on the Potomack also, in the occupation of father Ashby; both the last named places are in St. Mary's county.

Besides these there are several other very considerable establishments belonging to the Jesuits, in this province, where no person resides but the priests and their attendants. However at each of these places they seem to have a haram of female slaves, who are now become white by their mixture.

There are at this time numbers of beautiful girls, many of them as fair as any living, who are absolutely slaves in every sense to these priests, and whose posterity must remain in the same degrading unfortunate situation.

Since the dissolution of the society of Jesuits those that were there at that time remain in the undisturbed possession of all their immense property.

Maryland is divided nearly into two equal parts by the upper half of the vaſt bay of Cheſapeak, which comes up almoſt through the centre of this province.

This prodigious body of water and the multitude of large and fine rivers that empty themſelves into it on each ſide, all of which are navigable, ſome even to the extent of two hundred miles, render theſe two provinces of Virginia and Maryland extremely valuable, commodious, and delightful, by the amazing benefit and public advantages of water-carriage and communication throughout the whole.

In Maryland there are ſixteen counties, an equal number of which are on each ſide of the bay of Cheſapeak; theſe two parts or diviſions of the province being kept carefully ballanced, as a check one upon the other, that all the advantages of trade, legiſlature, &c. may be juſtly divided. By way of diſtinction one ſide of the Cheſapeak is called ſimply the Eaſtern Shore, and the other the Weſtern Shore;

Shore; of which the last however is considerably the best inhabited, the most beautiful, fertile, and polite.

By far the greatest number of Roman Catholics are on the Western Shore; and, what is very surprising, it was also the most violently rebellious and disaffected.

The principal Roman Catholic families in this province are generally better descended than is common to America, where they are most frequently ashamed to trace their ancestors a single generation back; but the chief of the families in this province, at least those of the Roman Catholic religion, came over with the first lord Baltimore, and were originally from good and respectable families in England.

About the period of the dissolution of the society of Jesuits, there happened a great confusion amongst them, as well as among all the Roman Catholics in the province, occasioned by a profligate priest of that order, who, after playing a number of tricks with many of the female part of his flock, thought proper to lay aside his habit and his vows, and enter into matrimony with a rich young Roman Catholic widow lady of weak intellects, along with whom he lives to this day, in open defiance of the Pope and his bulls, yet still professing the same religion. This I mention as an extraordinary occurrence, so rarely to be met with, that a similar instance I do not imagine can be produced.

Landed property, by being more divided in Maryland than in Virginia, is thereby enhanced in value, and sells at a much higher price, frequently for no less than three or four times as much, especially on the Western Shore, where the soil is also far superior to that on the other side of the bay.

On the Eastern Shore the land in general is neither good, nor valuable; being very sandy, light, and poor, excepting near the head of the Chesapeak, where it becomes more stiff, and fit for the culture of wheat,

The

The town of St. Mary's, upon St. Mary's River, in the fame county, once the capital of the province, is now no more, and exifts only in name. Its great inconvenience, being fituated in a peninfula, in an extreme corner of the province, was the reafon of its fall, and of the feat of government being removed to Annapolis, an hundred miles diftant, more in the centre of the colony, delightfully fituated on the river Severn, and in full view of the Chefapeak.

Annapolis is a beautiful town fomething larger than Williamfburg, and the ftreets are remarkable for their fingular and whimfical manner of being laid out from the province-houfe in directions like rays from a centre.

The foil in and around Annapolis is fandy, which renders it as agreeable in the winter as it is unpleafant in the fummer, although it contains a number of exceeding good buildings.

There is alfo a courfe or public race ground in the vicinity of this town, on which capital

races

races are performed twice a year; this being the central spot whereon the great contentions between the southern and northern horses are decided, in which however those from the south have evinced an undoubted superiority.

But even Annapolis will not continue much longer as the capital of Maryland. The seat of government must soon be removed to Baltimore, a large, flourishing and very fine town, lately erected, thirty miles farther back in the country than Annapolis; situated upon Patapsco River about fifteen miles from Chesapeak Bay, with an excellent harbour and commodious wharfs.

This town, built on a spot which but thirty-six years ago was covered with woods, contains already more houses than every other town in the province together, and between twelve and fifteen thousand inhabitants.

It carries on a very great trade, which is increasing in a surprising degree, chiefly in wheat, flour, &c. &c. But as every thing

thing has undergone a total alteration by the rebellion, Baltimore muſt alſo be a very great ſufferer thereby.

The number of inhabitants in Maryland were computed by the Congreſs at three hundred and twenty thouſand, which I alſo think exaggerated in the ſame manner as in the other provinces; for I am well aſſured that two hundred and ſeventy-five thouſand comprize all the ſouls in the province; of which more than half, perhaps two-thirds are Negroes. And the whites include a great proportion of Iriſh and Germans, eſpecially in the back counties.

CHAP.

CHAP. LXI.

The Rebellion breaking out. Harassments on account of Loyalty. Political Opinions, Sentiments, and Impartiality of the Author. The Manner of forming the first Congress's Committees, &c. and the Persons who composed them. Against the private Inclinations of a great Majority of the People. Politic Stroke or Measure. Severe Persecutions and extreme Hardships. Alexandria.

AFTER my return from this very fatiguing and disagreeable expedition to the back country, although I had so much need of rest and tranquillity, yet a very small share fell to my lot; for the flames of discord and rebellion, beginning to burst forth with violence all over the continent, likewise in my vicinity and through several counties around the inhabitants being extremely disaffected to British government, and my opinions and inclinations in favour thereof being decided and public, I was harrassed and

per-

persecuted beyond measure, by the demagogues of this formidable faction.

As the natural generosity of sentiment of the bulk of the people of Great Britain, and especially of those of an high rank, has prevented them from being able to form any idea of the illiberality of conduct of the Americans, and the barbarous treatment practised by them upon those unhappy persons who have had the misfortune of falling into their hands, especially if ever they were active against them, I shall here give a brief narration of what has fallen under my own observations, as well as what I have experienced myself; at the same time, utterly disclaiming every idea of personality, prejudice, and every vindictive sentiment.

And to evince my candour on this subject, it is necessary for me first to declare, that I was exceedingly attached to the country and the people, very many of whom I loved, esteemed, and respected; I was habituated to, and fond
of

their fociety, cuftoms, and manner of life; I delighted in their agriculture; in fhort, I was equally interefted in every event that could befall them, with any of them all, as I intended to end my days in that country, wherein every individual was happy and free, under the mild government of Great Britain; where plenty and contentment reigned, and not a beggar was to be feen, before the flames of fedition and revolt confumed this fair and noble fabric.

My political opinions alfo were decidedly in favour of civil liberty, and I equally detefted defpotifm and republican government. A mixed monarchy, fuch as that of Great Britain, was the government I approved of, and the object of my choice.

So that as my fentiments have been liberal, and my conduct actuated by principle alone, fo fhall my relation of the events, that occurred in confequence thereof, be candid and impartial.

In

In the county wherein I refided, at the firft meeting of the people to confider about electing committees, conventions, congrefs, &c. I oppofed the meafure with all my power, perfuafion, and influence; and then three-fourths of thofe prefent came over to my fide on dividing. But notwithftanding this, the other remaining fourth part, the abettors and promoters of fedition, appointed themfelves committee-men, &c. and had the effrontery to publifh in the news-papers that they were unanimoufly chofen by the people.

This was the cafe in general, as well as there; and it was in this manner, and out of fuch as thefe, that the firft committees, conventions, and congrefs were chofen and compofed.

From the firft I conceived this was a deep laid fcheme, that was greatly promoted by a number of favourable fortuitous events accidentally intervening, which as they occurred no forefight nor precaution could divert; for it is an undoubted

doubted truth, that not one tenth part of the people at large at firſt countenanced or approved thoſe violent and ſeditious meaſures that were afterwards adopted.

After the firſt general congreſs broke up, the people beginning to murmur, the boldeſt, deepeſt, and moſt politic ſtroke of all was now formed and executed. In ſhort, it was that on which the baſis of all their future authority, power, and ſucceſs, was eſtabliſhed.

A meeting of each county on buſineſs of great importance was deſired, on an appointed day, in anonymous hand-bills diſtributed and paſted up at public places. A very few people only met, and they were chiefly ſtrollers and idle perſons. However, the former ſelf-created committee now re-elected themſelves, and added eighty or ninety others, indeed every perſon of any influence in each county, though abſent, and although many of them had diſapproved of their

meaſures,

meafures. Of this number any five were impowered to act.

This meafure of increafing the number of the committee-men rivetted their influence, and effectually filenced thofe who oppofed their defigns.

Frequent meetings were afterwards held, wherein the former defigners always carried their own fchemes, and the laft nominal committee-men were fatisfied with the name and fhadow of power, for in fact they had none of the fubftance.

Although I had always openly and publicly difapproved, and oppofed the whole of their proceedings, yet now they nominated me alfo as one of their committee; propofed me to command three troops of light horfe, and the chairman waited on me with the offer of their commiffion, (and with four papers for me to fubfcribe, viz. one for the fupport of the feditious inhabitants of Bofton in New England, one for raifing a magazine, one for the payment of the members of the Congress, and the fourth was the association of revolt;) intending thereby to corrupt my principles, as they did those of many others, and expecting that this ostentatious though really lawless power would be so alluring as to fascinate me out of my loyalty. But in this however they were mistaken, for I positively refused the whole, giving him for answer, that I would sooner suffer death than be guilty of what they requested and have such a stain of what I considered as ignominy upon me.

Being then cited before them to answer for my conduct, I plainly and candidly informed them, " That I had no share in
" electing them; that they neither repre-
" sented me nor my principles; that I
" beheld them as an arbitrary, insolent,
" self-created, petty tribunal, to which
" I paid no obedience: but that I was
" always ready to answer in a legal and
" constitutional way to any accusation
" against me."

This

This incensed them highly; and for self-defence, as well as in support of his Majesty's government, I then drew up a loyal association, and exerted my utmost influence to promote it.

In two days, I obtained four hundred subscribers. We were to meet on the ensuing Saturday, in order to concert some effectual measures to support constitutional government, and avert the threatened oppression of the congress and committees.

However this attempt was rather too late; the mal-contents had gathered too much strength; and in the mean time having got intimation of it, they in one night and day had every person privately seized on, and compelled them to renounce his Majesty and his government even on oath; two Scotsmen, who refused, they tarred and feathered, and they sent a party after me: but I, being apprized of it, and being well provided with arms and ammunition at my own house, and resolute servants, resolved to

defend

defend myfelf. Apprehenfive of too warm a reception they returned without me.

After this however I was in continual dangers and alarms, and could not fleep in my own houfe in fafety. Several times parties of forty armed men, with two rounds each of ammunition, were ordered to take me, and if I refifted to fire upon me; but one of their officers always privately gave me timely notice of it, fo that I efcaped, and generally went over Potamack in my boat to Virginia on fuch occafions.

Happening there once before fome violent rebels to fay, " that inftead of
" blaming the conduct of his excellency
" the Earl of Dunmore, then Governor
" of Virginia, I thought he had always
" acted in a manner that did him infinite
" honour, and wifhed that all the reft of
" his Majefty's Governors had performed
" their duty with equal fpirit and refo-
" lution:" a Captain Weedon, from Frederickfburg, the innkeeper formerly

mentioned, (now an American General) came down to the river fide with his company, confifting of fixty rifle-men, to feize upon me, when I came over, but a lady, refiding on the banks, fent her maid to the fhore unfufpected to warn me of the danger, who called to me when within about three hundred yards informing me of their intentions and defiring me to return immediately. As foon as they obferved the boat ftand off again from the fhore, Weedon and his banditti ran down to the river fide ordering me to land immediately or they would fire upon me. Accordingly, on my refufal and difregarding their threats, they fired about an hundred fhot with their rifles at me, and having arms in the boat I returned their fire eight or ten times; but the diftance was fuch there was no great danger on either fide.

That fame day on my return home I was informed that three different parties intended on the morning following to befet my houfe on all fides, in order to prevent my escaping. About sun-set also I discovered a boat with eight or nine armed men coming over to my house; upon which I immediately went down to the river side with my fusée, and ordered them not to land there, threatening that I would certainly fire upon them if they attempted it. They persisting in it, I fired upon them three times from under cover of the root of a sycamore tree blown up, which they also returned; but it prevented their landing at that place, and they stood up the river to Cedar Point, about two miles above. This boat contained some of those who were to assist in surrounding me next morning.

I was now beset by them on all sides; but effected my escape in the night, by riding along in the river Potomack, upon the flats which extend in width near half a mile and several in length, with the water up to the skirts of the saddle, and so far in the river that I could not be discovered from the shore on that dark night; thus I proceeded for near ten miles up the river,

river, and thereby avoided the centinels and guards they had placed at every avenue leading to my houfe.

In the morning they were in fuch rage at miffing me, when they imagined they had me quite fecure, that they deftroyed above an hundred barrels of Indian corn, fhot two of my horfes in the plough, and beat all my people. It was the more inconvenient and diftreffing upon me at this time, as I had fold five hundred bufhels of corn to a Bermudian, whofe veffel was then at my landing receiving it, and I was forced, having no overfeer that year, to leave him and my fervants and negroes to do with it juft as they pleafed.

I had at this time a very large crop of wheat, having fowed about three hundred and fifty acres, befides an exceeding fine crop of Indian corn and tobacco, all of which were neglected, by my being continually harraffed and purfued by thefe ruffians; for I was determined not to be taken.

At

At this period alſo I was declared inimical to the Americans, and on that account was reſtricted from bringing any action, or even recovering the debts for which I had before this obtained judgments in court, and was obliged inſtantly to repay the money I had formerly received in part of payment of the debts that were due to me; as any perſons that pleaſed might bring actions againſt me, but I was prevented at the ſame time from commencing ſuits againſt any one.

That morning I reached Piſcataway, thirty miles diſtant, to breakfaſt, where an Iriſhman named Johnſon, a deſerter from the fourteenth regiment of foot, was exerciſing a company of gentlemen rebels all in ſcarlet. Here likewiſe I ſoon found myſelf in danger, and on that account went over to Alexandria.

This fine town, formerly named Belhaven, is ſituated on the Virginia ſide of the Potomack, upon the banks of this noble river which are here remarkably high and commanding.

Alexandria

Alexandria is delightfully situated in a most healthy and beautiful spot, is now the first, and before the destruction of Norfolk was the third, perhaps the second, town in Virginia for magnitude, opulence, trade, and elegance.

There are some good buildings in Alexandria, and excellent warehouses and wharfs. Besides a great many ships for Europe, the West Indies, and other places, several vessels sailed from this port annually for New Orleans with flour, which, as well as wheat, is the staple of this part of the country.

Ships as well as smaller vessels are built here; the town is in a most flourishing state, and it is in reality a very pleasant and agreeable place.

It may contain perhaps four or five thousand inhabitants; but, like every other town in America, this has also decreased since the general revolt.

The site of Alexandria is particularly strong and commanding, and better calculated

culated for a place of arms than any other town in Virginia or Maryland; being capable of receiving additional ſtrength from every exertion of judicious labour and expence; the ground on which the town is built being conſiderably higher than any in the adjacent country; the ſoil ſtiff, heavy, and well adapted for fortifications; the water of the river, which is here near two miles wide, being quite freſh and ſweet, as it continues for ſeventy miles below; and the whole country around producing the fineſt wheat, flour, and proviſions. The river is perfectly commanded by the banks, which are exceedingly high; and the water is ſo deep that the largeſt ſhip of the line could lay her broadſide to the wharfs.

This ſituation is the more uncommon, as almoſt all the towns in America are built on low grounds, at the falls of the rivers, for the convenience of water-carriage alone, without regard to ſtrength, beauty, or healthfulneſs, all of which

this

this fine town can boaſt of in an eminent degree.

About eight miles above Alexandria, oppoſite to George Town, are very valuable mills; and there are likewiſe ſeveral others very excellent in this vicinity, both above and below.

CHAP.

CHAP. LXII.

Alexandria. The Place where General Washington first began to countenance the general Revolt of the Colonies. A Loyalist tarred and feathered. Patuxent River. Benedict Town. Lower Marlborough. Upper Marlborough. Queen Anne. London Town. Annapolis. Severn River. A Hurricane. Baltimore. Patapsco River. Elk Ridge. Examined by the Committee. My Servant tarred, feathered, and killed. Obliged to fly for Safety. Travel an hundred and ten Miles on Foot in two Days. Nottingham. Exhausted and overcome with Fatigue. In extreme Pain. Taken very ill. Dangerous Situations. Betrayed by a false Friend. Taken by the Rebels. Rescued. Most perilous Escape.

IT was at Alexandria where George Washington first stept forth as the public patron and leader of sedition and revolt, having subscribed fifty pounds to these purposes when others subscribed only five, and having accepted the command of the first company of armed associators against British government, which he had clothed in his old uniform of the Virginia regiment last war, viz. blue and buff;

buff, a dress he has continued to wear until this time; and being likewise the first encourager of desertion from the British army, by publicly abetting and advising it, and promoting a large subscription to this Johnson already mentioned, a deserter from the fourteenth regiment, for the purpose of teaching the inhabitants tactics and military exercises.

Although there were a number of gentlemen of loyal principles in this place with whom I was very well acquainted, yet I could not associate with them, nor could we even converse together only with the utmost caution and privacy, lest I should be discovered, and we all should fall victims to the lawless intemperance and barbarity of an ignorant frantic mob.

I soon found that all my precautions to remain here undiscovered were fruitless, and the first intimation I had of this was from Colonel George Mason while at dinner, who desired me to take particular notice of an unfortunate loyalist, tarred and

and feathered by the mob, who were that inftant carrying him along as a public fpectacle, emphatically obferving *that it nearly concerned me.*

In the evening the deferter Johnfon (one of the moft complete fcoundrels in exiftence, and now a colonel in the American army,) endeavoured to caufe me likewife to be tarred and feathered, as an enemy to American licentioufnefs, but the gentlemen of moderation prevented it, by protecting me for that time, and turned the fellow out of the houfe with difgrace.

I had come up here for quietnefs, hopeful to be able to remain unnoticed until the ftorm at home fhould fubfide, but finding myfelf equally in danger every where; I gave up the idea of meeting with an afylum in any place, and fet out again privately for my own houfe that fame night, refolved not to ftir from thence, but to defend myfelf in it to the laft extremity.

I for-

I fortunately paffed fafe through Pifcattaway, and Port Tobacco; at both which places parties were waiting to feize on me as I returned, for they had notice from Alexandria of my being there.

I had fcarcely arrived at home when two gentlemen, perfonally my warm and fincere friends, came to me in private, and earneftly entreated that I would affect to comply with the meafures of the Congrefs, and pretend to join them if it was only in appearance; telling me it was nothing fhort of madnefs for me alone to refift, and the confequence would be that I muft be facrificed, and my whole property feized or deftroyed. My anfwer was, That as I had never countenanced them in the fmalleft degree, I would not now have the infamy upon me upon any account of joining them, although in appearance only; that ever fince the time I found myfelf overpowered I had no longer made any oppofition to them ; that I concerned not with them, and never vifited
them

them nor their meetings; but as I did not acknowledge their authority, I was determined not to put myself in their power, which I would sooner part with life than submit to; and that this was my final resolution, from which I would never depart.'

Upon this they left me in sorrow, saying that possibly they might never see me more.

Then they went to the president, who was once my intimate friend, and informed him of my determination. He, being very sensible that I would abide by my declarations to those gentlemen, connived at affording me some little respite; and for two months I was not so openly harrassed; but however they endeavoured to distress and surprise me unprepared.

For which purpose, during harvest, they frequently inveigled away my negroes, in order to obtain a favourable opportunity of taking me when I was searching after them. But in this stratagem they also failed.

Indeed

Indeed my preservation and safety during all this time, was chiefly owing to an opinion they had formed of my being poſſeſſed of a deſperate courage and reſolution.

I had purchaſed a large quantity of Indian corn, wheat, and flour, for which I had alſo paid half the purchaſe money, and freighted a brigantine, when the proprietor diſpoſed of her to a purchaſer: I then found it impracticable to freight any other veſſel before the time that exportation was prohibited, ſo that I loſt the whole of this by its remaining on my hands.

That year I made on my plantation between five and ſix thouſand buſhels of wheat, which coſt me above three hundred pounds in gold to cut down and ſecure, of this I was able to get only one thouſand buſhels ready for market by September, on the tenth day of which exportation terminated, and ſhipped them on board two ſmall veſſels bound for Baltimore; one of theſe veſſels was loſt in a ſtorm, and the other five hundred bushels I was compelled to dispose of for only one shilling and six pence per bushel.

I went up to Baltimore myself, by the way of a small town named Benedict, upon the south side of the river Patuxent.

This is a very pretty river about two miles wide, and the town is in a beautiful situation, containing about sixty houses.

There is no great trade at Benedict, and what there is consists chiefly of tobacco, of what is termed the bright species, which is the most valuable of any, and is produced upon light and sandy, but rich soil, being peculiar to the planters on the Patuxent, whose land is generally of that quality.

The inhabitants of this town are very violent in their disaffected principles, and I certainly should not have approached it, (for it was considerably out of my way), had it not been to recover a servant who had been enticed away from me to that place, where I found him, being juſt twenty-four miles from my houſe.

After ordering my ſervant home, I proceeded up the ſide of the Patuxent for Lower Marlborough, a little town, on the north ſide of the river, not ſo large as Benedict, and ſcarcely worth notice.

Here I joined company with a gentleman named Buchannan, a conſiderable merchant and ſhip-builder at Baltimore, and travelled with him through Pigpoint, and another town named Upper Marlborough, ſomething larger than the former, upon this river alſo, but of very little conſequence; from thence we paſſed through a ſtill more inſignificant town, named Queen Anne; and croſſing South River at another little town called New London, we arrived at night at Annapolis, from which the laſt place is only four miles diſtant.

The whole day was ſtormy, wet, and diſagreeable, but at night there was the moſt dreadful hurricane ever remembered to have happened in this part of America.

The shocking accidents, and strange effects, occasioned by this most violent gust, or tornado, it would be endless to enumerate; I shall therefore only observe, that the province house of Maryland, an elegant public building, just finished and covered with copper, had the whole roof laid bare, the sheets of copper being rolled up like scrolls of parchment.

We left Annapolis early in the morning, and found the roads rendered almost impassable by this dreadful storm.

We dined at a pretty town named Elkridge, situated at the falls of the southern branch of the Patapsco River, which we crossed, and arrived at Baltimore.

This route is by no means the nearest, or direct road to Baltimore; but Mr. Buchannan having business at these places, I went with him for the sake of company.

The town of Baltimore is built on a declivity in the form of a crescent, on the north side of a large bason, or rather bay, the water whereof is not deep enough

nough for vessels of any considerable burden.

The harbour of Baltimore is named Fell's Point, about two miles from the town itself, although the houses are now continued almost all the way. Here is water sufficient for the largest ships to lay their broadsides to the wharfs.

Almost immediately after my arrival in Baltimore I had the misfortune to be seized with a violent dysentery and was extremely ill.

But in the mean time the committee deputed three of their members, named Tolly, Colquhoon, and Levi a Jew, to inspect my papers, letters, and baggage; and it required no small share of address and precaution to get clear.

Next day the mob tarred and feathered my servant, and treated him with such barbarity that his death ensued in consequence.

I was incensed in the highest degree at this shocking instance of brutality, and having applied to a very worthy respectable magistrate, viz. Doctor Stephenson, senior, I obtained warrants; and by a bold and vigorous exertion of resolution seized on the ringleaders and securely lodged them in the common prison.

However they were released by the mob on the day following, and I was obliged to secrete myself notwithstanding my debilitated and wretched state of health; for I only held the dysentery under by taking great quantities of laudanum every half hour, which alone enabled me to keep out of bed.

In this dangerous and most distressed condition, a worthy friend, Jonathan Plowman, Esq. privately afforded me every comfort and assistance, although at the greatest risque to himself had it been discovered.

To enable me to escape with safety I concluded to leave my horses at the inn, and engaged a vessel to carry me round by water to my own house.

After I went on board, and the vessel was about two miles out from the shore, the she was quite becalmed and could not proceed; in this state we remained for twenty-four hours; the whole time in sight of the town, every boat from which alarmed me extremely, apprehensive that they might have received information of my being in the vessel, and were sending to seize upon me.

This state of anxious suspense and alarm I resolved to abandon, and after paying the master of the vessel his full freight, ordered him to land me early next morning just above the town; and I set out on foot for my own house, in as painful and weak a state as ever a man was that attempted to walk any distance, being reduced almost to the verge of death by this violent dysentery which continually afflicted me.

The distance I had to march was an hundred and ten miles, and the weather was extremely hot and sultry; but what will not a man undertake when life is in danger?

I set

I set out with a spirit and resolution very uncommon to a person in my enfeebled and sickly condition; however it was this spirit and resolution alone that supported me, my strength of body being quite exhausted.

In this journey I selected the most private and retired ways, crossing the Patuxent just by Nottingham, a small and very pleasant town upon the south side of the Patuxent river, eight or ten miles below Pig Point.

Here I rested for half an hour, and refreshed myself with a little wine and water, having taken no kind of nourishment before all the day; at night I slept at a house in the forest of Patuxent, having travelled this day fifty-five miles; but I was so extremely fatigued and overcome with this extraordinary exertion, that the violent pains through all my limbs, occasioned thereby, prevented me from getting but a very small share of repose.

I arose

I arose in the morning ſtiff, ſore, and very little refreſhed, and purſued my journey; dined at Allan's Freſh, and reached my own houſe in the afternoon; having travelled this day alſo fifty-five miles.

But I was taken ſo very ill, in an hour or two after my arrival, and was ſeized with ſuch extreme pains in all my limbs, that the excruciating torture occaſioned by this too arduous effort, could not be endured: and I was obliged to be put in a hot bath, and all my limbs conſtantly rubbed, that night, for three hours, before I obtained the leaſt reſt, or relaxation from pain.

My health and conſtitution received a ſhock from this which it never afterwards recovered; and on the ſecond day after my return, I was again ſeized with the moſt extreme pains, throughout my whole body, which nothing could remove nor allay, but copious bleeding and large doſes of laudanum. This I was conſtantly obliged

obliged to make use of, and repeat every two or three days, as the pains returned as often.

Having concluded to leave this part of America in October, and to remove to the Mississippi by land, on accouut of these troubles; and this being reported to the Council of Safety, they, apprehensive that I would prompt the Indian nations, through which I must necessarily pass, to make war upon and do the Congress every ill office, sent orders for me not to leave the province.

Soon after my return from Baltimore, one of my people, some of whom I was under the necessity of keeping as sentries day and night about a mile from my house, came running with information, that forty armed men were advancing to seize upon me, I desired him to go back, and acquaint them from me, that I would not suffer them to come near the house, for if they attempted it I would certainly fire upon them, let the consequence be

what

what it would. Their principal officer then sent me word that he and six men only would come up; requesting me not to fire, as he was far from wishing to hurt me, being only in execution of his orders.

I had three firelocks, three pair of pistols, all loaded, plenty of cartridges on the table, and two trusty servants. I stood in the door, and when they came within sixty yards called to them to stop, declaring if they advanced ten steps farther I would certainly fire upon them; the officer upon this ordered his men to halt, and as I consented for him to come up himself, he advanced alone.

He also was formerly a particular friend of mine, and now made use of every argument and persuasion to induce me to join them, informing me, that it was judged extremely improper to suffer such a public example of attachment to Great Britain as myself to be at large, either in the county or province; and that his orders were to bring me, by force, before the Council of Safety. But finding me fully determined

mined to lose my life rather than be taken, he said that my blood should not lie upon his head, some other person must execute their orders, and went away.

After this, being obliged to go into St. Mary's County, I fell into a snare laid for me, by shewing my arms to a person in whom I confided as a friend. Immediately he and twelve others fell upon me naked and defenceless, run me through the thigh with a sword, made me prisoner, and carried me thirty-six miles.

As we went along I met a Scots gentleman, Mr. M'Pherson, and several other loyalists, by whose assistance I recovered my liberty, my horse, and my arms; and parting from them returned home next night with inconceivable pain and difficulty.

On my way, being alone, two violent rebels laid in ambush to seize on me, thinking me quite disabled and my pistols empty, but finding that I had got them loaded again, they rode off with precipitation.

Before

Before I was taken I had fought againſt them all until I was dangerouſly wounded, and ſcarcely able to ſtand with loſs of blood; and in returning was under the neceſſity of paſſing through two places where two Captains and their companies laid in wait for me, but by travelling in a very dark ſtormy night, through bye-ways, among ſeveral dangerous precipices, and deep ravines, in ſome of which my horſe fell with me ſeveral times ſix or eight feet perpendicular, with many wounds and contuſions I eſcaped theſe ambuſcades, and reached home, but in a condition ſo wretched and miſerable, that I had almoſt died, not being able to leave my bed, and being in a continued agony of excruciating pain, during ſeveral weeks afterwards.

In that time a party came to take me away, but I was ſo very ill that they could not remove me, being covered with wounds, beſides that through my thigh which was extremely dangerous, unable to ſtir, and alſo being quite delirious with a raging fever, which then proved my preſervation.

Before

(Before I was half recovered from this illness, and before my wound was near healed, a gentleman came to inform me, that a captain with forty men intended to carry me to the Council of Safety as soon as I was able to be removed; and that their determination was to make use of force against me if they found it necessary.

On the night following, they carried away two of my servants for drummers, and hearing of them I went fifty miles after them in great pain, found them in a muster-field, and was bringing them home, when ten rebels, rushing suddenly upon me, deprived me of my arms, both servants, besides the servant that attended me, and two very fine English mares; and detained me until midnight, when I effected my escape, and with difficulty reached home.

Some nights afterwards they inveigled three more of my negroes from me; pursuing them next day, I found them, and was bringing them back, when I difcovered thirty of the rebels after me, fo was obliged to abandon my negroes to preferve my own liberty.

In fhort I found that if I ftaid among them much longer, it would be impoffible to avoid falling into their hands.

CHAP.

CHAP. LXIII.

Set out for the Miſſiſſippi. In a miſerable State of Health. Port Royal. Character of the Inhabitants. Anecdote of an unfortunate young Gentleman. Arrive at Blandford. Royal Standard erected at Norfolk. Repair to it. Seized upon at Surry Court Houſe. Eſcape. Sleepy Hole on Nanſemond River. Arrive at Portſmouth. Wait on the Earl of Dunmore. Informed againſt as a Spy. Leave Portſmouth. Suffolk. Overtake my People, &c. at Maherren. Taken Priſoner. Eſcape. Set out again for Norfolk. Country alarmed. Take Refuge in the Great Diſmal Swamp. A deſcription of it. Dreadful Conflagration. Aſtoniſhing Difficulteis. Arrive again ai Portſmouth. Suſpected again for a Spy. Servant carried on Board the Governor's Ship by a Guard. Servant examined and acquitted.

I Had made every preparation for my departure to the Miſſiſſippi, notwithſtanding their edict againſt it, had written, and ſent all my letters privately to Great Britain, deſiring my friends and correſpondents there to tranſmit their letters no more by the packet nor through thoſe revolted

volted colonies left they should fall into the hands of the Rebels, but to send them immediately to the Mississippi or Pensacola. And on the night of the fifteenth of October, in the year seventeen hundred and seventy-five, being informed that a great force was coming next morning determined to seize upon me, I privately crossed the Potomack in boats that I had secretly engaged for that purpose for some time before.

I carried along with me five servants well armed, besides a very considerable property; and notwithstanding this hazardous enterprize was still very sick, weak and emaciated, being by no means perfectly recovered of my wounds.

I travelled over the Northern Neck of Virginia, crossed the Rappahannock at Port Royal, where I arrived to breakfast, and having great need of rest and refreshment staid to dine there also.

Port Royal is a very pretty little town, on the south side of the Rappahannock which is here about seven hundred yards wide. It may contain eighty or perhaps an hundred houses, all of which are very pleasantly situated; but it has no great share of trade, and the inhabitants are remarkable for surliness and disagreements among themselves, which gave occasion to a merry facetious wag making the following observation, ' That he verily believed, that if only one person lived in Port Royal, he would quarrel with himself.'

A remarkable and affecting event happened in this town, singular indeed in America. A young gentleman became so lost in love with a very young lady, that understanding she was willing to marry another person in compliance with the commands of her mother, although he was sensible the young lady gave the preference to himself, he with the greatest deliberation secrecy and resolution swallowed such a quantity of opium that it ended his days; and on the same night that he took the fatal drug he died in great agonies.

I travelled about fifteen miles beyond Port Royal that evening, and next day was taken so extremely ill as to be unable to proceed. But my usual remedy, of being copiously blooded and taking large doses

doses of laudanum, enabled me again to pursue my journey, after being detained here for a whole day.

My state of health was so bad that this was my painful and unfortunate condition, thus repeated every other day, until I arrived at Blandford, upon the river Appamattox in Virginia.

At this time the Royal Standard being erected at Norfolk by the Earl of Dunmore, his Majesty's Governor, I thought it my duty to repair thither, which was about an hundred and thirty or forty miles distant, not only to make a tender of my weak services, but having heard his Lordship's life frequently threatened as I came along, and several plans laid to murder him privately, I was really concerned for his safety, and apprehensive that he might fall a victim by these ruffians and assassins, and for that reason went likewise to acquaint him of the danger.

Accordingly I sent my servants, horses, and baggage on before towards Carolina, and set out alone for Norfolk. It happened,

pened, that on that very day a rebel edict was published, ordering every person, travelling towards Norfolk, to be stopped, and carried to the rebel commander Patrick Henry, at Williamsburg.

At Surrey court-house I was seized on by a very dirty crew, who proposed carrying me prisoner to Williamsburg; but, plying them well with punch, I suddenly stepped aside, mounted my horse, and left them in full speed, whilst eight or ten of them were firing after me.

Twelve or fifteen miles from thence I fell in company with a rebel pay-master, and a commissary, named Wells Cooper who lived in Suffolk, and Solomon Shepherd, whose house is beyond Sleepy Hole on Nansemond River. These gentlemen I completely deceived, and in company with them passed safe, though not unmolested, through that infernal place Smithfield, as well as several places besides, where the inhabitants were very violent, otherwise I could not possibly have got down; for every half dozen fellows we met,
wanted

wanted me to give an account of myself, and proposed to carry me to Henry at Williamsburg; but these gentlemen always prevented them.

Mr. Shepherd, who was really very kind to me, accompanied me farthest on my journey, his house being within twelve or fifteen miles of Portsmouth.

As soon as I arrived at Norfolk, or rather Portsmouth, for it was there I staid, I waited upon his Excellency the Earl of Dunmore, on board an armed ship named the William, where I likewise conversed for a considerable time with Lieutenant-Colonel Connolly. I then acquainted his Lordship with my designs, and he observed that I would certainly find it impossible to pass along through the country, in its present distracted state, to the Mississippi. I also mentioned to his Lordship my apprehensions of his personal danger, but he seemed to pay little regard to his own safety.

I did not stay above an hour on board the William, and informed no person at
all

all of any thing, but his Lordship himself, on account of the hazard and danger I had to encounter in returning through the country in order to overtake my servants and proceed on my journey.)

My silence was suspected, and my being a perfect stranger induced two meddling worthless fellows to go on board the Governor's ship in the night to inform him that I was certainly a spy from the rebels, to which piece of intelligence his Lordship however paid no regard.

In the morning I waited again on his Excellency to take my leave, and set out from Portsmouth with a heavy dejection on my spirits at the disagreeable reflection of the danger of returning and perhaps falling into the power of a set of the veryest wretches, and most infamous ruffians in existence. I was also in pain for his Lordship's personal safety, on account of his easiness of access.

That night I lodged at Suffolk, and on the day following two men were sent from thence seven miles after me to bring me back

back to the Committee there: but by presenting a piftol at thefe fellows I quickly fent them away prodigioufly frightened.

With great difficulty I proceeded as far as Edward's Tavern, on Maherren River, in the county of Brunfwick, where I overtook my fervants, &c. but was fuddenly furprifed and feized on by a ftrong party of rebels, in confequence of one of my fervants (an Irifh fellow) having given information that I had been at Norfolk with the Earl of Dunmore.

Llewellin, Hopwell, and Stanton, the ruffians who commanded, treated me with illiberal infult and barbarity, (plundering me of my horfes, flaves, baggage, arms, and about three hundred and fifty piftoles in gold, befides a large quantity of filver in dollars; my Irifh fervant left me, and enlifted with them; but another, a Scotfman, remained faithful to the laft.

Moft fortunately for me two Scots gentlemen coming that way called, and in the night, by their very kind affiftance, I effected my efcape from this party, with my my Scots servant, three of my horses, and a considerable value besides.

These two worthy friends met me that same night eighteen miles from thence in North Carolina, and directed me the way to proceed to Norfolk.

Searching amongst the baggage which my servant had recovered I found arms and ammunition, which I now considered as one of the most estimable acquisitions.

My former journey and intentions being now entirely frustrated, I set out for Norfolk again next morning, with a very heavy and dejected heart, and in a condition so sick and feeble, and in so bad a state of health with the excruciating pains to which I was so subject, as to be obliged to be blooded and lay by every second day for some time.

For secrecy, and to avoid pursuit, I travelled on the North Carolina side of the boundary line, the inhabitants on that side not being very violent, and with the greatest difficulty and fatigue proceeded on

until

until I arrived within fifty or sixty miles of Norfolk.

Being quite exhausted with hunger and hardships, I was thereby constrained to call at the house of one Copland a Quaker for some refreshment, and to prevent suspicion I caused my servant to sit down at table along with me.

I did not tarry here an hour; and when I had travelled about nine miles farther my horses tired, and I remained that night and the day following at the house of a warm planter named John Harris, a very old man and a good friend of government.

On the second night I was alarmed by a Negro, and soon afterwards by a white man a relation of Mr. Harris, who informed me that friend Copland's wife head had imagined that I was Governor Martin, of North Carolina, travelling in disguise to Lord Dunmore at Norfolk; that this booby had raised the alarm throughout the country, and that in consequence of it three companies of militia
were

were in pursuit of me; that they had proceeded in search of me as far as Suffolk, and were now returning beating up the whole country as they passed; and that understanding I was well armed, they intended to shoot me down on sight.

Finding by means of several other friends to government that this intelligence was well founded, I gave the Negro two dollars to carry me immediately into a private place in the *Great Dismal* Swamp, where I lay hid during the day, and travelled every night.

This *Great Dismal* is the principal of all those dreadful places, called swamps, only to be met with in America, for there is nothing of the kind to be found in all Europe, Asia, or Africa.

It is in form of a vast oval, thirty miles in breadth, and fifty in length, with a lake, nearly in the center, seven miles diameter, abounding with fish.

From this lake there is no outlet or running water to any other place; nor can there be said to be any descent throughout

out all this immense fwamp, excepting a little without its outer circumference; all within being in a manner entirely covered with water out of which innumerable quantities of large ftraight and lofty cyprefs-trees are growing in almoft impenetrable clofenefs to each other throughout the whole extent; betwixt thefe trees infinite numbers of that ftrange production cyprefs knees arife above the water from three to fifteen inches, almoft as clofe as they can ftand together)

Throughout the whole of this truly *difmal* place, there is fcarcely the leaft appearance of any kind of foil; for even where there is no water nothing can be difcovered but cyprefs knees, clofely intermixed with a matted body of ftrong fibrous roots vines and vegetative productions every where, in a dark and dreary fhade altogether impervious to the rays of the fun. The trees, &c. growing fo clofe thick and lofty, that one perfon will lofe another therein, at ten yards diftance; and afterwards if they wander a few hundred yards asunder,

asunder, no noise, clamour, or hallooing, from either of them, can be heard by the other; for the woods are so close as to prevent the vibration of the air for any distance through them; even the report of fire-arms is smothered.

The only way of hearing any sound, for the least distance, is by laying one's ear close to the ground, by which means one can hear six times as far as any other way.

There is a kind of ridges, running throughout this swamp, from fifty yards to a quarter of a mile and upwards over, and one, two, four, and sometimes six miles asunder.

These ridges are without water, although no earth or soil can be seen, but all between them is covered with water from two to five and six feet deep.

On these ridges are astonishing numbers of bears, wolves, panthers, wild cats, oppossums, racoons, snakes, some deer, and every kind of wild beasts; between them
are

are vaſt numbers of otters, muſk'rats, beavers, and all kinds of amphibious animals.

In very dry ſummers ſome of theſe ridges have been accidentally ſet on fire, and cauſed moſt dreadful conflagrations the flames conſuming all before them, burning into the earth for a vaſt depth, and over-ſpreading the whole country around with thick ſmoke.

Theſe places are ſoon afterwards filled with water, and become ſmall lakes.

There was one fire in the *Great Diſmal* particularly horrid and tremendous. It happened on an extraordinary dry ſummer, and burnt with irreſiſtible fury for many weeks, ſpreading terror and deſtruction around.

The wild beaſts were ſo frightened, that prodigious numbers of them of all kinds forſook the ſwamp, overrunning the plantations for many miles diſtance, and the whole country was perpetually enveloped in thick ſmoke, during many weeks, for ninety miles around.

The

The effects of this horrible conflagration formed a lake, a mile and a half in breadth, and above three miles long, from four to eight, ten, and even twelve feet deep.

It is imagined that the great lake in the center was formed by fome former dreadful conflagration far beyond human memory; as burnt wood is frequently found in the bottom of it, even near the middle, and in the deepeſt places throughout.

This ſwamp belongs to a company of proprietors, who have begun to render it of advantage and profit to them. They commenced with getting lumber, cypreſs ſhingles, and boards, and with incredible labour they have now formed ſeveral plantations therein, which produce immenſe crops of Indian corn.

They have alſo cut a navigable canal, nine miles in length, from the great lake, for the conveyance of their lumber and produce, as near to the edge of the great ſwamp

swamp as poffible, and they have formed a caufeway of timber, as a road through it, from the end of the canal.

The land all around it is fomewhat higher than it is within it, and is flat, fandy, wet, and barren.

This is a fafe harbour and place of perfect fecurity for all kinds of wild beafts, as well as ftray horfes, cattle, hogs, and runaway Negroes many of whom live here to be old without the leaft danger of being difcovered.

This place is alfo called the *Great Defert*, on account of its being deftitute of human inhabitants, and being the general afylum for every thing that flies from mankind and fociety.

On the fecond night after the above mentioned alarm I had three rebel guards to pafs, who were pofted, to prevent any communication with Norfolk, at paffes through which every perfon that went towards that place were obliged to go.

The firft, at Meads Mill near Suffolk, I avoided, by fwimming the creek below.

The

The second, just by Nansemond Church, I passed without the least noise, and fortunately unnoticed, although I heard the centinels challenge in half a minute after I had passed them.

And the third guard, at Smith's Tavern, I also got past by moving on slowly in perfect silence; and afterwards by pushing briskly forward arrived at Portsmouth before day-break; with a heart and spirits now light and chearful, although almost exhausted with hunger and fatigue. Happy however, beyond expression, to be out of the power of the rebel banditti, although at the expence of the greatest part of all I had in the world.

On the day following, being excessively fatigued, I did not immediately wait upon his Excellency the Earl of Dunmore, intending to perform that duty as soon as I was a little refreshed.

But that same afternoon Captain Squire, of his Majesty's sloop Otter, threatened to carry me as a prisoner on board his ship, as a spy from the rebels, partly
upon

upon the former ridiculous suspicions against me when I was here before, but chiefly because I did not wait on him immediately upon my arrival. And at the same time a guard was sent by the governor to bring me and my servant before him, on another information of the same kind against me, by a certain fellow from mere pique and malevolence, because I would not suffer the assuming, ignorant wretch to brow-beat, bully, and insult me.

I was at this time along with Lieutenant-Colonel Connolly, who lodged in the same house, and with whom I had passed the greatest part of the day, when the guard came to the door, of whose orders or intentions I had not the most distant idea, nor did I know then of any of these suspicions or informations against me.

The guard indeed did not meddle with me, (in consequence I presume of secret orders from his Excellency, who never gave any credit to these insinuations, but acted thus at the pressing instance of the forward assuming fellow whom I have just mentioned), but they carried my servant on board before his lordship for examination, when this vile caitiff being present endeavoured to intimidate him, in order to induce him to bring some accusation against me; but his Excellency himself soon put a stop to such scandalous attempts. However, a gentleman, who had been also along with Colonel Connolly, waited upon his lordship with a letter from the Colonel, assuring his Excellency that the information against me was totally false and groundless, which the examination of my servant likewise evinced in the fullest and most satisfactory manner.

CHAP.

CHAP. LXIV.

Embark on an Expedition to the Back Country. Proceed up the Potomack. Pass through Maryland. Frederick Town, a Description of it. Funks Town. Taken Prisoners. Hagar's Town. Great Valley. Connigocheague. Extremely abused and maltreated. Robbed of our Money. Nature of the Expedition. A curious Manner of secreting Papers. Confined and in great Danger at Frederick Town. Escape. Fall through the Ice into the Potomack. Astonishing Dangers and Fatigue. Fly into the Mountains. Deep Snow. Break the Ice and wade deep Rivers. Wounded and Lame. Robbed by a Man that I had placed Confidence in. Continue to push forward for Detroit and Illinois. Fort Cumberland. Romantic Situation. Cross the Allegany Mountains. Retaken by mere Accident on the Yohiogeny River.

AFTER these groundless and most ridiculous suspicions were happily cleared up, the whole intention and substance of a secret expedition to the back country, under the command of Lieutenant-Colonel Connolly, then appointed Commandant of the Queen's royal regiment of Rangers, was difclofed to me, and I was earneftly folicited by the Colonel to accompany him, along with another gentleman named Cameron; to this I moft chearfully confented, and in the above regiment we all received our commiffions.

On the day following I received an order to take any veffel in the harbour, and alfo fuch of the pilots on board his Majefty's floop the Otter as I judged proper, for the ufe of this expedition.

This circumftance was no fmall fatisfaction to me, as I thereby convinced Captain Squire of my being no fpy, as he had alledged; and on going on board his fhip made choice of two of his beft pilots.

When we departed from Norfolk on this expedition, I was obliged to leave behind me my fervant and all the property I 'had been able to bring down there. My fervant and horfes, which were valuable, were to be fent to the plantation of Mr. Atchifon, at lord Dunmore's requeft; and the reft of my property

perty I left in the houfe of a Mr. Pierce at Portfmouth, but I have never fince that time heard the leaft account of any thing belonging to me.

We embarked on board a flat-bottomed decked fchooner, which I had engaged for that purpofe, with our horfes, and only one fervant who belonged to the Colonel.

Our fmall party confifted of Lieutenant-Colonel Connolly, Mr. Cameron, myfelf, and the fervant; and we intended to proceed in this veffel up the Chefapeak, into Potomack River, and land if poffible near to my houfe or Port Tobacco Creek, and afterwards to pafs through the country on horfeback until we arrived at Detroit in Canada.

It was propofed that I fhould pafs through Pittfburg, with difpatches to Mr. M'Kie the Indian fuperintendant, and to fome other friends of government, then proceed down the river Ohio to the mouth of the Siotto, and from thence up that river, through the Shawnefe, Delawares, and Wiandotts, and down Sandufki River to Sandufki Old Fort, from thence I was to crofs lake Erie, by the Rattle Snake Iflands, to Detroit. While the other two gentlemen were to crofs the Allegany River at the Kittanning, and proceed by the neareft and moft direct route to Detroit. Here a very confiderable force was to be collected from all the neareft pofts in Canada, and tranfported, early in the fpring, acrofs the lake Erie to Prefquifle, where I was to be employed during the winter with a detachment of two hundred men in covering and conducting the building batteaux, and collecting provifions, in order to proceed by the way of French Creek, Venango, and the Allegany River, to Pittfburg, which we were to feize on and eftablifh as head-quarters, until the difaffected intereft was entirely crufhed, and the whole ftrength of the country collected and formed into regular difciplined regiments.

After leaving a fufficient garrifon at Pittfburg, we were to advance acrofs the

Allegany Mountains with our whole force upon the back of Virginia; and after establishing a strong post at Fort Cumberland, it was proposed to fall down the river Potomack, and seize on Alexandria, where the Earl of Dunmore was to meet us with the fleet, and all the force of the lower part of the province. Alexandria was to be strongly fortified, as a place of arms, and the communication between the southern and northern parts of the continent thereby cut off.

If a misfortune, of such magnitude, should have happened, as to oblige us to give up this enterprize at any particular stage thereof, our retreat was then secured by these posts which we occupied in our rear; and if it should have failed in the first part of the expedition, by our finding it impracticable to seize upon Pittsburg, we were to fall down the Ohio in our batteaux to the Mississippi; where we were to be joined by the garrison, artillery, and stores from Fort Gage of Kiskuskias at the Illonois; and then to proceed

ceed down to the mouth of the river Miffiffippi in Weft Florida; where we were to embark in tranfports, and come round to Norfolk in Virginia, there to join the Earl of Dunmore.

For the execution of this well formed, judicious, and vaft undertaking, Lieutenant-Colonel Connolly was furnifhed with the proper and neceffary powers, both from General Gage the Commander in Chief, and from the Earl of Dunmore, and with ample inftructions for his future conduct, as well as commiffions for the formation of a complete regiment at Detroit, or Pittfburg; all of which, containing no lefs than eighteen fheets of paper, we carried along with us in a fecret manner invented by and executed under the infpection of his lordfhip.

All thefe papers were concealed in the mail pillion-fticks on which the fervant carried his portmanteau, they being made hollow, for that purpofe, and covered with tin plates, and then canvafs glued thereon as ufual; this was fo dextroufly and com-

completely executed that it could not be difcovered on the ftricteft examination.

We failed up the Potomack, almoft as far as Lower Cedar Point, when a moft violent gale came on from the north-weft, which obliged us to ftand down the river again, and run up into St. Mary's River in Maryland, where we landed on the twelfth of November, without occafioning the leaft fufpicion, having fent off the veffel again immediately after we had taken out our horfes.

Here I undertook to be the conductor through the country for above two hundred miles; and it was not without the utmoft addrefs, precaution, difficulty and danger that I carried them, and paffed myfelf quite fafe and unfufpected, through all that extent of thick fettled country, wherein my perfon and principles were fo well known, and without being once difcovered myfelf.

However we were frequently very much alarmed, particularly at Frederick Town, where we arrived on the evening
of

of a general muster, or field-day of the armed affociators. At the inn where we put up, each of us calling for fomething different from the others, caufed an enquiry, and of courfe a fufpicion concerning us, and it was propofed to bring us before the committee in the morning for examination. This plan we accidentally difconcerted by fetting out from Frederick Town in the morning at day-break; and as the committee had all got intoxicated over night, it was too late next day, before they arofe, and recollected any circumftances concerning us, to fend in purfuit after us.

We paffed through a village named Middle Town, about eight miles beyond Frederick; and in the South Mountain, four miles farther, we took the wrong road, which led us to another village named Funk's Town, after Jacob Funk a German, the proprietor.

We dined in this place, and paffed on through a confiderable town called Hagar's Town, named fo alfo after the

pro-

proprietor, a German; a few miles beyond which we unfortunately met a little man, a hatter, who knew Colonel Connolly at Pittſburg, where he had lived, and now recollected him again, and ſpoke to him.

This accident giving me great uneaſineſs, I mentioned to the Colonel my apprehenſions of our being diſcovered thereby, and propoſed for us to change our route. But he being of a different opinion, and thinking there was no danger, it gave me inexpreſſible concern, and had it not been for two reaſons which prevented me, I would then have left him and provided for my own ſafety.

The firſt was, that being under his command I could not diſobey; but of that I was ſenſible he had too much generoſity to take advantage, therefore it was not this that deterred me.

The ſecond reaſon was, the former ridiculous ſuſpicions againſt me at Norfolk; and it was on that account I determined

termined to stand or fall with him, and to wait the event with patience, should captivity, or even death be the consequence.

We lodged at one Doctor Snayvelley's, a German, about five or six miles beyond Hagar's Town, upon the banks of the river Connegocheague, and accordingly as I had dreaded, about midnight we were all seized on in our beds and made prisoners by a company of riflemen from Hagar's Town, who were ordered out for that purpose in consequence of the little hatter's information.

This company consisted of thirty-six men exclusive of officers, who rushing suddenly into our room, with their rifles cocked and presented close to our heads while in bed, obliged us to surrender. This happened in the night of the nineteenth of November, one thousand seven hundred and seventy-five.

This party consisting solely of rude unfeeling German ruffians, fit for assassinations, murder, and death, treated us with
 great

great ignominy and infult; and without the leaft provocation abufed us perpetually with every opprobrious epithet language can afford.

We were then carried to Hagar's Town, and examined feparately before the committee there, after being fearched for papers; our faddles and baggage alfo underwent a ftrict fcrutiny and infpection, but nothing was difcovered againft us. This committee was ignorant, rude, abufive, and illiberal, and ordered us to be carried to Frederick Town, under a ftrong guard, for further examination.

The fame ruffians continued to guard us, and were perpetually threatening to take our lives. As we rode along (for as yet they had not deprived us of our own horfes) fome of them in the rear every now and then fired off a rifle directed very near us, as I could hear the ball whiftle paft within a few feet of us, every time they fired.)

At Frederick town I was told that *I* need not expect to get clear, for *I* was a
noted

noted friend to Britain, and they had long endeavoured to get *me* in their power.

Here we were stripped and searched again, and examined separately before the committee, where one of the most illiberal, inveterate and violent rebels named Samuel Chase, (son to a respectable and very worthy clergyman of this province) a lawyer, and a member of the Congress presided.

At this place we were not a little alarmed lest they should discover our instructions, papers, &c. as they examined every thing so strictly as to take our saddles to pieces, and take out the stuffing, and even rip open the soals of our boots, in vain, for the object of their search was not found, although they so frequently handled what contained it.

However, by some neglect of Colonel Connolly's servant, an old torn piece of paper was found in his portmanteau, which discovered part of our design; and then Colonel Connolly, to prevent our

falling

falling immediate sacrifices to a frantic mob, acknowledged our commiſſions)

Upon this we were actually robbed of our money, by Samuel Chaſe and the committee, the chairman of which was named John Hanſon, and he has ſince then become a Preſident of the American Congreſs, who left us only one guinea each; and we were put under a ſtrong guard in the houſe of one Charles Beatty, in a cloſe room three ſtories high, with the windows ſcrewed faſt down, reſtricted from pen, ink, and paper, and no perſon allowed to ſpeak to us.

Thus were we confined, for ſeven weeks, all in one room, under a ſtrong guard, ſuffering every ſpecies of inſult daily, and in danger and dread of being murdered every night.

The ſervant however, who was faithful to his truſt, being allowed to go at large from the firſt of our confinement, took care to deſtroy the mail pillion-ſticks, containing the papers, commiſſions, and inſtructions, which we dreaded ſo much
being

being difcovered, as foon as he could effect it with fafety, which put an end to our anxiety and alarms on that account.

Fredrick Town is a fine large town, built of brick and ftone, there being very few timber houfes in it, it is an inland town, being at leaft fifty miles from George Town, which is the neareft navigation or port, and is not fituated upon any river or water courfe; the neareft to it being Monoceacy Creek, which is four miles diftant, and Potomack River, which is about eight miles from it.

The land around Fredrick Town is heavy, ftrong, and rich, well calculated for wheat, with which it abounds; this being as plentiful a country as any in the world.

The face of the country here fwells into beautiful hills and dales, and twelve miles beyond the town it arifes into mountains, named the South Mountain. The foil is generally of a deep rufty brown colour, and ftrongly impregnated with iron.

Frederick

Fredrick Town is not so large as Alexandria, but more confiderable than Williamsburg, or Annapolis, and contains upwards of two thousand inhabitants, who abound in provisions, and all the neceffaries of life.

Beyond the mountain Elizabeth Town, or Hagar's Town as it is generally called, astonishes you by its magnitude, beauty, and good buildings, chiefly composed of stone and lime.

It is situated on a plain, in the great valley between the two mighty ridges named the South Mountain, or Blue Ridge, and the North Mountain, or Great Ridge.

This valley is about thirty miles wide, extending many hundred miles in length, and contains a body of the richeft land in the world. It abounds with the moft clear and pellucid water-courfes, and all the ftones and rocks are lime-ftone.

Both Frederick Town and Hagar's Town, as well as the greateft part of the back country of Maryland and Pennsylvania, are inhabited chiefly by Germans and Irish, but the first are the most numerous; and carry on almost every kind of manufacture, as well as a considerable share of trade. Neither of them stand upon any large water-course; but there is abundance of mills, forges, furnaces, and iron works, all around them, throughout the adjacent country.

Many of the Irish here can scarcely speak in English; and thousands of the Germans understand no language but High Dutch; however they are all very laborious, and extremely industrious, having improved this part of the country beyond conception; but they have no idea of social life, and are more like brutes than men. They came to Frederick Town from all quarters to behold us, as if we had been some strange sight, and were always very liberal of insults and abuse, without the least cause or provocation.

On

On the thirtieth of December, orders were brought from the Congress, that we should be sent to them at Philadelphia; and they were preparing to set out with us next day.

It had been preconcerted, that if we should be taken prisoners by the way upon this expedition, we should attempt, either by escape or any other method, to inform the garrison of Detroit of an expedition the rebels intended against them from Pittsburg; and also to bring the garrison of Fort Gage at Kiskuskias Illonois, with the artillery, stores, &c. down the Mississippi to the Gulf of Mexico, and from thence by transports round to join the Earl of Dunmore and the troops under his command at Norfolk.

For this reason I had been long scheming an escape, and had engaged one of the inhabitants named Barclay to accompany me on this hazardous undertaking; and he was to be liberally rewarded for his services.

As we were ordered to set out for Philadelphia next morning, there was now no time to be lost in making this attempt.

For this purpose I watched all this night for the moment that the two centinels might fall asleep on their posts at our door, which they had also locked on the outside; at length the much wished-for period arrived; and that instant unscrewing the lock, I made my escape, with letters, dispatches, and every necessary order, but by an accident was obliged to leave almost all my cloaths behind. After some little difficulty I found Barclay's house, and he getting out of bed, we immediately set out on our journey.

There was a deep encrusted snow, and most dreadful roads, so that travelling was beyond expression fatiguing, especially as I went on foot, leaving my horse behind to prevent any suspicion of my route; as no one could imagine that a journey, over the Allegany mountains, to Detroit, and to the Mississippi, would be attempted

attempted during that rigorous feafon of the year, by any perfon alone, as they muft conceive me to be, and on foot.

In order to pafs on with more privacy, I endeavoured to crofs the Potomack, and travel up on the Virginia fide of that river, becaufe fo many people from Maryland had feen me while in confinement at Frederick Town and Hagar's Town; but in attempting to go over on the ice, I broke in, and it was with the utmoft difficulty my life was faved. Barclay would not venture.

It was fnowing and freezing at the fame time, and I had feven miles over the mountains to go before I came to a houfe to thaw, dry, and warm myfelf. At laft when I reached a houfe, there was no fire, the people could not fpeak nor underftand a fingle word of Englifh, and it was impoffible for me to ftay; fo I travelled on in that wet and frozen condition all day, and at night lay before the fire, at the houfe of a poor ignorant Dutchman; which I alfo did

did the night before, upon a bear's skin, at the house of a very violent Scotsman, a surveyor, on the side of the Potomack, after having undergone more than can be expressed in travelling round a town named Sharpsburg, the snow being deep and encrusted over, but not strong enough to support my weight, so that at every step I sunk down almost knee-deep, and cut my legs also by every movement in walking.

On the first day of January, 1776, at sun-rise, I came to the mouth of a river named Cunnigocheague, (where it enters the Potomack.)

(This river was frozen half-way over, and we were compelled to break the ice, strip, and wade through, with the water up almost to our shoulders.)

Hearing of a pursuit after me, we struck out of the road into the North Mountain, travelled all day through deep fatiguing encrusted snow, and staid during the night (for I slept not) under a rock in the mountain.

On

On the second of January, we likewise travelled all day in the mountain, and at night scraped away the snow by the side of a fallen tree, made a fire, and slept a little.

On the third of January I directed our course towards the road again, being then behind the pursuit, and staid all night at a miserable hovel by the fire. Here we procured some coarse food, which was extremely acceptable and delicious, having been entirely without any kind of refreshment for the last two days.

At this place I heard a thousand falsehoods told concerning me, and was obliged to join in the abuse against myself, which was generally equally groundless and illiberal; several of the people here said they knew me perfectly well, and attributed a multitude of singular actions and exploits to me that I had never before heard of; but they all united in insisting that we ought immediately to have been put to death when taken, to prevent escapes and future mischief.

Our journey was somewhat retarded, and rendered extremely disagreeable, by great numbers of large water-courses or rivulets in our way, which we were under the necessity of passing over, all of them being partially or entirely frozen, yet scarcely any able to bear us, so that we had to break the ice on each side, and wade through. Among the multitude of these, I still recollect the names of the Great Khonholloway and Little Khonholloway.

On the fourth of January, being under the necessity of crossing a river that was frozen over, (I had three violent falls on the ice) by which I received a deep wound in one of my feet, and a very bad strain in my ancle.

This rendered travelling intolerably painful and difficult; however to me there was no alternative, but death to stop, or life to proceed; and I continued to push on, although constantly in extreme

treme torture, until we arrived at a planter's houſe on the road, about a mile on this ſide of a large water-courſe named May's creek; where I was compelled to ſtop, unable to proceed farther, being abſolutely exhauſted, and quite overpowered with extreme pain and fatigue.

Here Barclay privately made off and left me, after plundering me of what little cloaths I had been able to bring with me, and every valuable article I had ſecreted from the rebels, viz. ſome ſilver and ſtone buckles, gold rings, and jewels, on which I depended ſolely for ſupport during this journey; for the committee, as I have obſerved before, had only left us a guinea a piece in money, of which one ſingle dollar was all I had remaining.

This fellow ſurely muſt have been influenced by the reflection, that in my wretched condition it would be impoſſible for me to accompliſh the hazardous and extenſive journey I had undertaken; and that conſequently ſooner or later I muſt

muſt be again apprehended; for which high rewards were offered, and the greateſt exertions made by the rebels.

For he never could be tempted by the ſmall booty he obtained to be guilty of ſuch a piece of villainy, after travelling ſo far, and ſuffering ſo much as he had done, along with me. This ſpoil from me however I preſume he thought proper to take to himſelf when he went off, as ſatisfaction for his trouble.

No event of my life ever ſhocked me more than the diſcovery of this wretch's treachery, when I found he was certainly gone.

A multitude of ſuſpicions crowded in my mind, and a thouſand fears alarmed me. Every moment I expected to be ſeized upon, in conſequence of information againſt me; and I diſtruſted every perſon I ſaw or met.

My mind diſtracted, my body enfeebled, emaciated, and tormented with excruciating pain, in an enemy's country, deſtitute of money or reſource, and without

without a single friend, I was in a condition truly to be commiserated, and not to be excelled in distress.

This was a trial the most arduous and severe I ever met with; but still my resolution did not forsake me, and I determined to proceed, notwithstanding every difficulty and danger.

I crossed May's Creek, and Wills's Creek, by breaking the ice and wading them, passed by old Fort Cumberland, which is in a beautiful and romantic situation, on the north side of the Potomack, amidst vast mountains and mighty torrents of water, that break through the mountains in dreadful and tremendous chasms, appearing very distinctly from this place.

The largest of these breaks in the mountains are those of the river Potomack and of Wills's Creek, which appear from hence superior to the rest in awful grandeur.

There is now only a little public house at Fort Cumberland, where that
immense

immense ridge particularly named the Allegany Mountains commences.

Here I began to afcend the mighty Allegany, and after travelling all day in an extremity of anguifh, pain, and anxiety, after having broken the ice and waded through a black and difmal river named Savage River, and a number of large and dangerous water-courfes befides, I arrived at Gregg's habitation, in the midft of the mountain; where I remained all night amidft the dreadful fcreamings and howlings of multitudes of every fpecies of wild beafts.

Here I was compelled to break in upon my poor folitary dollar, for, notwithftanding all my intended frugality, nature required fupport, which money alone could procure.

I fet out again next morning, and in this moft diftreffing and wretched condition continued to pufh forward, until I had got over the Allegany mountains; but, notwithftanding all my

circum-

circumspection and strenuous exertions, I had the misfortune to be retaken by mere accident on the Yohiogeny River, a branch of the Ohio, on the twelfth of January, by a party of nine ruffians returning from Pittsburg, where they had been dispatched in pursuit of me.

CHAP.

CHAP. LXV.

Cause of Life being preserved. Instances of singular Mal-treatment and Barbarity. Bound with Cords. Examined before the Committee at Frederick Town. A curious Description of the Committee and their Examination. Great Danger of being murdered. Confined in York Town Gaol, where a most worthy Loyalist Dr. Kersley was then a Prisoner. His Sufferings, and tragical Fate. Cross the Susquehannah on the Ice. An Account of Lancaster, York Town, and the Susquehannah. Arrival at Philadelphia. Carried before the Congress. Sent to Prison. Suffer unparalleled Barbarity. Health declining fast, and expect to be sacrificed. Wrote some Verses upon the Wall with Charcoal.

NOTHING preserved me from immediate death from the hands of these banditti, but the hopes of the reward they should meet with by carrying me to the Congress.

However there was no restriction to deter them from exercising the most wanton insult, the highest ignominy, and the most unaccountable cruelties upon me.

They

They set me upon a pack-horse, on a wooden pack-saddle; they tied my arms behind me, and my legs under the horse's belly; they took the bridle off the horse, and fastened a great bell around his neck; and in that condition they drove the horse before them, with me upon his back, along narrow slippery ways covered with ice, and over all the dreadful horrid precipices of the Allegany and Blue Mountains, for a distance little short of three hundred miles.

During the first day and night they never halted but for necessary refreshment, of which however they afforded me no share; and every night afterwards compelling me to lie upon the bare ground.

Thus travelling in this rapid manner very probably saved my life, as I have been informed since, for another banditti of thirty men from the vicinity of Pittsburg, upon an alarm that a person was taken on his way to raise the Indians against them, had pursued us under oath to kill me, but after following us for a

day

day and a half in vain, despairing to overtake us they returned.

I was carried in this inhuman barbarous manner past Tumbleston's, Grigg's, Fort Cumberland, Cressop's or Old Town, &c. &c. and at several places it was with the utmost difficulty my guard could prevent the ruffian savage inhabitants from murdering me in cold blood; but although they preserved my life, for the sake of the reward they expected for apprehending me, yet they never attempted to protect me from the most cruel and mortifying insults and mal-treatment at every place they halted; and I was frequently even exhibited as a public show, as if of a different shape and appearance from other men.

During all this time I tasted nothing but water, excepting one meal of indifferent food; this also contributed in some degree to my recovery, by abating the inflammation of the wound in my foot, and the strain in my ancle, both of which were

pro-

prodigiously swelled, and so intolerably painful, that, besides entirely depriving me of sleep, I was not able to walk an hundred yards even if it had been to obtain life and liberty as a reward.

I was then delivered up again to the Committee of Hagar's Town; who, after ordering me to be searched four different times in one day, made use of every artifice of promises to delude, and threats to intimidate, in order to corrupt my principles, and gain me over to their cause; and when all would not avail they ordered me to be carried to the Congress at Philadelphia in irons.

A fresh guard was added to the former, consisting of a Major, and two Captains, the rest being Lieutenants, Ensigns, and Serjeants, amounting to twelve in number, besides the former nine, who would not wait for the irons to be made, but set out with me, bound as before, and my horse tied also with two large ropes, and led by two of the guard, accompanied with fife and drum beating the rogue's march, which

which they seemed every where to be particularly fond of.

In this manner I was carried to Fredrick Town, and there dragged, bound with cords, before the Committee, which consisted of a taylor, a leather breeches-maker, a shoemaker, a gingerbread-baker, a butcher, and two publicans.

The greatest part of them being Germans, I really underwent a most curious examination, nearly to the following effect. "*Got tamm you*" (says one) "*howſh darſht you make an exſhkape from diſh honorablſh Committiſh?*" "*For flucht der dyvel* (says another) *Howſh can you ſhtand ſho ſhtyff for King Shorſh akainſht diſh koontery?*" "*Sacramenter* (roars out another) *Diſh Committiſh will make Shorſh knoa howſh to behave himſelf.*" " *By Goat* (bawls the butcher) *Ich vould kill all de Enkliſh tives, as ſoon as Ich vould kill van ox, or van cow.*"

After they had all exhausted themselves by haranguing in this manner, they insisted that I should answer them.

I replied, ' that I could have very little to say to them, having no intention of employing

ploying either of them; as when I wanted cloaths I should apply to another taylor; and to other persons also for leather breeches, as well as for shoes or boots; that I never eat gingerbread; and had an aversion to butchers and publicans, whenever they stepped aside from the line of their proper occupations; and, that as I conceived they had as little business with me as I with them, requested they would detain me no longer.'

This threw them in a most violent rage, and they ordered a guard of their own to take me to a dungeon.

But my former guard refused to deliver me up, and swore that they would not trust me in their hands, lest they should permit me to escape again, as they had done before.

This I confess gave me some satisfaction, and also prevented me from receiving abundance of abuse and mal-treatment for that time.

They left Fredrick Town with me early next morning, and at the distance of fifteen miles

miles from it we were overtaken by a Captain and fifty armed men, who had been sent after us to take *me* from my guard, and carry me back to two hundred more ruffians in arms that had assembled and marched into Fredrick Town, for the sole and avowed purpose of seizing on and putting me to death immediately, in order as they alledged to save the country expence; for they all appeared to be absolutely certain, that this would be my fate after I was carried to the Congress at Philadelphia.

This unexpected circumstance occasioned a very warm contest between the two parties, and detained us at least three hours.

My guard, it is true, seemed resolute to defend me, at the expence of their blood; because by giving me up they would be deprived of their expected reward, but they must certainly have been overpowered by numbers, if it had come to action.

However I myself found means to persuade this rabble from their first intentions, which required no small share of address to accomplish, as they were actually

tually sent by the rest on purpose for my destruction; but at length we were by this means suffered to proceed.

I was carried, in this manner, through Cressop's Town as I have observed before, as well as Hancock's Town, Hagar's Town, Middle Town, Frederick Town, Tawney Town, Peter Little's Town, Mc Allaster's Town, and at last arrived at York Town, commonly called Little York, in Pennsylvania, where they lodged me that night in the common gaol, being the first prison I ever entered in my life.

Here I was confined in an apartment adjoining to that where a most meritorious and respectable loyalist was then kept prisoner.

This gentleman's name was Doctor Kearsley, of the city of Philadelphia, who, on account of his loyal principles, was torn from friends, family, and fortune, and after being long and rigidly confined in different prisons, fell at length a sacrifice to the cruel and persecuting spirit of these iniquitous sons of barbarity.

Although

Although I was here locked up in a strong stone prison, yet a guard consisting of the inhabitants, was placed in the gaol below, and a centinel at the door of my room.

This night being excessively cold, the ruffian who was placed at my door got intoxicated, and after putting himself in a rage, by damning and swearing, began to fire at me through the door. Upon the report of the piece the guard came up and relieved him; but the next centinel acted in the very same manner, and this being relieved the third did just so likewise; so that I never closed my eyes all that night, and was heartily glad when we left Little York next morning.

We crossed the Susquehannah a large broad and beautiful river, upon the ice about two miles above Wright's Ferry, and at night arrived at Lancaster, the largest inland town in America, containing at least ten thousand inhabitants, chiefly Germans and Irish.

However it is neither handsome nor agreeable, although very plentiful, and abounding

abounding with moſt excellent cyder and proviſions.

York Town is much pleaſanter than Lancaſter, and ſtill farther diſtant from navigation. It is ſituated on Codorus Creek, a pretty ſtream which falls into the Suſquehannah, and contains between two and three thouſand inhabitants, chiefly Iriſh with a few Germans intermixed.

The river Suſquehannah, which falls into, and forms the head of the vaſt Bay of Cheſapeak, is one of the largeſt and moſt beauiful rivers in America, yet perhaps one of the leaſt uſeful, being navigable only about ten or fifteen miles at fartheſt, from the mouth, for veſſels of any burden; above which it is only navigable for canoes, and even they meet with many interruptions.

The weſt branch of the Suſquehannah riſes near and interlocks with the waters of the Allegany, and the north branch of the Potomack.

The eaſt branch heads near the long fall and portage on the Mohawks River, a branch a branch of the Hudson or North River which falls into the sea at New York.

The source of this branch of the Susquehannah is in the country of the Mohawks, a considerable distance north from Cherry valley, and from thence to its mouth, at the extremity of the Chesapeak, is not less than five hundred and twenty-five miles in direct lines, and about seven hundred miles along with its meanders.

In Lancaster I was also lodged in the common prison, with a guard at the door as at York; and with this information, to comfort me and promote my repose, viz. that some hundred barrels of gunpowder were lodged in the floor above; and yet they allowed me a fire.

Here also there was a loyalist confined, in the next room to me, named Mr. Brooks.

In this place I received no particular abuse nor insult, and we left it next morning on our journey to Philadelphia.

About two or three miles from Lancaster we crossed Conestoga Creek, which falls into the Susquehannah; and on the
second

second day about noon, after croffing the Schuylkill, we arrived in Philadelphia, after the moft fhocking and difagreeable journey that I ever experienced; being dragged all this diftance, which is between four and five hundred miles, bound with cords, and treated in the moft barbarous and ignominious manner, like a criminal or felon carried to execution.

At Philadelphia, the Congrefs, to exprefs their approbation of the cruelty and zeal of thofe ruffians who retook me, gave to each of them a commiffion in their fervice, and fifty dollars; and to the principal perfon among them two hundred dollars, and a captain's commiffion of rifle-men as a reward; befides a liberal gratuity to each of the officers, who came as the additional guard from Hagar's Town.

After being interrogated by the Congrefs, I was fent by them to the Council of Safety, (properly of deftruction,) and from thence to the common gaol, where a very large pair of irons were brought for me; but a gentleman prefent, named Courtney,

Courtney, one of the American artillery officers, went out in apparent indignation, and in a fhort time returned with an order to prevent their being put upon me.

I was then thrown into a cold damp vaulted room, or cell, in the criminal apartment for females, wherein at that time more than feventy were confined.

Both the iron and the wooden doors of my cell were conftantly locked and chained; no perfon even in the prifon was allowed to fpeak to me, nor to anfwer me if I called to them; reftricted from pen, ink, and paper, or the fmalleft communication with any creature living; without a chair, table, bed, blanket, or ftraw, and obliged to lie on the bare floor, with a log of wood under my head; in the midft of a moft fevere winter, without a fpark of fire, and the ificles impending from the arched roof of this horrid vault; and fometimes fuffered to remain for three days together without a drop of water, or any kind of drink; my fituation was too diftreffing for human nature to endure.

In

In this moſt wretched and dreadful condition I remained for three weeks, extremely ſick and very lame; and without having changed my linen, or had my cloaths off, for thirty-three days.

Indeed to think on all I ſuffered, one would imagine, that human nature could hardly ſupport it. But a man, under ſome circumſtances, and at certain times, can undergo more than would at other times deſtroy him.

Every loneſome ſleepleſs night that I paſſed in this dreary manſion of wretchedneſs and miſery, my ears were perpetually harraſſed with the moſt dreadful ſounds, and horrible noiſes, proceeding from the clanking of chains, the rattling of maſſy keys, the creaking of the vaſt and numerous iron doors, the reſounding of the bolts, bars and locks, and above all the moſt ſhocking ſcreams and howlings of the unhappy wretches confined in this horrible place of reſtraint.

Theſe diſmal ſounds, too dreadful for deſcription, were rendered a thouſand times

times more hideous and terrible, by the reverberation of the echo from the vaulted roofs.

If parching thirst and extreme cold could have allowed me any sleep, it would have been effectually prevented by the agitation of mind occasioned by these frightful noises that constantly broke in upon the silence of the night, in regular and melancholy succession.

If despair ever approached me, it was in this cruel situation; for I not only expected to fall a victim to their vindictive barbarity, but actually felt my destruction advancing by inches; as my health was lost, and my strength declining every hour.

Yet still my resolution did not abandon me, for the conscious integrity of my intentions and the justice of our cause supported the mind, and I determined to await my doom with patience and fortitude.

It was at this time that having accidentally obtained a piece of charcoal I wrote the following lines upon the wall, expressive of my situation and sentiments.

Verses

Verses written with Charcoal on the Wall in Philadelphia Prison.

CONFINEMENT hail! in honour's justest cause,
True to our King, our Country, and our Laws;
Opposing anarchy, sedition, strife,
And every other bane of social life.

These Colonies of British freedom tir'd,
Are by the phrenzy of distraction fir'd;
Rushing to arms, they madly urge their fate,
And levy war against their parent state.

Surrounding nations, in amazement, view
The strange infatuation they pursue.
Virtue, in tears, deplores their fate in vain;
And *Satan* smiles to see disorder reign;
The days of *Cromwell*, puritanic rage,
Return'd to curse our more unhappy age.

We friends to freedom, government and laws,
Are deem'd inimical unto their cause:
In vaults, with bars and iron doors confin'd,
They hold our persons, but can't rule the mind.
Act now we cannot, else we gladly wou'd:
Resign'd we suffer for the public good.

Success on earth sometimes to ill is given,
To brave misfortunes is the gift of Heaven:
What men could do we did, our cause to serve,
We can't command success, but we'll deserve.

CHAP. LXVI.

Insupportable Severity. Brought before the Congress. Promised better Treatment. Captain Campbell and General Prescot ill treated. Our lives endangered by rigid Confinement. A Committee of the Congress sent to visit us. Their Illiberality and Abuse. Greater Severities than ever. Subsisted only on Bread and Water. Thrown into the Dungeon where we almost perished. Philadelphia expected to be attacked by the British Army. Congress fly to Baltimore. Twenty British Prisoners marched in Irons through Derby, Marcus Hook, Brandywine, Wilmington, Newport, Christeen-Bridge, and the Head of Elk. Shocking Instance of Brutality at Newport. Description of Philadelphia and the Delaware. Opulence, Trade, and Number of Inhabitants in Pennsylvania.

THIS deplorable condition, to which I was reduced, at length moved even the iron heart of the Gaoler to compassion, and he intreated me to make application to the Congress for the preservation of life; observing that although he was restricted from allowing me pen, ink, and paper, he would send me a pencil and a card.

Determined never to acknowledge or submit to the authority of the Congress, unless by compulsion, I was much at a loss in what manner, or for what purpose to address them ; and I concluded only to request, that they would either render my confinement supportable, or order me to immediate execution, which I infinitely preferred to my present situation of being destroyed by inches. This I transmitted to them by the Gaoler, written with a black lead pencil upon the back of a common playing card.

They then ordered me to be brought before them ; and excepting some insidious attempts to corrupt my principles, behaved towards me very politely, making apologies for what was past, and promising better treatment in future ; at the same time declaring their astonishment at my desperate attempt, as they called it, of reaching Detroit or Illonois alone, (for I had not divulged the circumstance about Barclay,) and on foot, at that rigorous season of the year, through a barbarous and
hostile

hostile country, and without friends, money or resources.

But although they promised to render my confinement more supportable, yet I was ordered back to prison almost in the same situation as before; for my condition was very little amended by them.

However Captain Duncan Campbell of the eighty-fourth regiment, or the Royal Highland Emigrants, a gentleman possessed of considerable property, and Lieutenant-Colonel of the militia, in Dutchess County in the province of New York, being also confined in the same prison, and hearing of the cruelties exercised upon me, rendered me every service in his power, that my precluded situation would admit of; and I gladly embrace this opportunity of returning that worthy and much esteemed officer and friend my most grateful and sincere acknowledgments.

Captain Campbell was likewise extremely ill, having been in prison above four months, and it was only to save his life that they at last admitted him to parole.

I was

I was then removed into the room in the front lately occupied by Captain Campbell; and Major-General Prescott, being brought prisoner to Philadelphia about this time, was confined in the room in the criminal apartment out of which I had been just removed.

Here he also was kept, until the dampness of the walls, and the unwholesomeness of the place caused his wounds to break out afresh, when he was carried into the city, and placed under a guard.

To hear that Colonel Connolly and Captain Cameron were here did not surprise me, being only what I had reason to expect; but you may guess at my astonishment to understand that the worthless assuming ignorant fellow, who had been so forward at Norfolk in giving false information against, me was actually in this prison also.

Treachery from such a wretch is what might be expected; but the extent, and at the same time the absurdity of his treachery defeated its own purpoſes, and became truly ridiculous.

He had dealt out his informations and intelligence to the rebels, as liberally as he did before to the Earl of Dunmore and the commanding officers of his Majeſty's troops, and with nearly a ſimilar effect.

It ſeems that he had not only acquainted General Waſhington and the Congreſs with every tittle he had privately diſcovered of our expedition, thus rendered abortive, but had likewiſe contrived to deliver all the letters and diſpatches from the ſouthward, for General Gage and the army in Boſton, into the hands of the enemy, and thereby preſerved his own effects from being plundered.

This man however by mere dint of aſſurance contrived to impoſe himſelf upon a great many friends of government as a perſon of conſequence and loyal principles.

After ſome days the Gaoler brought me a paper containing a parole, which he ſaid was ſent for me to ſign, as they propoſed

posed now to atone for their former severity, and acquainted me that a Colonel Nixon had interested himself to procure it. But as the purport of the parole was of too illiberal a nature, and as Lieutenant-Colonel Connolly and Captain Cameron were not offered their paroles also, I refused to sign it, for three days succeffively, it being presented to me daily for that purpose, and severe threats made use of towards me on declining it.

I was then removed into the same room with Colonel Connolly and Captain Cameron, the windows of which were nailed down, and both the iron and wooden door locked and chained close upon us, so as not to admit a breath of fresh air; we were debarred the use of pen, ink and paper, no person whatever was permitted to see or speak to us, and we were thus totally precluded from the whole world as effectually as if we had been in our graves.

In this manner we were held for six months, until our lives were despaired of, which was represented to the Congress, by

Doctor Benjamin Rush, Doctor Cadwallader, and Doctor Bond, three eminent Physicians in Philadelphia, in written memorials; upon which that distrustful junto appointed a committee of themselves, composed of a Mr. Wilcot from Connecticut, and a Thomas Mac Kean of Newcastle upon Delaware, to inspect the prison, and see and examine into our situation and state of health.

Mr. Wilcot behaved and spoke like a moderate man, but the violent raging rebel McKean introduced himself by abusing in the grossest terms the King, Parliament and Ministry, the whole British army and navy, and particularly the Earl of Dunmore, and General Prescot.

He assured *us*, for our comfort, that *we* should be retained for retaliation; that if Allen, or Proctor, or any of their leaders, then in the hands of the King's troops, were executed, we should share the same fate; and that we ought to think ourselves very happy not to be in irons, as their prisoners were always kept in irons by by the British, (which was a most notorious and malevolent falsehood.)

In order to preserve us for the *laudable* and *humane* purpose of retaliation, he ordered our windows to be opened; and after some time an order also came from the Congress that we should be permitted to walk, for two hours every day, in the hot, nasty, suffocating yard of the prison, under the constant inspection of two centinels; but this last indulgence was allowed us only for a few days.

All this time the Gaoler charged us at an extravagant rate for diet, fire, and candle, besides an allowance that he received from the Congress for that purpose; by which means he extorted every farthing of money from us, as far as our credit then would go.

But being determined not to run in debt, I at length refused to pay him any more than the Congress allowed, and was obliged after this to subsist upon bread and water alone during seven weeks.

This goaler's name was Thomas Dewees, as tyrannical, cruel, infamous a villain as ever disgraced human nature.

Some time before this, Brigadier General M'Donald and twenty-five officers, chiefly Scots, among whom was the hospitable Dutchman, Michael Holt, mentioned in the former volume, were brought prisoners to this goal, compelled to march all the way from Carolina on foot. They were confined in three close rooms for six weeks, and were afterwards allowed the liberty of walking in the yard of the prison, only every third day.

In July the Congress appointed two new gaolers, brothers, of the name of Jewell, if possible more barbarous and tyrannical than the former, and removed him and all the debtors and criminals to another prison, keeping only what they denominated prisoners of state in ours.

The cruelties practised in this place were almost incredible, and not to be exceeded, perhaps not equalled, by that of the Spanish inquisition.

There

There was always a strong guard here, ready to inforce their most barbarous commands, the guard-room being in the prison, and a great number of centinels posted both within and without on constant duty.

The restrictions upon us were so severe that we were not permitted to speak to any in different rooms.

On the twentieth of September, the gaoler *Jewell* accused me of conversing with Colonel Connolly, and ordered a serjeant and nine men to carry me by force into a nasty common guard-room, and from thence into a damp, cold, empty vaulted room, where I was compelled to to lie on the bare floor, which gave me a violent colic and cold.

I was then extremely ill, without any care or notice taken of me; and remained in that sick helpless condition, locked up in a cold damp room by myself, without the least assistance whatsoever.

This produced a dysentery, which continued upon me for seven weeks, and
reduced

reduced me to the verge of death; yet still I was kept locked up, without any care, attendance, or notice.

Dr. Benjamin Rush, then a member of the Congress, a man eminent in physic, but as eminent in rebellion, and still more so in unfulfilled professions, after tantalizing me with the expectation of a parole, exchange, and assurances of very great regard and commiseration, came one day and informed me, that many members of the Congress declared they personally knew me to be so determinedly inimical to the independence of the American States, and to have always exerted such influence and interest against them, that I need not expect nor hope for any kind of indulgence whatsoever, not even to save life.

However after this, thanks to heaven, I recovered: then Captain Cameron, Captain M'Lean, and I were confined in a room together, selected from the rest to experience the dire effects of their inhuman malice; and a centry extraordinary was
posted

posted at our door, to prevent our having the least intercourse or communication with any one.

In December the gaoler came with a guard, and plundered us again, under pretence of searching for papers; and abused us in the most injurious manner.

About this time the British army approaching through the Jerseys towards Philadelphia, the Congress were struck with a panic, and fled to Baltimore.

On the tenth of December the North Carolina prisoners were sent off to Baltimore under a guard; and on the eleventh sixty Jersey men, from Shrewsbury, chiefly Quakers, were also sent away, every two bound together with cords, under a small guard likewise.

Our confinement was now become so insupportable that even death would have been an agreeable deliverance.

This set us on a desperate scheme of breaking out; and with incredible danger, difficulty, and labour, we made way through the strong arched vaulting, cut afterwards with our penknives through a

two

two inch oak plank door, and got up through the cupola, on the top of the prison; intending to defcend by a rope, to crofs the Delaware, and pufh forward to the Britifh army then at Burlington and Mount Holly, only eighteen miles diftant.

But our rope, which confifted only of fheets and blankets tied together at the corners, gave way with Captain Cameron, who defcended firft, and he fell forty-eight feet perpendicular on the pavement. His life was miraculoufly preferved, but his bones were crufhed, and he fuffered amazingly in confequence thereof.

Captain M'Lean and I were then ftripped of our money, papers, and of every individual thing we had, not excepting even my journal, and were thrown into the dungeon for condemned felons, without light, bed-cloaths, or ftraw, or even our great coats to preferve us from the intenfe cold, and without food or drink for thirty-fix hours.

Here I expected nothing but to end my days in mifery; but the goodnefs

and

and juftice of our caufe fupported my fpirits, and difregarding my own fituation I felt nothing for myfelf, all my concern and diftrefs was for poor Captain Cameron, as they all cried " Let him die " and be damned," when I intreated them to affift him, offering them two hundred dollars (all the money I then had) to fave his life; upon farther enquiry concerning him, they immediately robbed me of all my money, telling me, " that he was dead, and in hell, and " wifhing me in the fame condition."

In this horrible fituation we remained until orders were given for our immediate removal to Baltimore, as they every day expected an attack upon Philadelphia.

They then brought out of prifon twenty of us in all; viz. feven gentlemen, eight ferjeants and privates belonging to the twenty-third and other regiments, and five failors.

They put us in irons, every two chained clofe together, and with a guard of fixty chofen Dutchmen (Germans),

fet

set out on the march to Baltimore on foot, crossing the Schuylkill, going through Derby, and that night lodged us in the common goal at Chester, without taking off the irons at all.

The irons prevented me from sleep every night; besides they were too small, cutting into my flesh, causing me to swell prodigiously, and were excessively painful.

Yet in this condition, with fixed bayonets they forced us to march on until ten o'clock each night, which was particularly severe on me, who had been close confined thirteen months without any kind of exercise, so that my feet were covered blisters, which breaking, my boots were filled with blood; yet still I was compelled to push forward.

The names of several of my fellow-prisoners were, Mess. William and Bridger Goodrich, and Bridger Jones, of Virginia; Mr. Abraham Wynant, of Staten Island, New York; Thomas Slater, of Baltimore; Captain Neal M'Lean of the
eighty-

eighty-fourth regiment; John Gee, son of Mr. Gee, of Stockport near Manchester, in England; Serjeant White of the twenty-third regiment; and Kirby and Barlow, &c. of the sixteenth light dragoons; Colonel Connolly being permitted to remain at Philadelphia, and Captain Cameron being incapable of being removed.

We passed by Marcus Hook, and the famous mills, near the mouth of the river Brandywine, the most extraordinary and valuable perhaps in the world, and through the beautiful town of Wilmington without halting; and came to Newport about ten o'clock, where we remained for the night.

This Newport, although a paltry little place, stands high in the rank of iniquity, for it is the very nest of sedition, where rebellion sits brooding over the demons of licentiousness, discord, persecution, cruelty, and outrage.

There happened at this detested place an instance of savage brutality, that the

greatest

greatest barbarians would blush to be guilty of. There was a friendless unfortunate English servant girl at the house where we were confined, who, greatly shocked at seeing us in irons, and being well affected to her king and country, happened to drop some expressions that betrayed those sentiments; this poor friendless girl, for this crime alone, after being severely beaten both by her master and mistress, was turned out of doors in the street at midnight, in a degree of cold not to be conceived in England, and, being seized upon by our ruffian guard, was dragged into their guard-room, where she was forcibly abused by seventeen of the villains, in the most gross, brutal, and injurious manner possible.

We left this detested place in the morning, and after passing through a small town named Christeen Bridge, arrived at another pretty town in the province of Maryland, at the head of Elk River, at the extremity of the Bay of Chesapeak, that afternoon.

The province of Penfylvania, through which I had juft paffed, contains eleven counties, and generally confifts of ftrong land well calculated for farming, which is the culture made ufe of, wheat and other grain compofing the ftaple of the province.

The whole country is finely diverfified by hills and dales; there are valuable farms, good buildings, plenty of water, and excellent mills throughout the whole country.

Nothing can be more beautiful than the banks of the Delaware, particularly below Philadelphia. Wilmington efpecially ftands in a fituation that cannot be excelled.

There are a great number of fine towns in this province; but they are all totally eclipfed by the beautiful, large, and elegant city of Philadelphia, as well as every other town is in North America.

This city is fituated on the neck of an ifthmus formed by the rivers Schuylkill and

and Delaware, which are here juft two miles diftant.

The town is laid out from river to to river, with the ftreets ftraight, wide, exactly regular, and croffing each other at right angles; but only that part bordering on the Delaware is as yet built upon: and at prefent it contains about thirty-five thoufand inhabitants.

The ftreets have fingular appellations, being named Firft-ftreet, Second-ftreet, Third-ftreet, Fourth-ftreet, Fifth-ftreet, &c. which are thofe that run lengthways of the town, or parallel to the rivers, excepting Water-ftreet, and Front-ftreet, which are neareft to the Delaware; whilft thofe that run from river to river are called after every different fpecies of trees, fuch as Chefnut-ftreet, Spruce-ftreet, Vine-ftreet, Walnut-ftreet, Cedar-ftreet, Pine-ftreet, &c. excepting Market-ftreet, which is in the center, and Mulberry or Arch-ftreet, and Saffafras or Race-ftreet, which are parallel to it.

The

The houses in Philadelphia are of brick, and well built; the public edifices are elegant and expensive, the New-Prison, in which we were confined and were also the first inhabitants, having cost no less than thirty thousand pounds.

But this fine town, whose inhabitants were once justly famed for universal philanthropy, and for the exercise of every humane and social virtue, has been so totally altered by the effects of the rebellion, that it is now a perpetual scene of discord and confusion, instead of the friendship, harmony, and order that once prevailed. And the entire change of their dispositions, the illiberality of their principles, and the cruelty of their inclinations, are sufficiently evinced by the shocking and barbarous treatment we experienced therein for almost twelve months.

This province includes two of the largest and most beautiful rivers in North America, viz. the Susquehannah and the Delaware; the last of which is navigable near two hundred miles, including the Bay.

At Philadelphia the Delaware is a mile and three quarters wide, and becomes broader all the way down, some parts of Delaware Bay being above thirty miles over, and at the mouth, viz. from Cape Hinlopen to Cape May, it is about eighteen or twenty miles; just below Wilmington this river is five miles over.

The Delaware heads not far from Albany; and from the source of the Mowhawk's branch to the mouth at Cape May and Cape Hinlopen it is about three hundred and fifty miles. This river is the boundary between Pensylvania and the province of New Jersey.

Although the heats in summer are excessively violent, yet the cold and frosts in winter are as severe, even to a degree of rigour not to be conceived in Britain; and this extreme cold extends also through Maryland and part of Virginia.

I have seen the vast rivers of the Delaware and the Potomack freeze quite over in one night where they were five or six miles wide.

When

When we croffed the Sufquehannah upon the ice, horfes and waggons made a common road over it, and it was above half a mile wide. The Delaware and the Potomack are alfo croffed in the fame manner conftantly every winter for the fpace of two months.

When a thaw comes, and the ice breaks entirely in thefe vaft rivers, the fight is dreadful and tremendous. The rivers rage, and the ice roars, arifes, and tumbles in immenfe cakes, with a hideous noife and bellowing not to be defcribed.

The rivers are totally impaffible on fuch occafions, and they generally continue in that condition for feveral days.

The trade of this province was very confiderable, which all centered in the city and port of Philadelphia, and amounted annually to feven hundred and twenty thoufand pounds in exports; and about fix hundred and twenty thoufand pounds in imports; which employed three hundred and ninety-five fail of fhipping inwards, and three hundred and fifty outwards; maintaining and giving bread to seven thousand five hundred seamen.

The trade of this province consists of grain, flour, timber, provisions, lumber, ships built for sale, copper ore, iron in pigs and bars, besides almost every commodity of Europe, Asia and America, this being a large and general emporium of commerce; but wheat and flour appear to be the staple or principal produce.

The merchants of Philadelphia are opulent, and carry on a very extensive trade.

The warehouses, quays, and wharfs are excellent, with water sufficient for ships of five hundred tons to load and unload close to them, but in the winter it is dangerous for large vessels to remain in this river on account of the driving of the ice.

Here is also a large and commodious market-place; and a college, that was very flourishing before the war.

There

There are barracks alfo, convenient and handfome, which were erected for the king's troops; and, befides feveral others of different kinds, there was an hofpital for lunatics in Philadelphia, the only one in America.

In the enumeration of the inhabitants made or rather publifhed by the Congrefs, this province is fet down as containing three hundred and fifty thoufand, including the three lower counties of Newcaftle, Kent, and Suffex upon Delaware.

I conceive this to be over-rated about fifty thoufand or upwards; and above one third of the number are blacks. A great proportion of the whites in this province are Germans, Swedes, and Irifh.

CHAP.

CHAP. LXVII.

Description of the Guard. The Captain by Trade a Porter. Their Behaviour. Meet several Companies of Rebels. A curious Scene. Put on board of a Privateer, and thrown into the Hold in Irons. Insulted and maltreated by two American Colonels, by Trade, one a Hatter, the other a Lighterman. Arrive at Baltimore. Irons taken off. Kindly and generously treated by the Inhabitants. Congress disapprove of this Lenity, change the Guard, and order us to be treated with great Severity. Effect an Escape, one retaken. Set sail down the Chesapeak. Land on the Eastern Shore. Most alarming Situation. Find Friends. Meet with a most welcome Reception.

OUR guard, which consisted of dismounted dragoons, was officered with a captain, a lieutenant, and a cornet; but the serjeants appeared to have the principal command, the officers themselves being obliged to obey their orders in preference to their own.

The captain was named Jacobs, by trade a *porter* of Philadelphia, by birth a German, a German, and by inclination, difpofition, and infenfibility, almoſt a brute.

Seven of us, although in irons, were delivered to this fellow as gentlemen, with orders to treat us with attention and refpect; this really was performed in an exemplary manner, as the captain, lieutenant, and cornet, always waited upon us in perfon in every menial office, and never prefumed to fpeak to us without cap in hand; notwithſtanding all this, they at no time relaxed a tittle in their feverity and rigour, which they exercifed upon us equally ſtrict as on the privates, during the whole journey; and they really had orders, in cafe of a refcue, efcape, or any other danger, to put us all to death immediately, which at one time they had almoſt actually put in execution.

During this march we met feveral companies of rebels, all in rags, going to reinforce Waſhington's army, and among the reſt a Captain Cook from Maryland

land, with two hundred men, all as drunk as lords.

This motley crew, perceiving our scarlet cloaths at a distance, took us for an advanced party of the British army, cocked their pieces, intending as usual to fire and run away; but, after they discovered that we were prisoners, they forgot to uncock their firelocks, or to form their line of march, and as they passed us a great many of their pieces went off by accident.

Several of them who were sailors, bawling out to us, "What chear, bro-"thers?" and staggering drunk, blundered into the midst of our ranks, until their heels were brought up by our irons. As they fell their firelocks went off, more to their own surprize than ours, and fortunately without doing us any injury.

They got up again on their feet, as well as they could, wondering to see us in that condition, and cried out, "D—n "my eyes, brothers, don't be afraid,

" We are sorry to see you belayed toge-
" ther though. By G—d, you are good
" fellows, and so is King George; but no
" matter for that now. D—n my eyes,
" brothers, you shall drink some grog
" with us," &c.

Upon this Captain Cook, their doughty commander, began to harangue our poor fellows with all the pomp, formality, and froth of self-consequence, noise, and folly, in order to prevail on them to enter into the rebel service.

He received for answer a general huzza for King George, which incensed him to such a degree that he drew his sword against our poor fellows in irons; but our guards drove him off.

When we arrived at the head of Elk, being unable to proceed farther by land, we were put on board a privateer bound for Baltimore; and, surely it must be to mortify us and render us uncomfortable, they sent our little baggage and cloaths on board of another privateer.

But

But all this not being sufficient to glut the malevolence of these savages, they suffered two of their colonels to take possession of the cabin and steerage of the vessel, and thrust us down in the hold amongst the ballast, which consisted of pig iron and stones, on which we were obliged to repose, without great coats, straw, or bedding of any kind, still in irons, every two being chained close together, although we were guarded by these sixty Germans, besides the privateer's crew.

They even carried their cruelty so far as not to suffer the hatches to be shut over us, although it was excessively cold, and the snow was falling fast upon us.

In this condition did they keep us, for two days and nights, until we arrived at Baltimore, without abating the least of their rigour, having had but one scanty meal of indifferent food, during all this time, which we brought along with us; and through the whole journey we were
obliged

obliged to bear our own expences, and that of the guard likewife; while the two colonels, and the reft of the rebel officers, were caroufing in eafe, plenty, drunkennefs, and riot, and were perpetually infulting and maltreating us the whole time. Thefe fellows were Colonel Price, a hatter in Fredrick Town, and Colonel Gunby, an illiterate rude fkipper of a common bay craft, fomething refembling the coal lighters in the Thames.

On our paffage up the Patapfco, we paffed a fort, which had been erected, and a chain or boom, cheveaux de frize, &c. thrown acrofs the river, about five miles below Fells Point, or Baltimore, where we arrived very foon after.

The committee of Baltimore being much difpleafed at our being in irons, ordered them immediately to be taken off, and pofted a captain's guard of the Maryland matroffes over us; but the two Meffrs. Goodriches were feparated from us, and thrown into the common prifon,

where

where the North Carolina officers were alſo confined.

I found Baltimore very much altered ſince the laſt time I was there; the friends to government having increaſed ſurpriſingly, and even the diſaffected being become more moderate and liberal in their ſentiments.

In a few days the Baltimore militia relieved the Maryland matroſſes, and mounted our guard; but ſo generous and friendly were they to us, and ſuch confidence did they repoſe in our words, that they not only carried us home with them to their houſes, but likewiſe permitted us to go at large for any length of time, and to any place, we pleaſed; indeed all the inhabitants of Baltimore ſeemed to vie with each other in ſhewing us every civility and kindneſs.

This indulgence however was but of ſhort duration, for as ſoon as the Congreſs heard of it they ordered the militia to be removed, and the artillery again to mount

our

our guard, which consisted of fifty-two men, of these nine were on constant duty.

Our restrictions were again rendered very severe; for John Hancock, then President of the Congress, and Charles Thompson their Secretary, came in person every day, to the house in which we were confined, to see that the rigid orders issued from Congress concerning us were strictly executed.

This Christmas was the second I had passed in this province while a prisoner; the first being at Fredrick Town.

Our windows were now nailed down, and the same severities attempted to be exercised towards us as were made use of in Philadelphia; but as we were not in a prison, and as the individuals of our guard were generally friendly, our confinement was not rendered half so rigorous and intolerable as it was in that city.

Indeed all the inhabitants of Maryland, especially such as were not Germans, and even many of them likewise, treated us
with

with more humanity, liberality, and frequently even generosity, than we experienced elsewhere; and it is no small satisfaction to me to be able to give this testimony in their favour.

As for our guard they were chiefly Europeans, and in general so friendly to us, and so well affected to his Majesty, that could I have brought them clear off, the greatest part would gladly have come away with me.

Being informed that his Majesty's ship the Pearl was in the bay of Chesapeak, we resolved to make a vigorous attempt to escape, that we might get on board of her: and for this purpose I privately engaged a sloop to remain at anchor waiting for us, about seven miles below the fort chain and chevaux de frize, for which I paid at the rate of three pounds a day, to convey us down the bay.

On the night of the tenth of January, 1776, having provided cords, and every necessary implement for our purpose, and having engaged a guide to wait for us at a

friend's

friend's houfe in town, we bribed the two centinels at our door to allow us to go into an adjoining empty room, and from thence we defcended to the ground with ropes, which being very fmall cut burnt and lacerated my hands exceffively. This rifque was very great, as there were three centinels below who had not been bribed, and from whofe vigilance we had every thing to apprehend.

The danger was evinced by the event; for only three of us got clear, the fourth being taken in the attempt.

It was Captain M'Lean and Slater that efcaped along with me; Jones was retaken, and Wynant was left fick.

After the greateft rifques imaginable, for we met both the patrole and the grand rounds whom we avoided by lying flat on the ground, and after a very fatiguing and circuitous route, we got on board the floop a little after midnight, hoifted fail with a fair wind, and ftood down the river.

At day-break we found ourfelves below Annapolis, about fifty miles by water below Baltimore,

Baltimore, having by sailing in the night escaped the observation of the forts there and the privateers and spy-boats constantly cruising off the harbour.

About noon we were much alarmed by a little privateer that kept hovering about us, but we stood boldly on, without appearing to regard her, and at night anchored in Hooper's Straits, near the Tangier Islands; at least an hundred miles from the place of our escape.

Here we received the disagreeable intelligence that there was no King's ship in the Chesapeak, which effectually disconcerted all our schemes.

This piece of information determined us to land on the Eastern shore, and proceed across the country to Lewes Town, and Cape Hinlopen, at the mouth of the Delaware, where we heard his Majesty's ship the Roebuck was stationed. For this purpose I ordered the sloop into Nanticoke River, where I left her and my companions with a promise to send for them next day, if I found friends.

At

At this place I hired a poor man to carry me in a canoe down the Nanticoke, and up Wicocomico River where I underſtood a great many friends to government reſided; and I told him that I wanted to purchaſe a quantity of proviſions and plank. Although this man was loyal, I did not truſt him with our ſecret, leſt, on a diſcovery of his having afforded me any aſſiſtance, the poor man might be ruined.

It was dark when we ſet out, the night was exceſſively cold, freezing even the ſalt water, which was ſix or ſeven miles acroſs; we had eight miles down the Nanticoke, and five miles up the Wicocomico to go, and I never ſuffered much more with cold in my life, having got wet and frozen, and the river being covered with ice which greatly impeded our progreſs.

The houſe we were bound to was the old man's ſon's, and when we arrived there, about midnight, not a living creature was within; we were obliged to break open the window to get in to make a fire;

a fire; and the old man then set out in search of his son, leaving me alone in the house, and was to return in an hour.

That time elapsed without any appearance of his return; the second, and even the third hour passing in the same manner, I began to be exceedingly alarmed, especially as there was a wind-mill at this place, and if the old man did not betray me, which I really apprehended, so many people would come to the mill in the morning that I must certainly be discovered.

My situation here was so extremely uncomfortable, that, although this was the fourth night and day I had passed entirely without sleep, I never closed my eyes. In the midst of an unknown hostile country, with a very high reward offered for apprehending me, and in the power of utter strangers, whose poverty alone might induce them to betray me, if they themselves should happen to entertain any suspicions concerning me, every anxiety and dread was justified.

After

After another hour of the greateſt uneaſineſs, the old man at length, at four
o'clock in the morning, returned, bringing with him his ſon and all his family.

In the morning the young man and I
ſet out on foot for the ſettlement where
the loyaliſts chiefly reſided, leaving the
old man to remain there until the return
of his ſon, and then ready to execute the
orders he brought from me.

We travelled ſixteen miles before breakfaſt, and then found friends, to whom I
revealed myſelf, and who gave me a moſt
cordial and kind reception.

I then ſent the young man back immediately, to deſire his father to bring over
my two companions to his houſe that
night, where I ſent horſes for them; and
before day they arrived at the place where
I was.

I acted thus purpoſely to diſconcert the
enemy in caſe of a purſuit, which it effectually did; firſt by ſending them up the Nanticoke, where our ſloop lay at anchor all
this time, and after the moſt ſtrict ſearch

after

after us there in vain, for we came down the Nanticoke again in a canoe and went up the Wicocomico, they gave up the purfuit.

About a year afterwards, our route being accidentally difcovered, when they apprehended the poor old man whofe name was Timmons, he cleared himfelf by making an affidavit that he had not the leaft knowledge or conception who we were that he had been employed by, which was indeed ftrictly true.

CHAP.

CHAP. LXVIII.

Offered a Guard of two hundred Men. Decline it, and accept of two Guides. Receive the kindest Assistance from many of the principal Inhabitants. Arrive at Indian River. The Roebuck left that Station. The Falcon touched there, but would not take us on board. Cruel Disappointment. Ardour and Zeal of the Loyalists. Insurrection of the Loyalists. Persuade both Sides to disperse. Friendship and Kindness of the Men, and great Goodness of the Women. Character of the American Ladies. Deep Snow. Discover some Ships. Set out in a Canoe. Driven out to Sea in a dark stormy Night. Dreadful Situation. Accidentally discover the Preston in a prodigious thick Fog. Received on board by Commodore Hotham and all the Officers of the Preston. A Hurricane destroys the Canoe, and blows the Ship out to Sea.

THE friends to government here were happy beyond expression at this proof of my confidence, and that it was in their power to assist us; offering us a guard of two hundred men to convey us safe on board the Roebuck at Cape Hinlopen.

This offer, more consistent with zeal than prudence, I declined, and desired only the assistance of two guides to conduct us privately in the night; and of a great many that offered, each seemed more desirous than the other to be made choice of.

Two resolute and zealous loyalists, well acquainted with the country and inhabitants all the way, accompanied us, and rendered us every service imaginable. They were named Mr. Hugh Dean and Mr. Robert Campbell, both Scotsmen; the first now resides in Nova Scotia, and the latter is an officer in the seventy-first regiment.

The place where we were thus kindly received was in the vicinity of a small town named Princess-Ann, the court-house and chief place in Somerset County, which abounds with loyalists throughout.

Every night we were visited by some respectable friends of government, among whom were Mr. Ingram a most worthy loyalist, a merchant late of Norfolk in Virginia,

ginia, Mr. Sheriff, a merchant alfo, both natives of Scotland, and Mr. Jones, then high fheriff of the county, now a Captain in the Britifh fervice.

The diftance to Cape Hinlopen was about eighty-five miles, and we travelled in the night for privacy.

After feveral difficulties we arrived at Rehoboth Bay, at the mouth of Indian River, and there to our extreme concern and mortification we were informed that the Roebuck had failed from Delaware Bay on the eighth inftant, juft a week before our arrival.

But on the day following his Majefty's floop of war the Falcon having landed fome prifoners, and burnt a fchooner at the mouth of Indian River, we fent Slater on board of her, in a little canoe or punt that could carry but one perfon, to defire the Captain to fend his boat for us, and for two gentlemen of the firft confequence, property, and intereft, in the county and vicinity of Suffex, named Thomas Robinfon and Boaz Manlove, Efqrs. who
were

were also persecuted for their loyalty, being forced to abandon their families and homes, and hearing of us had joined company.

But Captain Linzee of the Falcon, though he had landed some prisoners near the place where we were, could not be prevailed upon, either to send his boat, or to wait only two hours for us; although he was most earnestly intreated to do so by Slater, whom we sent on board for that purpose, and who also particularly and repeatedly informed him, "that we were British prisoners escaped at the certain hazard of our lives from a long and most cruel confinement, and that two of the first gentlemen of property and interest in the country were along with us, extremely anxious to get on board, being driven from their homes to avoid the persecution of the rebels."

This was inexpressibly discouraging to all the friends to government; and one of the most truly mortifying disappointments to us that we could possibly have experienced.

Next

Next morning we viewed the ocean with many a longing earneſt look, ſtill flattering ourſelves with hope that the ſhip might return, but all in vain.

I continued with the two gentlemen I have juſt mentioned, all well armed; and we intended to keep concealed until another ſhip of war ſhould arrive an the coaſt. But from that time, which was the twentieth of January, none of his Majeſty's ſhips, nor any Britiſh cruiſer touched at that important ſtation, until the twelfth of March.

During this time the American frigate the Randolph came down the Delaware from Philadelphia, proudly cruiſed off and on the Cape for three days, being really a very fine lofty veſſel, then ſtood out to ſea. Taking her for a King's ſhip we had almoſt gone on board, but ſoon were undeceived by our friends, who were indefatigable in aſſiſting us.

It is impoſſible to do juſtice to the ardor and earneſtneſs with which the loyaliſts
endea-

endeavoured to serve us, and to support and defend his Majesty's interest.

I am confident that there was not one of them but would have chearfully lost the last drop of his blood for the King, and for British government.

The principal gentlemen of the country for sixty or eighty miles around came constantly to us, in the dead of night, in order to assist us, and to furnish us with all the intelligence of the country. They acquainted me with the very favourable disposition of a great majority of the inhabitants to his Majesty's government, and requested my directions for their future conduct.

They also intreated me to represent many circumstances of great importance, of which they informed me, to the Commander in Chief, should I be so fortunate as to reach New York.

I advised them to cherish, by every means in their power, the laudable zeal of the well-affected, but to restrain their ardor, and at all events to avoid or prevent

any

any infurrection of the friends to government, until such time as they were properly fupported, which period I imagined, and earneftly hoped, could not be far diftant.

But every exertion for this neceffary purpofe was fruftrated by the rebels having received intimation of our being in fome manner affifted by Mr. Dean, whom in confequence of this they fhot through the thigh, and began to commit feveral acts of violence and oppreffion towards the friends to government.

Upon this eleven hundred of the loyalifts affembled, and encamped at Parker's Mill, near a fmall town named Salifbury, upon the river Nanticoke, in Somerfet county, Maryland, where they blocked up the rebels, who had alfo collected in Salifbury to the number of three hundred well fupplied with artillery, ammunition, and fmall-arms, of which the loyalifts were utterly deftitute; yet the rebels did not dare to face them.

On the eleventh of February about midnight, a meſſenger arrived from the loyaliſts with the above mentioned intelligence, and requeſting me to go there and take the command.

Upon this I conſulted with the principal gentlemen in his Majeſty's intereſt in the county of Suſſex upon the Delaware, and it was concluded by every one that we ſhould endeavour to keep all quiet, until a proper ſupport ſhould arrive; as ſuch a number of undiſciplined men, without order, ammunition, officers, or arms, and without tents, forage, or proviſions, taking the field and entering upon action at this rigorous ſeaſon, muſt draw upon themſelves the whole ſtrength of the Congreſs from all quarters; and they would not only be cut off, but all the loyaliſts, and the whole of his Majeſty's intereſt on this ſide of the Cheſapeak, (which was very conſiderable) muſt by this imprudent and ill-timed meaſure be inevitably ruined.

For theſe reaſons I wrote to the leading men among the loyaliſts in Somerſet to uſe

their

their utmost endeavours to persuade both sides to disperse, without injury to the persons or property of any of our friends; yet by all means to be prepared against the worst, as the faith of rebels was not to be relied on; desiring them to send us notice, by a faithful messenger, if the rebels would not consent to this proposal, that we might then exert our utmost efforts for the common cause, and for the general advantage of his Majesty's interest; intending, if the rebels were determined on bloodshed, instantly to seize on the magazines and artillery in Lewis's Town, to raise and embody all the loyalists in Sussex, and to make use of the most active and vigorous exertions against the common enemy in all quarters.

An original copy of this letter was laid before and approved of by the Commander in Chief.

As the whole country was infested by marauding parties, to prevent a discovery I put the letter, rolled up like a scroll, into a hollow made in the end of a crooked
stick,

stick, plugging up the end so as to render it imperceptible; and in this manner sent it by Hoffington, the messenger, (who was to use it as a switch to ride with.)

He was taken five or six times, searched and examined by different parties of the loyalists as well as of the rebels, but was discharged, and at last delivered it safe to the persons for whom it was intended; after going into Salisbury, and discovering the posture, strength, and disposition of the rebels there.

On the sixteenth, Hoffington, the messenger, returned with information, that in consequence of this letter, and the earnest endeavours of those to whom it was sent, both the loyalists and the rebels had dispersed, and each returned to their respective habitations; which proved to be a most judicious and fortunate measure, as the Congress soon afterwards dispatched General Smallwood, and Colonel Guest, with five companies of artillery, six field-pieces, and six armed vessels, from the Western shore against them, besides two

regi-

regiments from the Eaſtern ſhore of Virginia, to quell the inſurrection; who, upon their arrival, finding all quiet, returned, after committing a few depredations.

Although there were ſo many loyaliſts in this country, all of whom I verily believe would have chearfully afforded us any aſſiſtance in their power, yet we thought it moſt prudent to diſcover ourſelves to as few as poſſible; neither did we inform but a very ſmall number of our beſt friends of our ſecret places of retreat, and for the greater ſecurity we kept cloſe concealed during the day, making our removals and excurſions in the night; nor did we ever remain three days together at any one place.

For my own part I went conſtantly well armed, having procured a firelock and bayonet, a pair of piſtols, and a ſword, with plenty of ammunition made up into cartridges; and I never went to reſt without all theſe at my ſide, nor did I ever part with them for a moment.

As from what I had already experienced, I infinitely preferred death to captivity, I was moſt reſolutely determined to defend myſelf to the laſt extremity, even if five hundred men ſhould attack me, for they ſhould never have taken me alive. This reſolution rendered my mind tranquil and eaſy, and furniſhed me with calmneſs and confidence in the midſt of every danger.

Our ſituation unavoidably rendered us liable to many alarms.

One night in particular, the maſter of the houſe wherein we were concealed awaked us about midnight, and informed us that we ſhould all be taken for we were ſurrounded wtth the enemy, and by the moon-light we could plainly perceive that a formidable number of men had actually encompaſſed the houſe ; we immediately prepared for defence, and were levelling our pieces againſt them, when Mr. Manlove diſtinguiſhed one of them to be his brother.

By this we diſcovered that they were friends, who had given us greater ſurprize by by endeavouring to avoid it, and had collected in fuch numbers, from a great diftance around, altogether by accident, to furnifh us with intelligence concerning the rebels.

But although the men in this loyal country were friendly and true, and ready to afford us every affiftance, it was from the goodnefs, care, and fidelity of the women that we received our principal comfort. Their endearing fociety, kindnefs and attention were beyond example, and made us ample amends for all the hardfhips and dangers of our perilous fituation.

In what has been formerly mentioned about the ferocity and favage brutality of the Americans, the ladies muft always be excepted, for they in general are truly humane and benevolent.

Excepting a very few inftances, during my captivity and efcape, the conduct and fentiments of the American women have been conftantly amiable and good.

Throughout the whole of this country they excel the men, beyond comparifon, in every appearance and accomplishment, nor are they equally contaminated with rebellion; for it is by no means uncommon to see the wives of the most violent rebels, even of their Generals, perfectly loyal and well-affected, and ready to furnish intelligence and assistance to the friends of government, at every hazard to themselves and the greatest risques imaginable.

I always reprobated the idea of the fair sex being incapable of keeping secrets, and here it was my fortune to experience the falsity of it in the most ample manner, and in hundreds of instances; being in the power of a great many women of every description, and not one of them ever betrayed me: but on the contrary they have frequently concealed me in their bed-chambers, whilst their rebel suitors (to whom sometimes they were even engaged in marriage contracts,) paid them visits, which they contrived to render as short as possible, for female ingenuity is never at a loss.

On the feventeenth of February we were joined by Doctor P. Kennedy from Baltimore, who alfo wifhed to take refuge on board a King's fhip from the perfecution of the rebels. And on the firft of March there came on a violent fnow ftorm, which lafted three days, and was then three feet deep, a circumftance very uncommon in this part of America.

On the day after the fnow ceafed falling, there were no lefs than thirty-two deer killed in the vicinity of the place where we were concealed.

Apprehenfive of being difcovered, our fituation having now become particularly irkfome and dangerous, not only from the fnow, which enabled our footfteps to be traced, but alfo from this long delay near one place, although we were perpetually changing our hidden retreats fometimes to very confiderable diftances from each other, and defpairing of a fhip of war arriving on the coaft in any reafonable time, we were forming many fchemes of proceeding to New York; fometimes of croffing the Delaware Bay, and travelling by land through the Jerseys, sometimes of rowing in a canoe all along the coast, and many others equally hazardous and enterprising; when at last, on the eleventh of March, we discovered two lofty ships and a sloop standing in for the Cape, and without waiting to hear what they were, immediately prepared for our departure.

At night, on the twelfth of March, after taking a tender and affectionate farewell of these truly meritorious and inestimable friends, who at every possible risque had rendered us such great and essential services, we set out, in a canoe, from the head of Rehoboth Bay, bound for the men of war at the Cape.

There were eleven of us in the canoe, viz. Thomas Robinson and Boaz Manlove of Sussex, Esquires, Doctor Kennedy of Baltimore, now a Captain in his Majesty's service in the regiment of Maryland Loyalists, Mr. Kollock of Sussex, now a Captain in the regiment of Loyal Americans, and myself, besides three more white men, and three Indians.

Our

Our canoe was formed out of the trunk of a fingle tree hollowed or dug out, and we depended folely upon oars, as thefe kind of veffels are at beft very dangerous, and never carry a fail.

We had to row over Rehoboth Bay fix miles to Indian River, thence four miles over the bar at the mouth, then eighteen miles upon the Atlantic Ocean, and afterwards three or four miles within Cape Hinlopen to Whorekill Road, in the entrance of the Delaware Bay, where we expected to find the fhips.

When we came to the mouth of Indian River, there was a dangerous bar to crofs, and the breakers or waves were running prodigioufly high. The fky was overcaft, the night was lowering, and threatened a ftorm. It was about dark when we approached the bar, and the breakers had really a dreadful appearance.

Every one but myfelf wifhed to return; I promifed, perfuaded, and intreated them to proceed, but in vain, they all were averfe to venture. However being at the helm

I would

I would not give up my place, and before they were aware of it steered the vessel into the midst of the breakers.

There was then no possibility of turning back. We were compelled to stand on, and cross the breakers obliquely, as had we attempted to change our course the canoe would have been instantly overset, and every soul of us must inevitably have perished.

By this manœuvre I got them over the bar against their inclinations; but the tossing of the vessel caused most of them to be sea-sick.

It being a strong ebb tide we were inadvertently carried out of sight of land; but after some time perceiving the light in the light-house on the Cape, we steered for it.

When we had rowed about eighteen or twenty miles from Indian River, and were only three or four miles south-east of the light-house, a violent squall came on, from the north-west, with incessant thunder, lightning, wind, and rain.

Every

Every one, excepting myself who was silent, unanimously resolved to return and make for land; and they rowed back for the distance of seven miles with all their might before they took time to reflect, how, in that dark stormy night, they could distinguish the right channel over the bar again; and if we missed it, which was almost certain, the canoe must be dashed to pieces by the breakers, and we could not possibly be saved from destruction.

This reflection suggested by me caused them to stop all on a sudden, and they next proposed running the vessel on shore upon the beach, and carrying her across it to Rehoboth Bay.

I took this opportunity of persuading them to return in search of the men of war; representing the danger of landing on the beach, where, the breakers running prodigiously high, the canoe must be staved before we reached the shore, and many of us thereby must be inevitably lost. Should we even escape that fate, we would not all be able to carry the
vessel

vessel acrofs the beach, which was a mile and a half wide over deep sand hills, to the bay; and that, as we must then land in the midst of our enemies, they would certainly discover us, and the whole country of the rebels would be in pursuit of us, so that we could not possibly escape them.

They were then totally at a lofs what to do, as there seemed to be nothing but death before us on all sides.

Taking advantage of this, I prevailed on them to attempt once more to get round to the Delaware. I cheared up their drooping spirits, and took an oar myself.

With amazing fatigue, and very great danger, we at length doubled Cape Hinlopen, and rowed all over Whorekill Road, without hearing or seeing any appearance of a ship.

The night was very dark, and it was one continued storm of thunder, lightning, wind, and hail, the violence of which

which forced us to the shore; glad to get to any part of it within the Cape for shelter.

At three o'clock in the morning we reached land, and found ourselves close by Lewis Town, within a few hundred yards of a rebel guard; so that we dared not kindle a fire, or make the least noise, lest we should thereby be discovered.

In this situation we remained upon the open beach during the rest of the night, exposed to the snow, wind, and rain.

In the mean time we sent Captain Kollock and one of the Indians to the lighthouse, in disguise, to make enquiry about the ships.

In about an hour they returned with an account, that two ships had been in the road that afternoon, that one of them had stood out to sea, and the other lay at anchor, off the light-house, abreast of the Cape.

At five o'clock, just about break of day, we embarked again in our canoe,

left

left this hostile shore, and once more launched out into the Atlantic.

About half a mile from land there came on a prodigious heavy thick fog, so that we could not see twenty yards around.

Just before the mist came on I imagined that I discovered the looming of a ship at a great distance, and by the assistance of a small pocket compass steered towards the place where she seemed to be. Having continued that course for an hour, without hearing or seeing any thing, they all began to murmur and despond; our hands likewise were so blistered with rowing, that the blood ran down, and we were quite exhausted with cold and fatigue. Just then we heard something like a grampus spouting, and rowed with all our might towards the sound: the noise was soon repeated, and we were then sensible it proceeded from spunging a gun: this, together with some chips and trash floating on the sea, revived our hopes, and cheered our drooping spirits;

and

and foon afterwards the crowing of a cock put it out of doubt that a ſhip was nigh.

Some of us obſerving that it might be a rebel frigate it alarmed our fears, and we concluded, if we found it ſo, that we would paſs ourſelves for ſome people croſſing from Cape May to Lewis Town, who had got loſt in the fog, and were driven out to ſea.

In the mean time all on a ſudden the ſhip appeared near enough for us to diſtinguiſh the name of PRESTON on her ſtern.

Never until this moment did I conſider myſelf out of danger ; and I now felt ſuch a tide of happineſs and joy, that it almoſt overpowered my ſenſes.

Every perſon in the ſhip was aſtoniſhed at ſeeing us ; and the worthy Commodore Hotham, as well as all the officers, received us on board in the moſt hoſpitable, kind, and friendly manner; ſo that it almoſt effaced the remembrance of our diſappointment from the Falcon.

We

We had not been half an hour on board, when a perfect hurricane came on from the land at north-weſt. It was ſo ſudden, and ſo violent, that, before our canoe could be hoiſted on board, it tore out the iron ring-bolt from her head, forced her from the ſhip, filled her, and ſent her out of ſight in an inſtant.

It alſo drove the Preſton out to ſea; and every officer on board repeatedly congratulated us on our moſt fortunate and hair-breadth eſcape and deliverance: becauſe had we not found the ſhip, which it was really aſtoniſhing that we did in ſuch a fog, we muſt every man have inevitably periſhed, as ſhe was four or five leagues from land, and we could not have rowed one league farther before the ſtorm came on.

CHAP. LXIX.

Take a fine Prize. Singular Circumstance attending the Capture. Go on board the Daphne. Excellent Regulations on Board. Affecting Story of a beautiful young Lady. Set sail for New York with the Prize Ship in Tow. Arrival at New York. Wait upon the Admiral and General. Meet with many Friends and Acquaintances.

THIS gale, which had instantly dispersed and carried off the fog, was extremely violent, and soon forced us out of sight of land; but it abated towards evening, and the Daphne with the Hotham sloop tender and two prizes came up with us.

Mr. Brown a midshipman and I went on board the Hotham sloop, and we all steered towards the Cape.

As we were all close hauled we in the sloop went considerably nigher the wind than the ships, and at break of day they were out of our sight; but we discovered a fine

fine ship standing in for the mouth of the Delaware, to which we gave chace.

We found ourselves gain upon her very fast, and coming up with her just off Cape May, perceived her to be very handsome, large, and formidable; and we could also distinguish with our glasses the men on board drawn up with small arms preparing for defence, yet still she stood on towards Cape May, where the channel is shallow and hazardous. But the wind dying away as soon as we came pretty close to her, I went in the boat with the sailors and marines to board her.

When we approached along-side we saw eighteen men with small arms just ready to fire into the boat, when Mr. Graves, who commanded the Hotham, observing it, at that very instant fired one of his two pounders into the ship amongst them, which lucky shot determined her fate.

All her hands, twenty-six in number, immediately jumped into their boats and rowed

rowed to land, after lafhing the helm hard up in order to run the fhip on fhore on Cape May, being then within two hundred yards of it, where two or three hundred rebels were drawn up under arms ready to protect her when fhe drove up. But the fhip wearing quite round ran back into the very hands of the Hotham floop, who immediately boarded and took poffeffion of her.

Taking this prize gave us greater fatisfaction and pleafure, becaufe the Hotham herfelf was but a trifling fmall floop of no force, carrying only two little guns, two pounders, befides a few fwivels.

We found on board the fhip eighteen new French firelocks lying upon the deck all loaded; befides five hundred ftand of fmall arms in her hold, three hundred and fifty barrels of gunpowder, fiftytwo tons of lead, a large quantity of fail cloth, tents, camp equipage, medicines, books, and even all their papers, letters, and manufcripts. A moft valuable prize; not fo much on account of what it would

pro-

produce at fale, as the lofs the enemy fuf-
tained by the capture.

This fhip was named the Sally, (bound from Nantz to Philadelphia, of two hundred and thirty tons burden, a beautiful veffel Philadelphia built.

A fine breeze fpringing up, we immediately ftood out to fea with our prize, and foon came up with the two men of war and the other three prizes; but ours was by far the fineft and moft valuable.

The wind blowing very frefh, and all the veffels lying too, I went on board of the Commodore, and foon after Captain Chinnery of the Daphne came on board alfo.

As the Daphne was to proceed immediately to New York with the prizes, I went on board of her along with Captain Chinnery, to whom the Commodore had introduced me, after returning my moft grateful thanks to the worthy Commodore Hotham, and to all the officers on board the Prefton, for their attention,
civi-

civilities, and favours, and after taking an affectionate farewell: thefe polite, worthy, and very refpectable gentlemen having honoured me with the requeſt that I would keep up a correfpondence with them; and, although that has been interrupted, I fhall never forget their kindnefs, nor my obligations.

The officers then on board the Preſton, befides Commodore Hotham and Captain Uppleby, were the three Captain Graves's, Captain Totty, the honourable Captain De Courcy, Captain T——, Captains Chriſtian and Hart of the marines, Dr. Steedman, chaplain, Dr. Cliffon, furgeon, Mr. Holwell, maſter, Mr. Titus Livius, fecretary to the commodore, &c.; and a fet of more agreeable, accomplifhed and deferving gentlemen never ferved his majefty in one fhip.

I was received and treated on board the Daphne, by Captain Chinnery, Lieutenant Paul, Lieutenant Campbell of Marines, &c. with equal attention and kindnefs to what I had met with on board the Preston; but a constant and severe indisposition destroyed all relish for pleasure, and deprived me of that exquisite joy and satisfaction, which otherwise I should have felt at my fortunate escape out of the power of an illiberal, vindictive, and barbarous enemy.

To my very great concern I perceived that my constitution was quite broken, and this bad state of health occasioned, by long and rigorous confinement among the rebels, and by the hardships of every kind I had experienced in different attempts to escape; especially in the last cold, wet, and stormy night, before we got on board the Preston.

This indisposition, which had been constantly increasing upon me for eighteen months past, was now become so extremely severe that I really did not expect long to survive it.

Had it not been for this sickness I should have been exceedingly happy indeed on board the Daphne, for Captain Chinnery was one of the best of men,

and

and his ſhip was under the moſt excellent regulations. Both whipping and ſwearing were ſtrangers on board, and every one obeyed the commands of his ſuperior with an alacrity and chearfulneſs that made their duty a pleaſure, and rendered the ſervice endearing.

To meet with a lady, young, handſome, and graceful, on board the Daphne out at ſea, it may well be imagined occaſioned to me no ſmall ſurprize.

As the ſhort but melancholy ſtory of this unfortunate young perſon is uncommonly affecting, I cannot forbear relating it, as one of the multitude of ſhocking inſtances of barbarous brutality that ſo frequently occur in the country which is the ſeat of war; in order that the people of Great Britain may be ſenſible of their good fortune and felicity, in being ſo long, and ſo far, from the obſervation and experience of ſuch lamentable and wretched ſcenes.

This unfortunate lady, deſcended from a good family in New Jerſey, was married

ried while very young to an American officer, who was daſtard enough to abandon her at Fort Waſhington in York Iſland, where ſhe was taken in the powder magazine by a private ſoldier of the Heſſians.

This unfeeling wretch, deaf to all her prayers and entreaties to be reſtored to her friends, and blind to her beauty and tears, only as they inflamed his luſt, retained her as his abſolute property, and compelled her to be ſubſervient to all his brutal deſires and drudgery.

None but a ruffian, deſtitute of ſenſibility and common humanity, could have been capable of ſuch barbarity to a moſt beautiful and delicate young creature, not then fifteen, whoſe tears, entreaties, and diſtreſs would have procured protection and aſſiſtance from a ſavage.

The Heſſian finding his captive unfit for his principal purpoſe, viz. carrying his plunder, and having ſufficiently gratified all his deſires with her, actually

ſold

fold her to a British officer, while upon the march to New York, for a shilling.

This officer, being made acquainted with her distress and cruel treatment, not only gave her her liberty, but sent her to New York to his quarters, and supported her decently therein.

This worthy man being slain in a skirmish, the poor unhappy young lady was thrown upon the wide world, destitute of friends, money, cloaths, and almost of the common necessaries for the sustenance of life.

In this deplorable condition she was truly to be commiserated, and fell a victim to the avarice and iniquity of one of those, I had almost said beasts of prey, of her own sex, that always contrive to make a property of unfortunate beatuty.

It was in this situation that she had come on board the Daphne on a visit; and the ship being ordered out immediately on a cruise, she was carried to sea without the knowledge of Captain Chinnery.

This lady was named Sukey *Washington*, after the fort wherein she was taken, and by that she is pretty well known in New York.

But I am apprehensive there have been many more such instances of misfortune and brutality, although the unhappy victims have not become so public.

On the fifteenth of March about noon, we took the prize ship in tow, and steered our course for New York, with a stiff breeze; having made an observation this day, and found ourselves in thirty-eight degrees thirty minutes north latitude; the longitude was seventy-four degrees fifteen minutes west.

The wind continuing to blow fresh and fair, we came in sight of Never-Sink Hills (the first high land on the American coast to the northward of Cape Florida,) on the morning following about nine o'clock; and soon afterwards arrived off Sandy-Hook and the light house,

within

within which we came to anchor, with all our prizes fafe, and remained there that night.

On the day following the Daphne beat up to New York, the wind being a-head, and anchored in the North River.

On the eighteenth I went on fhore, where I found Caleb Jones, of Princefs Anne, Somerfet county, Maryland, Efq. who had arrived at New York before me in the Brune frigate, from the Chefapeak.

(At New York I immediately waited on Lord Howe, and Sir) William Howe, then his majefty's Commanders in Chief, &c. and had the pleafure of meeting with Brigadier-general Mac Donald, Captain Campbell, and feveral more of my much efteemed friends; who, after the mutual congratulations on our being fo fortunate, contrary to every former expectation and probability, as to meet together once more in the much prized enjoyment of liberty and real freedom, under the mild and benign influence of

British government, and in the protection of his majesty's arms, after the unexampled hardships, severities, and cruel maltreatment we had all experienced from a rude, illiberal, and barbarous enemy, continued in honouring me with every attention, civility, and kindness, until our duty in the different lines and scenes of action in his majesty's service interrupted this agreeable intercourse of friendship by separation, being ordered to different and very distant parts of the vast continent of America.

CHAP.

CHAP. LXX.

Visit the British Posts and the Works thrown up by the Americans. Danbury Expedition. New England. Account of the Country, Inhabitants, &c. Their Inhospitality and Inquisitiveness. Connecticut River. Hartford. New Haven. Number of Inhabitants in Connecticut, Rhode Island, Massachussets Bay and New Hampshire. Newport. Providence. Boston. Salem. Portsmouth.

NOTWITHSTANDING the continuance of my bad state of health, I immediately visited all the posts in the vicinity of New York occupied by the British troops, and viewed the multitude of works, all over the island, thrown up by the rebels, which will remain lasting monuments of American folly and fearfulness, notwithstanding they have so unexpectedly, even to themselves, succeeded in their wild and fatal pursuits, far beyond their most sanguine and presumptuous hopes.

Contrary to the advice of all my friends I also accompanied an expedition to Danbury

bury in Connecticut, where we destroyed a great quantity of stores, &c. collected by the rebels, and deposited there as in a place of absolute security.

But as the particulars of this excursion, as well as of all the other expeditions, campaigns, engagements and skirmishes in which I had the honour of serving his majesty during the war, will be given in the regular chain of events as they occurred, in a separate volume or appendix, I shall pass it over here, and only mention the appearance of the country, and the inhabitants, to a person totally a stranger and unacquainted with them.

However from the very disadvantageous occurrences and events attending my visit to that province, during the circumscribed distance and stay I made therein, this account must unavoidably be incorrect, cursory, and superficial, and cannot be placed in competition with that already given of the more southern provinces, through which I had

very

very often travelled under more agreeable and favourable circumstances, and had frequent and ample opportunities of becoming much more intimately acquainted with their inhabitants, customs, dispositions, sentiments, commerce, produce, agriculture, and soil, as well as the appearance of the country, the beauties of the perspective, and the extent of the rivers and settlements.

The whole face of nature, as well as the manners and dialect of the people here are widely different from that of the southern provinces, and greatly to the disadvantage of New England.

The land in general is broken, poor, and stoney, excepting on the banks of rivers, where there is a narrow slip of rich low grounds on each side, commonly converted into meadows.

The timber is inferior in magnitude and height, the Indian corn itself is of a diminutive growth, and every other produce of a worse quality, as well as less in quantity.

The

The inhabitants too are possessed of narrow principles, bigotted and illiberal. Almost universally fanatics in religion, their manners, customs, and opinions are strongly tinctured with puritanism, their sentiments confined, and their benevolence of mind extremely limited.

At the same time that they are destitute of that hospitality, and generous openness of heart, so prevalent in the southern provinces, they super-abound in impertinent curiosity, and troublesome inquisitiveness. A stranger may travel in New England many a day without being once asked to eat or drink; but he cannot call at any house whatever without being required to give an account of himself by every person therein, and indeed frequently by those that may overtake him as he rides along the road. They will desire to know ("Whence he "came? Where he is going? What his "business is there? How long he in- "tends to stay? Whether he will return "that way? Likewise his name, estate, family,

" family, situation in life, general opi-
" nions, and future intentions?"

But on Sundays he muſt not travel at all, not even to change his inn for the ſake of better accommodations.

Property in this country is very much divided, and even ſubdivided; ſo that you will ſeldom ſee a conſiderable farm, although almoſt every houſe or family in the towns or townſhips have a few acres annexed to them, yet theſe ſmall portions of land are by no means cultivated to the beſt advantage as might be expected; for agriculture here is ſtill in its infancy, and not equal to the ſtate thereof in any of the reſt of the provinces.

Excepting Boſton, Newport, and a very few others, the towns in general are no better than ſtraggling villages, yet theſe undoubtedly are numerous, conſidering the inferiority of the ſoil as well as climate.

However it muſt not be imagined but that there are ſome tracts of good land, as well as a few hoſpitable people to be

met

met with, throughout the whole four of these wide extended and thick settled provinces of New England: it would be a very strange thing indeed if it was not so; but certain it is, that the generality of the inhabitants, and bulk of the land is far otherwise.

The New Englanders are disliked by the inhabitants of all the other provinces, by whom they are called *Yankeys*, by way of derision, and they seem to return a similar kind and degree of affection towards all the rest; yet at the same time appear to acknowledge a kind of an inferiority, for they actually depend upon the southern provinces for the principal part of the bread they eat; and for that purpose every winter their sloops, schooners and small vessels are swarming in all the ports and rivers south of New York, where they purchase Indian corn and other grain; for which in return they give rum of an inferior quality, molasses, cordials, dried fish, and all kinds of European goods

but

but always of the worst and cheapest kinds.

In fact they are the Dutch of America; and have engrossed the same share of commerce there, as the others have done in Europe; deriving their subsistence also in a similar manner from fishing and trade.

In the fishing season they repair to the banks of Newfoundland, where they seldom fail of loading their vessels; and the rest of the year they trade to the southern provinces, the West Indies, and even to Europe.

In these fishing as well as trading voyages it is their general custom for every man in the vessel to have some concern or share in the cargo, and consequently in the profits of the trade.

Although New England abounds with excellent harbours for small vessels, yet there is no considerable river in all the four provinces, excepting Connecticut River in the province of that name, and Merrymack River, Sagahadock River, Kenebeck River,

River, and Penobſcot River, in New Hampſhire.

Of all theſe, Connecticut River is much the fineſt, largeſt, and moſt valuable, as well as the beſt ſettled and the longeſt; being about three hundred miles from its ſource, not far diſtant from lake St. Pierre in the river of St. Laurence in Canada where it interlocks with the head branches of the river St. Francis, to the mouth between the inconſiderable villages of Saybrook and Lyme in the Sound which ſeparates Long Iſland from the Continent.

This river is navigable for ſmall craft as far as the town of Hartford, which is about thirty-five miles from its entrance into the Sound.

The courſe of the Connecticut, from its ſource being nearly ſouth-by-weſt to its mouth, includes ſeveral degrees of latitude, viz. from forty-five degrees two minutes to forty-one degrees fifteen minutes north.

In the exaggerated calculation of the number of inhabitants publiſhed by the Congreſs,

Congrefs, the province of Connecticut was said to contain one hundred and ninety-two thousand; the province of Rhode Island fifty-nine thousand six hundred and seventy-eight; the province of Massachuset's Bay four hundred thousand; and the province of New Hampshire one hundred and fifty thousand; being altogether eight hundred and one thousand six hundred and seventy-eight.

This undoubtedly is very considerably beyond the truth; for in the last actual numbering of all the inhabitants in the United States of America, by order of Congrefs, for proportioning the affeffment for taxes, in 1783, Connecticut contained two hundred and six thousand; Rhode Island fifty thousand four hundred; Massachuset's Bay three hundred and fifty thousand; and New Hampshire eighty-two thousand two hundred; amounting to six hundred and eighty-eight thousand six hundred souls in all the four New England governments, of which about one twentieth part are Negroes and civilized Indians.

The capital of Connecticut is Hartford, but the towns of New London and New-haven are certainly more confiderable than it; the reft of the towns, as has been obferved before, are nothing better than fcattering villages, yet many of them containing a number of inhabitants nearly equal to thofe of the towns above mentioned.

Of the government of Rhode Ifland, Newport is the capital, and is a large and very beautiful town, with an excellent harbour. Excepting Providence, which is alfo a confiderable town, there is none elfe of note in this province.

Bofton, the capital of Maffachufets Bay, is one of the largeft, moft populous, and fineft cities in North America; poffeffing an excellent harbour, and a multitude of delightful perfpective views from every fide.

Salem in this province is the next in magnitude to Bofton, and the reft of the

towns

towns are similar to those of Connecticut, but considerably larger.

New Hampshire is still in its infancy, and its capital Portsmouth is but a small insignificant place, not near so considerable as many of the towns in the other provinces which have not been thought sufficiently deserving of notice even to be named here.

CHAP. LXXI.

Description of New York. Its delightful and advantageous Situation. Fort Washington. Long Island. Description of it. Hell Gates, a dreadful and dangerous Strait. Description thereof. Hampstead Plains. An Account of them. A very singular Insect. Dangerous Sand Banks. Loss of the Liverpool. Description of Staten Island. Account of the North River. Mohawks River, and Hudson's River. Albany. Trade of New York. Fire. Dutch Inhabitants. Number of Souls in the Province.

HAVING made many excursions over the greatest part of Long Island, as well as Staten Island, York Island, and West Chester County on the continent, in the government of New York, I shall embrace this opportunity of giving a sketch of these places, in a manner that has not been generally described.

The city of New York, the capital of the province, is beautifully situated on the southern extremity of an island of the same name, which is about sixteen miles in length, and not more than three miles wide in the broadeſt part.

This iſland, being a county in itſelf named after the capital, is formed by the Hudſon or North River on the weſt; the Eaſt River, which is the name of the narroweſt extremity of the Sound, or arm of the ſea, that ſeparates Long Iſland from the Continent, on the ſouth-eaſt; and a ſmall branch or natural canal named Haerlem River, King's-Bridge River, or Spiking Devil, on the north, which communicates between the North River, and the Eaſt River, near a place on the laſt mentioned River named Hell Gates.

Nothing can be more delightful than the ſituation of New York, commanding a variety of the moſt charming proſpects that can be conceived.

It is built chiefly upon the Eaſt River, which is the beſt and ſafeſt harbour and is only ſomething more than half a mile wide.

The North River is better than two miles over to Powles Hook, which is a ſtrong work oppoſite to New York, is expoſed

posed to the north winds, and to the driving of the ice in the winter, whereby ships are prevented from lying therein during that season of the year.

The land on the North River side is high and bold, but on the East River it gradually descends in a beautiful declivity to the water's edge.

The town is entirely commanded by a considerable eminence in Long Island, directly opposite to it, named Brookland Heights, on which a strong regular fort, with four bastions, has lately been erected by the British troops.

About a third and it is said the most beautiful part of this town has been destroyed by a fire, which happened soon after it was taken possession of by his Majesty's forces: and it is beyond a doubt, that this most iniquitous and abominable action was committed by the American incendiaries, several of whom were detected in the infamous fact of setting fire to combustibles purposely placed in the houses, and immediately

diately were thrown into the flames by the enraged foldiery.

This city, while in poffeffion of the Britifh troops, might contain about thirty thoufand fouls, but the numbers muft be diminifhed at leaft one-third, perhaps one-half, or more, by the evacuation.

There is a great number of moft delightful fituations in the vicinity of New York, which is really a very beautiful country.

The harbour, efpecially the Eaft River, is one of the beft in the world, being fheltered from every wind, having excellent anchoring ground, and fufficient depth of water for fhips of the line, which could almoft lay their broadfides to the wharfs.

To defcribe the works thrown up by the Americans upon this ifland would take up more room than this volume can afford, or the fubject deferves, as they actually cover the whole ifland.

Two only I fhall take notice of, viz. a ftrong work on an eminence, juft at the entrance into the town from the land,
which

which is named Bunker's-hill; the other is fort Washington, or Kniphausen, on the North River, whose banks are every where very high and particularly so at this place, just ten miles north from New York.

The situation of this fort is singularly strong and advantageous, so as to be capable of being rendered almost impregnable; but all this country abounds with strong and commanding situations.

King's-Bridge which joins the northern extremity of this island to the continent, is only a small wooden bridge, and the country around is mountainous, rocky, broken, and disagreeable, but very strong.

Amongst the multitude of elegant seats upon this island there are three or four uncommonly beautiful, viz. Governor Elliot's, Judge Jones's, 'Squire Morris's, and Mr. Bateman's.

And opposite upon the Continent, just above Hell-gates, there is a villa, named Morrisania, which is inferior to no place in the world for the beauties, grandeur,

and

and extent of perspective, and the elegance of its situation.

New York is just thirty miles north from the sea, which is at Sandy Hook; and there is no place in the world that enjoys the advantages of every kind peculiar to the finest navigable rivers more amply than New York.

The land in the country adjacent is strong, stiff, rocky, and broken, the inclosures being generally made of stone.

Long Island, which is in this government, is the largest island from Cape Florida to Cape Sable, and is indeed a very fine and most valuable one. It is an hundred and thirty miles in length, and about fifteen miles broad at a medium, extending from opposite Staten Island, and Sandy Hook in the Jerseys, to Montock Point, which is opposite to the boundary line between Connecticut and Rhode Island.

All the south-east side of Long Island, or as it is called therein the south side, next to the Atlantic Ocean, is low, level, sandy, and infertile, having extensive bays
running

running within the land almoſt the whole length of the iſland. The north-weſt ſide, or as it is there called the North ſide, next to the Continent, is high, hilly, and broken, with numbers of fine harbours, creeks, and bays, and abundance of excellent ſituations, and rich land. Through the middle of the iſland length-ways, there runs a chain of high hills, which command a view of the ocean, and a great variety of the moſt delightful and extenſive proſpects.

Two-thirds of the inhabitants of this iſland, eſpecially on the weſt end, are of low Dutch extraction, and continue to make uſe of their cuſtoms and language in preference to Engliſh, which however they alſo underſtand.

But they differ materially from the Hollanders in the article of cleanlineſs, thoſe in Long Iſland being not only conſtantly inveloped in dirt and naſtineſs, but their houſes and food are often rendered almoſt intolerable with filth and uncleanneſs.

There

There is no such thing as society amongst these people, at least for a Briton, for they and their constant companions the hogs and cattle appear to possess an equal share of sensibility and sentiment. Many of them however are opulent, and they all live well, or rather plentifully.

In the whole province of New York there are fourteen counties; of which three are in Long Island, viz. King's County, Queen's County, and Suffolk County. The two first are in the west end of the island, and the last includes all the middle and east end, being above half the island.

The inhabitants of King's County are almost entirely Dutch. In Queen's County four fifths of the people are so likewise; but the other fifth, and all Suffolk County are English, as they call themselves, being from English ancestors, and using no other language.

The towns in this island, as upon the continent in New England, are little better than scattering villages, and the manner

manner of living of the inhabitants is pretty much similar, but destitute of that degree of illiberality and narrow-mindedness, which proceeds from the fanaticism of the New Englanders; for in Long Island there is some small share of hospitality, and sometimes indeed of generosity, to be met with. This however is much more prevalent among the English inhabitants than among the Dutch.

Although considerable numbers of the inhabitants of this island have acquired much money during the late war, yet many more have been most cruelly oppressed, and vast numbers of them repeatedly plundered by the depredations of both sides.

Such shocking instances of barbarous brutality have frequently occurred in different parts of Long Island, during this unfortunate conflict, that the bare recollection of them is painful in the extreme, therefore a relation of them could not be acceptable.

There are two very extraordinary places in and adjoining to this island, the like
of

of which are not to be met with in all America besides, and are well deserving of the observation of travellers.

The first is a very dangerous and dreadful strait or passage, called *Hell-Gates*, between the East river and the Sound; where the two tides meeting cause a horrible whirlpool, the vortex of which is named the Pot, and drawing in and swallowing up every thing that approaches near it, dashes them to pieces upon the rocks at the bottom; at one time of tide this tremendous whirlpool boils furiously like a pot, and at another time it sucks like a funnel every thing into it.

Opposite to this is another dreadful reef of rocks, named the Frying Pan, over which the tide rages with great violence, making a noise resembling water poured upon red-hot iron; this also draws vessels towards it, to their certain and utter destruction.

In an oblique direction between these two, there lies another sharp ledge of rocks, as dangerous as either of the former,

named

named the Hog's Back, which proves fatal to as many veffels as any of the others.

It requires the greateft fkill and care imaginable to pilot fhips through this moft dreadful and dangerous ftrait, and there is fcarce a tide paffes but fome veffel is dafhed upon the rocks; for in endeavouring to avoid the Pot, they frequently are carried directly upon the Frying Pan; and if a veffel is fo fortunate as to pafs clear of both thefe, fhe has ftill the utmoft difficulty to avoid being wrecked upon the Hog's Back, which lies almoft in the middle of the narrow channel between the others.

The tide here likewife rufhes on with an impetuofity and fury dreadful to behold, and both fhores, as well as the whole bed and channel of the ftrait, confift of vaft, horrible, dark brown rocks, with fharp edges pointed in every direction, and are generally covered with wrecks.

The fafeft time for paffing through this moft perilous and horrid Strait is at high water with a ftiff breeze; yet
even

even at this time a skilful pilot is absolutely necessary, in order to avoid the sharp ledges and reefs of rocks, then just sufficiently covered with water to render them the more dangerous.

Before the late war, a top-sail vessel was seldom ever known to pass through Hell Gates; but since the commencement of it, fleets of transports, with frigates for their convoy, have frequently ventured and accomplished it: the Niger indeed, a very fine frigate of thirty-two guns, generally struck on some hidden rock, every time she attempted this passage.

But what is still more extraordinary, that daring veteran, Sir James Wallace, to the astonishment of every person who ever saw or heard of it, carried his Majesty's ship the Experiment, of fifty guns, safe through Hell Gates, from the east end of the Sound to New York; when the French fleet under D'Estaing lay off Sandy Hook, and blocked up the harbour and city of New York, some ships of the line being

also

also sent by D'Estaing round the east end of Long Island to cruize in the Sound for the same purpose. So that the Experiment must inevitably have fallen into their hands, had it not been for this bold and successful attempt of her gallant commander.

The other remarkable place is Hampstead Plains, which begin about fourteen or fifteen miles from New York, and including what is called the Brushy Plains, extend near twenty miles in length, and from three to eight miles in breadth.

These plains are perfectly level, and destitute of timber, not a tree growing upon them throughout their whole extent, which in America is a very striking and singular phænomenon.

They are said to be incapable of producing either trees, or any other growth or vegetation, excepting grass of a coarse and inferior quality; only about half of them, which are named the Brushy Plains, is covered with a production of brush or shrubs, extremely thick and low, being not more than about three, four, and five

feet

feet in height above the surface of the ground, and never grows higher.

The soil of these plains consists of a thin covering of a mossy kind of black earth, of a spungy contexture, over an universal bed of gravel, which immediately absorbs the heaviest rains, and prevents water from remaining upon the ground. From this it may be naturally and readily concluded, that in wet seasons they throw out great quantities of grass, and consequently in dry years they are entirely parched up.

These plains are a kind of common, and support an immense number of sheep, black cattle, and horses, which are supplied with water from ponds made in different places and the bottom covered with clay to collect and retain the rain; for there are no springs or running water to be met with throughout their whole extent; and they are entirely unenclosed, and almost totally uninhabited, excepting some few houses for the accommodation of travellers.

Their great extent, and the perfect equality of their surface, renders the appearance of the horizon around, to a person travelling over them, very much resembling that to be observed at sea; and in the same manner the inhabitants bordering on these extensive plains direct a person, enquiring the way to any particular place, to proceed south, southwest, east, or north-east, or some other point of the compass, according to the situation of the spot to which he is going.

On the north side of these plains the ground begins to swell into ascents, and even little hills, the soil being stiff, strong, and stony. On the south side the land is perfectly level, sandy, and rather poor.

Around the edge of Hampstead or the Great Plains, besides the towns or townships of Jamaica, Hampstead, &c. the places have singular names, selected from the scripture it is true, but still very uncommon, such as Jerusalem, Jericho, Barsheba, Bethsaida, &c. where the inhabitants are chiefly Quakers. And in the

the weft end of the ifland the firft Dutch fettlers named their villages after the different towns in the United Provinces in Europe from whence they came, as Flufhing, Brooklyn, Wolabacht, Haaerlem, &c.

There is a very fingular infect in this ifland, which I do not remember to have obferved in any other part of America. They are named by the inhabitants here *Katy did's*, from their note, which is loud and ftrong, bearing a ftriking refemblance to thofe words.

They are from an inch to an inch and three quarters in length, of a moft beautiful vivid green, as thick as a lady's finger, with two large and almoft tranfparent wings: they are perfectly inoffenfive, but extremely clamorous and noify: they generally appear about the middle of fummer, in great numbers, and fix their refidence among the leaves and fmall branches of young lively fruit-trees, but the cherry is their favourite, and their green colour renders them difcovered with great difficulty; but their noife is loud and inceffant, one perpetually and regularly anfwering the other in notes exactly fimilar to the words *Katy did*, or *Katy Katy did*, repeated by one, and another immediately bawls out *Katy did'n't*, or *Katy Katy did'n't*. In this loud clamour they continue without ceafing until the fall of the leaf, when they totally difappear.

The whole fouth-eaft coaft of Long Ifland is particularly dangerous for fhipping; being deftitute of a fingle harbour for any thing but boats and very fmall coafting veffels, throughout its whole extent. At the fame time there are a great many very fine bays and harbours on the north fide of the ifland.

On the fouth fide, fand banks and bars prevent fhips from approaching within two miles of the fhore: this, together with the great extent of the inland bays all along this coaft, which are generally from five to ten miles wide within the beech that feparates them from the Atlantic Ocean, whereby the appearance of the land, which is naturally low, is thus alfo rendered very diftant, and the prodigious feas seas that run along this open coaſt, renders all this ſide extremely dangerous, eſpecially in the night when the wind ſets violently on ſhore, and the ſhips have not previouſly made the land in the day.

This occaſioned the loſs of his majeſty's ſhip the Liverpool, the remains of which are ſtill to be ſeen on Rockaway Beech, ſo cloſe to the ſhore as great part of her to be dry at low water.

From the weſt end of Long Iſland I paſſed over, at what is called the Narrows, to Staten Iſland, which is about three miles from the neareſt part of Long Iſland, and nine miles due ſouth from New York.

This iſland belongs to the government of New York, and contains juſt one county named Richmond. It is ſixteen miles long, and between eight and eleven in breadth. Like Long Iſland, the north ſide of this alſo is high land, broken and ſtony, while the ſouth ſide is low and level. The ſoil is more light, and not ſo fertile as upon Long Iſland.

O₂

On Staten Island there is but one town, which is named Richmond, and it is the county town and principal place on the island. At the Narrows, next to Long Island, the land is very high, and commands an extensive view of land and water, and very beautiful prospects.

This being the place of residence of my poor old fellow-prisoner Abraham Wynant, whom I left dangerously ill in Baltimore when I effected my escape, I called at his house to make enquiries concerning him; and greatly to my surprize and satisfaction found him there himself, where he had arrived long before I had got on board the Preston.

He informed me that he was indebted to the people of Baltimore for his liberation, who had exerted themselves in his behalf for that purpose, on account of his ill state of health, and quiet inoffensive conduct.

Poor Wynant was happy beyond measure at seeing me, having understood that I had been killed during my escape.

The

The North or Hudson's River is the boundary between the government of New York and that of New Jersey until it reaches a large bay formed therein named Topham Sea, about thirty miles above the city of New York. The boundary line of the province of New York then crosses the river, and runs in a north-west course, until it touches the river Viskill, or the upper part of the eastern branch of the Delaware.

The land upon the North River is of various qualities, but generally stony, stiff, and strong, excepting in the high lands or mountains, where it is rocky and barren.

Beyond Albany, upon the Mohawks River, the land is in general very rich and fertile, but the country is chiefly inhabited by Germans, and the climate extremely incommoded with cold during the winter, which is there long and rigorous.

The shores of the North River are entirely different from any other on the continent, being remarkably high, bold, and even

even mountainous, to the water's edge, in general as far up as the high lands or mountains, at West Point, through which this noble river passes, above fifty-five miles above the city of New York. Beyond the high lands there are large bodies of very valuable low grounds on each side.

This noble and mighty river is navigable as far as Albany, which is an hundred and sixty miles above New York, and the tide flows about ten or fifteen miles still higher, to the confluence of the river Mohawk with the Hudson, which are the two great branches of the North River.

By the Mohawks River, which heads near Lake Oneyda, there is a communication with Lake Ontario and Canada, only a few portages intervening. On this river is a large cataract, called the Cohoes, the water of which is said to fall seventy feet perpendicular, where the river is a quarter of a mile in breadth.

By the Hudson's River, which is the northern branch, there is an immediate and ready communication, through Lake George,

George, Lake Champlain, and down the Sorel and St. Laurence rivers, into the heart of Canada, which is the shortest, best, and most generally made use of.

The source of the Hudson is not far distant from the Cadarakui or St. Laurence, and interlocks with the head waters of a small branch thereof named Swegatchi River, from whence to the entrance of the North River into the ocean at Sandy Hook is not less than three hundred miles in a direct course, of which this noble, grand, and beautiful river is navigable almost two hundred miles, the tide also flowing nearly that distance within it.

Albany is a large and very fine town, being the second in the province, and contains near six thousand inhabitants. Excepting Montreal in Canada, and Augusta in Georgia, Albany possesses the greatest share of the Indian trade of any place on the continent. All the rest of the towns in this province are actually nothing better than scattering villages.

Before

Before the late unhappy war the trade of New York was very confiderable. Their commodities were wheat, flour, barley, oats, fome Indian corn, beef, pork, fkins, and furs. Their exports then annually amounted to five hundred and thirty thoufand pounds fterling, and their imports from Great Britain to five hundred and thirty-five thoufand pounds.

In the firft computation of the number of inhabitants, publifhed by the Congrefs, this government was faid to contain two hundred and fifty thoufand: this was undoubtedly exaggerated about fifty thoufand, as is afcertained by their laft enumeration, in 1783, for the purpofe of proportioning an equal affeffment of taxes, when the number of fouls was then calculated at two hundred thoufand, of which number about one third may be Negroes.

CHAP. LXXII.

New Jerfey. Defcriptiion of it. Perth-Amboy. Burlington. Prince Town, &c. Produce fhipped from New York and Philadelphia. Different Towns in New Jerfey. Remarkable Cataract. This Province has fuffered greatly during the War.

THE only province now remaining to be noticed is New Jerfey: of this likewife I am enabled to give but a fuperficial account, obtained and collected during feveral excurfions and expeditions therein along with detachments of the Britifh army, both from New York, Staten Ifland, Perth Amboy, and Brunfwick, and from Philadelphia and the Delaware, in which I had the honour of a command; as well as in the march of the grand army, acrofs that country, from Philadelphia to Sandy Hook and New York.

The inferior province of New Jerfey ftands in the fame predicament with its two powerful neighbours of Penſylvania and New York, as North Carolina does with South Carolina and Virginia, For a great proportion of the produce of New Jerſey is exported from the cities of Philadelphia and New York, to which places it is carried to market.

Perth Amboy, the capital of Eaſt New Jerſey, and Burlington upon the Delaware, the capital of Weſt New Jerſey, juſt began to emerge from obſcurity, and to reap ſome of the advantages which they might have obtained earlier, from the proper management of ſo fine ſituations: for as the people of New Jerſey had been accuſtomed to ſend their produce to the markets of New York and Philadelphia, to which they are contiguous, they find it hard, as it always is in ſuch caſes, to draw the trade out of the old channel; for there the correſpondences were fixed, the method of dealing eſtabliſhed, credit given, and a ready market for needy dealers, who in all countries are ſufficiently numerous; ſo that the trade of Perth Amboy, which is

the

the more confiderable of the two, is ftill fcarcely worth notice.

Perth Amboy is delightfully fituated upon a fine bay at the mouth of the Rariton River, contains near two hundred houfes, and has a moft excellent harbour. The land about this place is high, the foil ftiff and ftrong, and the country in general extremely pleafant. But this town, as well as Brunfwick, Prince Town, Newark, Elizabeth Town, Bergen, Woodbridge, &c. have fuffered extremely by the ravages of the war.

In Eaft New Jerfey there are only five counties, viz. Monmouth, Middlefex, Somerfet, Effex, and Bergen. But in Weft New Jerfey there are eight counties, viz. Cape May, Cumberland, Salem, Gloucefter, Burlington, Hunterdon, Suffex, and Morris. Of thefe Burlington is the capital, which is very pleafantly fituated on the banks of the Delaware, about eighteen miles above Philadelphia; although it is only an infignificant place, being

being inferior in every respect even to Perth Amboy.

The adjacent villages, or, as they are all denominated in America, towns, of Borden Town, Trenton, and Mount Holly, are scarcely inferior to Burlington itself, and the towns of Freehold and Shrewsbury in Monmouth county, as well as Greenwich, Salem, Morris Town, &c. are likewise equal to the capital.

At Prince Town there is a college, which is in a very flourishing condition, and at this time is one of the best in America. It was established by Governor Belcher in 1746, and has a power of conferring the same degrees as Oxford or Cambridge.

The southward part of this province and the eastward part of it also, as far as Shrewsbury River, is low, flat, level, and sandy, exactly resembling the lower part of North Carolina, Virginia, &c. already described, from which this part of New Jersey scarcely differs in any one article,

ticle, excepting the inferiority of the foil.

There are also inland bays, all along the coaſt, from Cape May at the mouth Delaware Bay, to Shrewſbury River a little diſtance to the ſouthward from Sandy Hook, which communicate with each other for the greater part of the way.

The high lands in this province begin at Never-Sink hills, upon the coaſt, which are the firſt and only appearance of the kind from Cape Florida to Montock Point, and at Ancocus River on the Delaware ſide, to the northward of which the whole country is hilly, broken, and mountainous, with a ſtrong, ſtiff, ſtony foil.

Among theſe eminences there are ſeveral very ſtrong and commanding, viz. the heights above Mount Holly near Burlington, and the heights of Middle Town near Sandy Hook, both of which were occupied by the Britiſh troops in their march from Philadelphia to New York; and

and the Short Hills or the mountains near Morris Town on which Washington formed his strong camp his constant place of refuge and retreat in the Jerseys; besides Fort Lee on the cliffs of the North River, opposite to Fort Washington; and a multitude of others not rendered remarkable.

The rivers in this province are too insignificant to merit any particular description. Their names are the Rariton, which is the principal, Shrewsbury River, Squan River, Meltcunk River, Monro's River, Ferke's River, Mullicus River, Great Egg River, Maurice River, Salem River, Ancocus River, Muscanctcunk River, Pegue's River, Tochookanctcunk River, Raway River, Hackinsack River, and Passaick River; on the latter of which is a remarkable cataract; the height of the rock from which the water falls is said to be about seventy feet perpendicular, and the river there eighty yards wide.

The commodities of New Jersey are bread, flour, wheat and other grain, beef, pork,

pork, butter, hams, cyder, flax, hemp, flax feed, bar iron, and lumber.

It is altogether impossible to ascertain the annual value of the exports of this province, as much the largest proportion of the produce is carried to the adjacent markets of New York and Philadelphia, from whence they likewise draw the greatest part of their imports every year.

This province has suffered extremely by the war, much more in proportion than any other; and it must be many years before it can possibly recover its former flourishing state.

CHAP. LXXIII.

Climate extremely cold in Winter. The Winds and Weather peculiar to North America. Particular Description of the Mountains. Number of Inhabitants in New Jersey. The Whole Number in all the United States of America. Great Proportion of Negroe Slaves. Astonishing and alarming Decrease in Population. Extreme Weakness of the American States, and their Want of Resources. Absolutely unable to defend themselves in any future War.

IN the northern part of New Jersey and Pensylvania, as well as throughout all the governments of New York and New England, the climate in the winter is so intolerably cold that it will freeze up the largest and broadest rivers in one night and renders those countries much less pleasant and agreeable than the more southern provinces; for the summers are likewise almost equally as hot and sultry, notwithstanding the extreme severity of the rigorous winters.

In

In regard to the winds and weather that generally prevail, it is obferved that in America all the great ftorms begin to leeward; thus a north-eaft ftorm fhall be a day fooner in Virginia than at Bofton.

There are generally remarkable changes in the degrees of heat and cold at Philadelphia every three or four days, but not fo often to the northward.

The navigation of the Delaware is almoft every winter ftopt by ice for two or three months, and the North River is longer frozen than the Delaware; yet New York, being on falt water, affords better winter navigation. Both Delaware and New York Bays are quite free from the fhip worms that infeft all the harbours and falt water rivers to the fouthward.

Land winds in dry weather raife the thickeft fogs, attracting the moifture on the rivers and coafts they come in contact with, in fuch large quantities, that until they are difperfed, by the fun and other caufes, they obftruct the rays of light in direct lines. After the dissipation of these vapours, the most intense heats are produced, and very often thunder gusts towards evening.

Thunder generally proceeds from the meeting of sea and land clouds. Those from the sea coming fraught with electricity, and meeting others less so, the equilibrium is restored by claps of thunder, eruscations, cracks, and flashes of lightning; the more opposite the winds, and the larger and compacter the clouds, the more dreadful and tremendous are the shocks.

These clouds, thus suddenly bereft of that universal element of repellency and expansion, immediately contract, and their water gushes down in torrents.

Land winds, passing over a large shaded and very often frozen continent on both sides of the vast and stupendous Apalachian or Allegany Mountains, are always dry and cold; and the sea winds on the contrary wet and warm. The north-east is a settled high wind, and mostly wet;

and

and the south-west wind is squally and unsettled. The hottest weather is with a south wind and calms, and the coldest with north-west winds. Snow comes from north to north-east, rainy storms come from north-east to east, and high dry wind from the west. However the land winds in America blow above three quarters of the year.

There is an immense ridge of mountains on the back of Virginia, Maryland, Pensylvania, and New Jersey, extending above nine hundred miles in length, and from seventy to a hundred right across, named the Endless Mountains, sometimes also called generally the Blue Mountains, of which scarce one acre out of ten is capable of culture. They are not confusedly scattered, and here and there promiscuously in lofty peaks overtopping one another like most of the mountains in Europe, but they stretch in long uniform ridges scarce half a mile perpendicular in any place.

These furnish innumerable funds for speculation, and systems and theories of the world: but the moſt obvious is, that this earth has undergone many changes, and is now compoſed on the ruins of its former ſtate. Bones and ſhells, which eſcaped the fate of ſofter and leſs durable ſubſtances, are frequently found here mixed with other materials, and elegantly preſerved in the looſe ſtones and rocky baſes of the higheſt of theſe vaſt ridges.

Theſe mountains certainly exiſted in their preſent elevated height before the general deluge, but probably not ſo bare of ſoil as now.

The farther ridges, which are much the largeſt and higheſt, proceeding from the inclination of the whole towards the ſea, are covered with very rich land even to the ſummits; whilſt all the ſoil ſeems ſwept from the very valleys on this hither ſide. Their great height, it may be preſumed, rendered them leſs expoſed to that general devaſtation, and preſerved them unhurt; while the ſoil and the looſe part of the lower hills and valleys, agitated by a greater weight of water, were
borne

borne away, fuspended in the dashing waves, and thrown downwards in stratas of different kinds, as the billows fluctuated and rolled from different parts, still obvious in the lower lands northward and westward of the Rariton and the Delaware.

But in New Jersey, on the other side of these rivers, the land is made by an accumulation of sand from the ocean. Digging there about eighteen feet, through white worn sand, you come to a stratum of sea mud intermixed with shells and other drift trash; and in some places vast beds of shells in pairs, entire, thirty miles from the sea.

Beyond the Endless Mountains, the vast ridge, particularly named the Allegany Mountains, begins, which are sixty miles from thence to their highest summit. There is a very extraordinary report among the natives, the Senekas and Onondagaes. It is said, in a tradition of the Indians, that at the foot of one of these mountains named Onugarexnae, near the source of a small river that enters the eaft branch of the Sufquehannah at Ofewingo, in Penfylvania, Indian corn, tobacco, fquafhes, and pompions, were firft found.

After thefe general obfervations concerning the weather, winds, &c. which I flatter myfelf will be thought ufeful, if not entertaining, it may be proper to recur to the former fubject of the ftate of population of New Jerfey, that of all the other provinces being already fpecified.

The number of inhabitants in New Jerfey are faid to be an hundred and thirty thoufand, which I believe to be pretty exact. Of thefe about one half are Negroes.

I have thus given not only the exaggerated account of the number of the inhabitants in all the Thirteen United States, as firft publifhed by the Congrefs, at the commencement of the revolt, in order to magnify the appearance of their refources and thereby deceive the different European powers, who were then awaiting with aftonifhment for the event of this unprecedented and formidable rebellion;

rebellion; but have stated also the real number of the souls in each of the provinces, as nearly the truth, and from as good authority, as could be ascertained.

According to this first calculation of the Congress, which I have considered as erroneous, the whole number of the inhabitants amounts to three millions one hundred and thirty-seven thousand eight hundred and sixty-nine, including the Negroes, Mulattoes, and civilized Indians, which, even according to this exaggerated statement, bear a formidable proportion in number to the whole.

For in Georgia two-fifths of the inhabitants are Negroes, and amount to eighty-eight thousand eight hundred and sixty. In South Carolina the slaves bear nearly the same proportion to the whites, and amount to one hundred and eighty thousand and ninety-three. In North Carolina two thirds are blacks, being two hundred thousand. In Virginia the same proportion makes four hundred and thirty-three thousand three hundred and thirty-four;

four; and in Maryland two hundred and thirteen thousand three hundred and thirty-four. In Pensylvania, and the three lower counties on Delaware, one third only being slaves, amounts to one hundred and sixteen thousand six hundred and sixty-six. In New Jersey about half are Negroes, which is sixty-five thousand. In New York there are more than one third blacks, making eighty-three thousand three hundred and thirty-three; and in the four provinces of New England there being upwards of one twentieth slaves and civilized Indians, they amount to forty thousand and eighty-three.

These numbers added together come to no less than one million four hundred and twenty thousand seven hundred and three, of useless, or rather burdensome inhabitants, when considered as the strength and resources of the state, and being deducted from the whole, there appears to be only one million seven hundred and seventeen thousand one hundred and sixty-six whites remaining, which confist of men, women, and children.

Three-fourths of thefe muft be women and children, and at leaft half of the remainder of the males unable to bear arms; which leaves juft two hundred and fourteen thoufand fix hundred and forty-five.

From this fmall number, all the artificers, labourers, manufacturers, failors, and foldiers, neceffary throughout the whole of the Thirteen United States, muft be furnifhed.

But as the foregoing calculation is manifeftly magnified beyond the truth, no lefs than four hundred and feventy-four thoufand two hundred and fixty-nine in the whole, the reft of the deductions being made in the above proportions, leaves a ftill lefs number to fupply the neceffary purpofes juft fpecified; viz. only one hundred and eighty-two thoufand two hundred and two; of thefe if every fifteenth man was taken to form

and

and keep up an army, which indeed would be more than could possibly be spared from the other necessary exigences in the œconomy and support of the state, it would only consist of about twelve thousand men; and any accidental diminution would with the utmost difficulty indeed be recruited or replaced.

From this view, our surprise will immediately cease at the inferiority of numbers of the American army, and the extreme difficulty with which it was kept up to any appearance of respect.

But at the same time our astonishment will be excited beyond measure at this trifling force, not only being suffered so long to remain in existence, but even ultimately to accomplish a degree of power and success they themselves never even dreamed of, and in the face of the finest army in the world, of five times their number, and fifty times their strength.

But I shall drop the curtain over this subject, being determined in future never to hazard or entertain any kind of political speculations.

The amazing decrease in population of these provinces, since the commencement of the late war, is evinced by a comparison between the first calculation of the number of inhabitants, made and published by the Congress in 1775, and the following one in 1783, made by order of the Congress also, for levying a proper proportion of taxes in each state.

According to the first computation the number of the whole in the year 1775 was 3,137,869. In 1783 their numbers stood as follows:

New Hampshire	82,200
Massachuset's Bay	350,000
Rhode Island	50,400
Connecticut	206,000
New York	200,000
New Jersey	130,000
Pensylvania	320,000
Delaware Counties	35,000
Maryland	220,700
Virginia	400,000

North Carolina — 200,000
South Carolina — — 170,000
Georgia — — — 25,000

In all (2,389,300)

From a comparison of the above statements, there appears to be a decrease in population of 748,589, within eight years; an event that surely ought to be sufficiently alarming; and both these calculations are supported upon the authority of the American Congress themselves.

By the enumeration which I have mentioned as nearest the truth, there also appears to be a very considerable decrease in population, viz. the difference between 2,663,600, which I considered as the real number of inhabitants in 1775, and 2,383,300, the number in 1783 : by this there appears to be a decrease of 280,300.

By this last computation, made by the Congress in 1783, it appears that the resources of the American states in men, the surest strength and only actual means

means of defence, are still inferior to what has been already mentioned; weak indeed, insignificant, and very inadequate to support the dignity and honour of independent and sovereign states, being, according to the foregoing proportion and deductions, only in the whole one hundred and sixty-three thousand and twenty-six males able to bear arms; from which, after supplying all the other exigences of the state, an army could not be raised of more than ten thousand men, for the purpose of guarding and defending a coast of one thousand five hundred miles in length, and a frontier on the opposite side no less exposed, and much more extended; besides detachments for observation, exclusive of any for carrying on offensive operations, if ever they should again be involved in war.

CHAP. LXXIV.

Brief Account of what befel several of the Persons formerly mentioned in the Course of this Work. The Fellow who robbed me in the Mountains. The poor friendless English Girl. The tyrannical barbarous Gaoler. The brutal Dutch Guard. Captain Cameron exchanged. Extraordinary Resolve of the American Congress and the Answer to it. Col. Connolly in Consequence thereof returned a Prisoner of War and exchanged.

AS in the course of the war I was so fortunate as to obtain ample satisfaction of many of the individuals of the Americans, who had been the instruments, and sometimes the occasion of the indignities and wanton barbarity exercised upon me while in captivity, I shall give a brief recital of a few of these occurrences here, as well as of what befel my unfortunate fellow-prisoners, along with whom I was first taken, and from whom I had been separated they being left at Philadelphia, before I close this volume; as the curiosity of my readers may have been excited by

the

the foregoing relation to be anxious to know their fate.

SOME few weeks previous to the embarkation of the grand army for the Chefapeak and Philadelphia, as I was returning from fort Wafhington to New York, I met a man whofe face was familiar to my mind, and in a few moments recollected him to be Barclay, the fellow who had privately made off after robbing me in the mountains, when in the moft extreme diftrefs imaginable, during my former attempt to efcape.

Having ftopped him, and called him by his name, he was almoft petrified with furprize, terror, and guilt at feeing me, and immediately fell on his knees intreating my forgivenefs.

I myfelf being equally aftonifhed at finding him at New York defired him, if he expected pardon or mercy, to be candid and acquaint me with the motives that induced him to commit fo bafe an action as to rob and abandon me when in the very greateft need and diftrefs, and in fo dreadful and wretched a fituation.

As his explanation and motives were both originals, and peculiar to himfelf, I fhall give them as nearly as poffible in his own words. " Arrah now" (fays he) " your honour knows, that I went many " a weary mile with your honour, and " waded many a deep, broad, frozen river, " with your worfhip, and laid many a " cold night in the fnow in the mountains " with your honour; and ftarved without " a mouthful to eat for many a day with " your worfhip; until I began to think " I could never hold it out much longer " at all at all; but at laft when both your " honour's legs were difabled, yet ftill " your worfhip would keep pufhing for-" ward, I then thought it would never " do; and that your honour would not " be able to go much farther at all at all; " and that by and by we fhould all be " taken; and that they would, for cer-" tain, murther me alive, if ever they
" catched

" catched me along with your worſhip;
" and ſo I thought I would fling them
" there; for I would leave your honour
" in time. And as I was certain they
" would plunder your worſhip, I thought
" I would fling them there too; and ſo I
" took every thing along with me, to
" take care of for your honour, and to
" keep it all from the rebel thieves, who
" would not have thanked your worſhip
" for all you had. Now, arrah, by my
" ſhoul, pleaſe your worſhip, this is all
" my reaſons, and motions, and more
" too; and I hope your honour will
" think them good enough, and enough
" of them; and pardon, and forgive me,
" for the ſake of my wife and weans;
" and we'll all pray for your worſhip as
" long as we live, and longer too; for
" arrah, by my faith, I am doing very
" well here; and have got all my wife
" and weans together, in a rebel houſe
" that had nobody in it; and I have got
" ſome rebel land, and we make pota-
" toes."

Being

Being diverted with his strange reasoning, and finding him loyal in principle, although otherwise a great rogue, I assured him of my forgiveness, gave him a dollar, and left him.

THE next circumstance that occurred, relating to any person that has been formerly mentioned, was at Kenneth's Square, in Pensylvania, where the army halted for a night, the very one preceding the action at Brandy-wine. Here observing a number of officers crowding around a young woman, at a house which had been abandoned by the inhabitants, to whom they were behaving rather improperly, looking in her face and recollecting the poor unfortunate English girl who had been so barbarously treated and basely abused by her Master and Mistress and our brutal Dutch guard at Newport only for mentioning her concern at seeing us in irons, I pushed away the officers rather rudely, and asked her if she recollected me? After a few moments consideration she remembered me, and the poor creature's joy was beyond measure

measure excessive to see me alive, and with my friends, as she imagined the Americans had destroyed us.

Her pleasure was not diminished by my requesting she would do me the favour of accepting of three guineas as a trifling compensation for her former commiseration and regard for us, as well as for her loyalty and sufferings.

The officers, whom I had so rudely pushed away during my first impulse of surprize, were all this time divided between resentment at my conduct towards them, aud wonder at this adventure: but on being made acquainted with the story they gave way to compassion and generosity, and amongst them made up a contribution of two guineas more for the poor unfortunate young woman.

Understanding that I had no tent, and slept only in a temporary wigwham upon the ground, which was indeed my situation all this campaign, this grateful kind-hearted creature pressed me to accept of her apartment, and feemed really much concerned and hurt at my declining it.

Next morning, the army having moved very early, fhe watched the line of march for my paffing, and when I came along moft earneftly wifhed me health, fafety, and fuccefs : and her prayers had their defired effect, for on that day, in one of the hotteft actions that has been in America, numbers fell on each fide of me, and I remained untouched.

ON the morning of the day that a detachment of the Britifh army firft entered Philadelphia, a number of the rebels fell into my hands, and amongft the reft Thomas Dewees, the cruel, tyrannical gaoler, under whofe iron talons I had fuffered fo long and feverely.

As foon as this wretch found that I was the officer commanding the party, his terror is not to be defcribed, as he expected nothing lefs than immediate death ; falling on his knees he begged for his life, and for mercy. I defired him to confider,
what

what he merited from me? He acknowledged that he deserved neither favour nor compassion, said that his orders respecting me had been more rigorous than against any other, and owned that he had executed them in their full severity; but still most earnestly intreated forgiveness.

I told him that for the sake of his innocent wife and children (for he had a large family) and to convince the deluded infatuated rebels that Britons were not of that vindictive disposition he had expected and represented us to be, I would forgive him, as he professed sincere contrition, and proposed to take the oaths of allegiance to his Majesty: this he readily performed; and had the audacity afterwards of applying to Earl Cornwallis to be appointed Deputy Provost Marshal over the rebel prisoners in Philadelphia, in the accomplishment of which pursuit however he very justly failed.

The other prisoners I had taken proved to be Capt. Jacobs, and the brutal Dutch guard, who had carried us in irons from Philadelphia to Baltimore.

When thefe fellows were brought to me, and difcovered that I commanded, their horror and difmay is inexpreffible. In an agony of dread and defpair, they fell upon their knees, and moft earneftly intreated for " one half hour to fay their prayers."

I could not conceive what they meant, and defired to know why they were fo violently determined on going to prayers juft then, at fo unfeafonable a time? They anfwered, *" Bee fhure they fay their prayers bevore they tay*;" and I found that they really expected immediate death.

A Highland officer, that was along with me, on being informed the caufe of their ftrange requeft and the occafion of their fears, drew his fword at Captain Jacobs, and terrified him moft unmercifully, defiring to know, " *hoo feck a fallow as he was, could dare to put a Breetifh Officer in eyrons?*" Jacobs replied, " *Bee fhure tvaz der dyvel's own Vork: Ich knowfh no beterfh. Poor ignorant Dytcherfh knowfh no beterfh,*" and then they all exclaimed, " *Yaw, Yaw, Ich knowfh no beterfh; Ich fery*

fery fhorry; vor fhure tvaz der Dyvel's own vork."

I told them they need not be in such haste to go to prayers, for their lives were in no danger: that I freely forgave them their ill treatment and injuries to me: that such of them as were really sorry for their past conduct might return to their homes upon taking the oaths of allegiance to their Sovereign. And that none need do even that, but such as chose to do it freely, of their own accord, for those who declined it should only be made prisoners, their persons being perfectly safe.

Upon this their joy and gratitude seemed equal to their former terror; and every man of them gladly took the oaths of allegiance, and returned to his home, where I am well convinced they would have continued as loyal and peaceable subjects, had they not been abandoned, and thrown back into the hands of the Americans.

IN regard to what befel Colonel Connolly and Captain Cameron, the following

lowing brief account will be sufficient. During the time the British troops were in possession of Philadelphia, Captain Cameron was permitted to come in there on parole, and was soon after regularly exchanged for an American officer of equal rank, who had been allowed to return to his friends on parole likewise. And the hard treatment and severe usage Colonel Connolly afterwards experienced is sufficiently ascertained and authenticated by the following resolve of the American Congress, and the answer to it also made public, the veracity of which answer, in in every single article, has never been nor can be controverted.

An extraordinary Resolution of the American Congress.

In CONGRESS, Nov. 12, 1778.

The Committee to whom was referred a letter from John Beatty, Commissary of Prisoners, dated September 15th, 1778, together with two letters from Joshua Laring, Esq. of the 1st of Sep-

September and 28th of October, and sundry letters from John Connolly, report the following state of facts.

That Doctor John Connolly (now stiling himself Lieutenant Colonel in the British service) was, in the latter end of November, 1775, apprehended in Fredrick county, in Maryland, in company with a certain Allen Cameron, and J. F. Smyth, by the Committee of Inspection of that county.

That at the time he was taken, he was not in arms, or at the head of any party of men in arms, but was clandestinely making his way to Detroit, in order to join, give intelligence to, and otherwise aid the garrison at that place, as appears by his own intercepted letters of the 16th of December, 1775.

That a number of officers in the British service, who were made prisoners, long after the said John Connolly was apprehended, have been exchanged in course; and no demand has been made (till within these few months past) by any British General, for the release or exchange of the officer last mentioned.

With respect to the treatment of the said Lieutenant Colonel Connolly, the Committee report,

That at the time when he was first apprehended, he was confined under guard, by the Committee of Inspection in the town of Frederick, in an apartment separate from his associates,

without

without any circumstance to aggravate his captivity, except the being debarred the use of pen, ink, and paper:

That, notwithstanding this restraint, he contrived to write several letters of intelligence to the British officers commanding at the posts of Detroit and Kuskuskis, which letters were found on the person of Dr. Smyth, one of his associates, who, having escaped from the town of Frederick, was again apprehended:

That by the resolution of Congress, of the 8th of December, 1775, he was ordered to be confined in prison at Philadelphia; that being brought to that city, he was confined in the new gaol, wherein he continued till about the month of November 1776, when he was permitted, on account of a declining state of health, to reside on his parole, at the house of his brother-in-law, on the river Susquehannah, where he continued for about two months; when on information being given to the Council of Safety, of the State of Pensylvania, of certain suspicious circumstances relative to him, he was remanded to his former place of confinement, in which he continued till about the spring, 1777, when he was again permitted on his parole, and the security of his brother-in-law, to return to his former place of residence on the river Susquehannah:

That during these periods of his confinement in the new gaol, he had, for the greatest part of the time, a separate apartment to himself, the privilege of walking in the yard, a person allowed to attend him in his apartment, and his own servant permitted to fetch him such necessaries as he chose to order:

That during the short period, when he had not a separate apartment, there were never more than two persons in the same room, seldom more than one, and those, some of his associates, or in consequence of his particular request:

That during these periods of time he made two attempts to escape, in which he was detected:

That an authentic information being given to Congress, at York Town, that the said Lieutenant-colonel John Connolly, was acting in a manner not consistent with the spirit of his parole, and the frontiers being threatened with a barbarous war, in which there was reason to apprehend he was designed as an instrument, he was ordered into confinement in the gaol at York-Town, on the thirteenth of October:

That on the 17th of May, the said J. Connolly, with several others confined in said gaol, made a representation to Congress, setting forth in the strongest colouring, the hardships and cruelties which they declared they were then suffering:

That on the result of a strict enquiry, and after the gaol had been visited by Colonel Pickering, one of the Members of the Board of War, it appeared that the suggestions contained in the said representation were scandalous and groundless;

less; and the report of the Board of War, was, on the 23d day of May ordered to be published:

That since the evacuation of Philadelphia, the said J. Connolly was remanded to the new gaol in that city, where (excepting the space of about fourteen days, when two persons were necessarily obliged to sleep in the same room) he has had a separate and commodious apartment of his own choice, the privilege of his own servant to attend him constantly, and to bring him whatever he may require, and the unrestrained use of a spacious yard to take the air in during the day:

That in his letter of the 12th of October, 1778, the said J. Connolly declared, "That the common rights of humanity are denied to him," and paints his situation in such terms, as would tend to induce a belief, that the most wanton cruelties and restraints are imposed upon him:

That in consequence of a request of J. Connolly, to be heard in person by a Committee of Congress, this Committee have complied with his request, when he declared, in presence of your Committee, "That excepting the restraint of his person, under the limits above mentioned, which however indulgent they might appear, he conceived unfavourable to his state of health, he experienced every other relief which could be extended to a person in confinement."

That Joshua Loring, Esq. British Commissary of Prisoners, in his Letter to Mr. Beatty of the
first

first of September, 1778, threatens to retaliate on an American prisoner of war, of equal rank with Lieutenanant-colonel Connolly, for the suffering which it is pretended that officer endures."

Whereupon Resolved,

That Lieutenant-colonel John Connolly cannot, of right, claim to be considered and treated as a prisoner of war: but that he was, at the time he was apprehended, and still is, amenable to the law martial, as a spy and emissary from the British army:

That the repeated representations made by Lieutenant-colonel John Connolly, of the grievances he undergoes, are not founded on facts:

That General Washington be directed to transmit the foregoing resolutions and state of facts, to the Commander in Chief of his Britannic Majesty's forces in New York; and to inform the said officer, that if under the pretext of retaliating for the pretended sufferings of a person, who, by the law of nations, has no right to be considered as a prisoner of war, any American officer, entitled to be considered and treated as a prisoner of war, shall undergo any extraordinary restraints or sufferings, Congress are determined to retaliate on the person of an officer of the first rank in their possession, for every species of hardship or restraint on such account inflicted.

Extract from the minutes,

CHARLES THOMPSON, Secretary.

This

This very extraordinary resolution of the American Congress produced an answer from one of the officers concerned and named therein, which was transmitted to the Congress at Philadelphia, and a copy of it inclosed to the British Commander in Chief, along with the following introductory letter.

To Sir Henry Clinton, Commander in Chief, &c. &c.

"Having seen a resolve of the American Congress, wherein they order their General to transmit to your Excellency by letter the report of one of their Committees concerning the case (and their conclusions thereon) of Lieut. Col. Connolly, for whose exchange I preferred a Memorial to your Excellency in August last, as that report is either totally false, or a misrepresentation of facts, which being known only to two, viz. Mr. Cameron and myself, and as Mr. Cameron is now gone to Britain, I conceive it would be an unpardonable neglect to me to allow that unfortunate officer, Lieut. Col. Connolly, to suffer through these misrepresentations, or to let such a notorious perversion of truth pass unnoticed and undetected.

Therefore by a plain and impartial relation of facts, for the truth of all which I will be answerable;

able; I have confuted their shameless and false assertions, thereby depriving them even of the shadow of an excuse for the perpetration of this last daring instance of intended cruelty; an insult on reason, humanity, and the law of nations.

This answer I have presumed to lay before your Excellency, imagining the necessary information in this matter might possibly be wanting, from that officer's situation and circumstances not being explained or sufficiently known, and flattering myself that your Excellency's wisdom and humanity will endeavour to preserve my unhappy fellow-prisoner's life, and enforce his exchange.

I have the honour to be, &c. &c.
J. FERDINAND D. SMYTH,
Capt. Q. R.

Oyster Bay, Long Island,
December 17, 1778.

To the AMERICAN CONGRESS at PHILADELPHIA.

WHEN an enquiry after truth is set on foot, from whomsoever the enquiry originates, it becomes the duty of every individual to promote the discovery of it; and, as far as comes within his own knowledge and observations, to make it public.

But when the name of an enquiry after truth is prostituted to the purpose of concealing it, when false assertions are published to the world, facts misrepresented, and conclusions thereby formed totally void of foundation, and inconfiftent even with that humanity which is now fupported by powers at open war with each other, it then becomes an indifpenfible duty on every perfon, in whofe power it may be, to fet thofe matters enquired into, in a true and proper light ; and it is alfo the duty of thofe who ordered the enquiry to attend to every fuch well-fupported information, that is, if they wifh to fulfil avowed good intentions.

From thefe motives I am induced to endeavour to fet you right, in regard to the report of your Committee to you, concerning the cafe of Lieutenant-Colonel John Connolly, a prifoner with you :—which report being founded on error and wrong information, may have mifled you ; and as reprefented by you, would induce the world to believe things that are not.

That officer's cafe, even as your Committee report it, with all their foftnings and difguifes, is fufficiently diftreffing and cruel. But when impartially related, as it fhall be by me, muft intereft humanity itfelf, and of courfe all mankind in his favour, to alleviate his fufferings.

That this is in my power is well known to you, being, as you are pleafed to ftyle me, one of his affociates, who was taken prifoner and fuffered along with him, under your iron rod, for the fpace of one year and three months. Nor am I unacquainted with the futility of your Committees of Enquiry, having in that time had three upon me, me, from your Congress, on account of insupportable confinement. Yet, notwithstanding the most clear and satisfactory proofs against those I complained of, I was still left in the custody and power of my tormentors.

At the same time I must do three of your members the justice to say, that they behaved with politeness, and appeared much shocked at our treatment: they are a Mr. Wilcot, from Connecticut, a Mr. Morris, and a Colonel Ross, of Pensylvania: but the injurious cruel measures of the persecuting, violent incendiary, M'Kean*, overpowered moderation and humanity.

Your Committee report. " that Lieut. Col. John Connolly, with his two associates, A. Cameron, and J. F. Smyth, were apprehended by a committee of inspection as spies, not in arms, &c. amenable to your law martial, &c." An assertion void of truth.

The fact is, that on the 20th of November, 1775, a time when you publickly disclaimed all intentions of independence or separation from Great Britain, avowing allegiance to your Sovereign, and affecting only to resist the Ministry and Parliament, we were made prisoners by a company of riflemen, consisting of a Captain, a Lieutenant, an Ensign, two Serjeants, and thirty-six rank and file, armed with rifles, tomahawks, &c. Lieut. Col. Connolly, and we also, were in arms against

* Since then President of the Congress for some time.

you, but were overpowered by numbers, our arms taken from us, which are still in your possession, and we were taken, and always styled by you as prisoners of war. That you beheld us in that light is put beyond a doubt, by your exchanging Lieut. Alan Cameron, one of these associates, as you are pleased to term us, of Lieut. Col. Connolly, for one of your officers of equal rank, in the latter part of 1777, or the beginning of 1778, at Philadelphia: and in September, 1776, a Committee of your Congress came to us in prison, desiring us to prepare to be immediately exchanged as ' prisoners of war,' which you also called us in all your writings.

You say, " that no exchange was demanded for Lieut. Col. Connolly until within these few months."

This assertion is also without foundation; for even in 1775, and also in 1776, Lord Dunmore frequently offered officers of your's, of equal rank, in exchange for Lieut. Col. Connolly and us, to your Virginia Governors, of which province you affected to call us prisoners. But your bugbear fears of us prevented you from exchanging us, and are still the occasion of that unfortunate officer's rigid confinement.

You say, " that he was clandestinely making his way through the country in order to join, give intelligence to, &c, and otherwise aid the garrisons of Detroit and Kiskuskes ;" and as a proof of this

assertion,

assertion, you mention " a letter from him, found on the person of Doctor Smyth, who escaped from Frederick Town, and was again apprehended," which letter you acknowledge, was written after he was taken prisoner.

The truth is, that Lieut. Col. Connolly was to proceed from Norfolk in Virginia to Detroit in Canada, there to take the command of an expedition, and he had his instructions from his Majesty's Commander in Chief. It lay with him to choose, whether he would proceed to Canada, round north by the St. Laurence and Quebec, or south by Cape Florida and the Mississippi, for which purpose an armed vessel awaited his commands, or to travel by land across the country to Detroit. The lateness of the season (it being then November) determined his choice of the last mentioned route, it being not one-sixth of the distance of the others. We conceived ourselves very able to pass through the country in arms, and the event shewed, that we were equal to the task, having passed safe above four hundred miles, and through every place where there was danger; our being taken at last being merely accidental; events which frequently disconcert the best planned and best conducted enterprises.

The name of " Spy" applied to either of us, is perfectly absurd, as we knew the country, and the minds of the inhabitants, as well as we could desire. Your proof of our being spies too is equally preposterous, being "a letter found on me written by Lieut. Col. Connolly near a month after his captivity," and the substance of the letter was, only for the commanding officers at Detroit and Kiskuskes to give implicit credit to my informations to them. That we wished to be as much unnoticed as possible is certain, as we were not sufficient to resist the attack of any numbers, yet by rapid marches we were superior to any force that might accidentally oppose us. But that we went in a "clandestine manner," as you say, is utterly void of foundation, as will appear by tracing our route.

That we were "amenable to your laws," because we once resided in these revolted colonies, not even the most sophistical reasoning can reconcile; because you know, that we opposed your measures, from the very commencement of this rebellion, even in arms; that none of you represented us, or our principle; nor did we claim any protection from you or your government, having publickly renounced your society, and abandoned our homes, to avoid your lawless and usurped domination.

The demand of the exchange of Lieut. Col. Connolly, in August and September last, was occasioned by a memorial from me to Sir Henry Clinton, whom, being our last Commander in Chief, I thought it my duty to remind of the sufferings of my unfortunate friend.

But

But the idea of a retaliation of cruelty I utterly disclaim; however neceſſary, I ſhudder at the thought of an emulation in ſavage barbarity. In that, your fertile reſources and ingenuity will enable you very far to excel us.

As to his treatment—you ſay, " he complains to you, that the common rights of humanity are denied him."

That they have been withheld from him I can very juſtly aver. The following ſtate of facts I can vouch for of my own knowledge.

That, after we were taken priſoners, excepting two or three days when we were ſeparately confined, we were all kept in the ſame room; that, during the firſt ſeven weeks, his ſervant was taken from him, and we ſuffered every ſpecies of inſult daily, and were in danger and dread of being murdered every night.

That, when he was thrown into Philadelphia gaol, in January 1776, his ſervant was again taken from him and ſent entirely away; and for a long year afterwards, he ſuffered a more ſevere and rigid confinement, than any perſon can have an idea of, except thoſe who have felt it; a confinement ſo inſupportable, as to juſtify the moſt deſperate attempts to eſcape.

That it was never in his power to ſend out for the moſt trifling neceſſary without paying court to your iron-hearted gaoler; and he had not permiſſion to ſpeak, even to us, whom you are pleaſed to ſtyle his aſſociates, although in the ſame priſon.

That his sharp talon'd ravenous keeper, by the most flagrant and iniquitous charges, continually extorted from him all the money he could possibly raise.

After his health had been effectually destroyed by your most horrid confinement, you say, "That he was then permitted to his parole about November, 1776." An assertion I must also deny; because on the 16th of December, 1776, when I and twenty-five other officers and soldiers were brought out of your dungeons, and drawn up in irons before his window, I then saw that unfortunate officer Lieut. Col. Connolly in tears in his cell at seeing the irons cut our flesh, and to prevent it he threw out of his grates a pair of gloves to Capt. M'Lean and me.

In that situation we left him. But I suppose, a few months imprisonment, even in a dungeon, is, by you, overlooked as a trifle of no consequence.

Having myself been then carried to a distant place of confinement, I can ascertain nothing farther concerning him, of my own knowledge. But you confess, "that you threw him soon afterwards in York-Town gaol, on an information of his acting in a manner inconsistent with the *spirit* of his parole." A most jesuitical subterfuge, whereby every officer on parole might, with equal propriety, be close confined, whenever it was found convenient.

If a prisoner complies with the *letter* of his parole, it has always been thought sufficient. And
let

let me acquaint you, that if acting contrary to the *spirit*, or even the *letter* of their paroles was noticed or punished here, not an officer of your's, now at large on Long Island, but would long ago have been close confined.

It too plainly appears, that this unfortunate officer has been equally injured by you throughout his whole captivity. And now,—*Finis coronat opus*, your sole, your mighty *fiat*, your last resolve breaks all bounds, and strikes at his life, as 'a spy, and emissary from the British army,' rendering him amenable to a motley government, and mock laws, originated, framed, and constructed since his captivity, months, and even years. And to conclude the whole, as an insult on human understanding, on British humanity, and on the law of nations, you order your General to transmit these resolves, acts, and conclusions of iniquity of yours, by letter to the Commander in Chief of his Majesty's forces; which, even as represented by yourselves, carry absurdity and falsehood in their face.

Your General, who wants not sense nor discernment, I conceive never had a more disgraceful or unwelcome task imposed on him. If he has a sense of honour or shame left, or that amiable and diffident merit for which he was once distinguished, he would much more gladly undertake another Brooklyn, Brandywine, German Town, or Freehold affair, than such a task of flagrant iniquity.

It is almost unnecessary to take notice, that your finishing " resolve of making retaliation on a British officer of the highest rank in your possession," is only worthy of your cause, and of the motives and men from whence it originates.

It has always been observed, that men are fond of entering on that particular line in which they are conscious they can excel :—hence your eagerness after retaliation.

But here again your thirst after barbarity and blood has betrayed you into the bare-faced avowal of that unequal and unjust retaliation, of " causing a British officer of the highest rank in your power, to suffer in the supposed manner of one of your Lieutenant-Colonels," whose restraint you yourselves are also the occasion of, by your treatment of our unfortunate Lieut. Col. Connolly.

However, this threat, and the execution of it, is of a piece with the whole of your proceedings.

The horrid idea of an emulation in cruelty is shocking to human nature, and is totally inconsistent with generous sentiments.

Those who are influenced by good principles can contend, even with an enemy, in disinterested generosity, and in actions shewing greatness of soul. An idea that will probably astonish you, being so far out of your line of conduct.

Notorious it is to the world, that you have long sported with the lives of men.

Britons, even as enemies, have been more merciful to your ill-fated defenders, than you have been

been, under the specious, but pretended name, of friends and protectors.

The oppression and death of the innocent has long been familiar to you, and you have also imbrued your hands in the blood of the peaceful Quaker, the inoffensive citizen, and the harmless, ignorant rustic, whose lives and religion you affect to defend.

At last, if possible, to add to the measure of your guilt, you are preparing to shed the blood of an innocent man, who has the honour to bear his Majesty's commission as Lieutenant-Colonel, after above three years cruel imprisonment in your gaols, under the sanction of tribunals, and by convenient laws, made for the purpose since his captivity.

But, for the sake of humanity, I could wish you would first consider the dreadful consequences of such a step.

Yet, as nothing of the kind from you can surprise me, I hope, if that should be my friend's unhappy fate, that he will bear the stroke with a fortitude becoming the dignity of *your* much injured *Sovereign*, whom we have the honour to serve, and the justice of the cause we maintain.

J. FERDINAND D. SMYTH.
Capt. Q. R.

Oyster-Bay, Long-Island,
December, 17, 1778.

The Congress, in a very short time after the above answer had reached them, ordered the officer in question to be returned as a *prisoner of war*, and soon afterwards in consequence thereof permitted him to be regularly exchanged.

CHAP.

CHAP. LXXV.

Fatal Termination of the War. Inauspicious to both Countries. Consequences to America of Separation from Great Britain, and of Independence. Consequences of their Connections and Alliance with France. Oppression, Depopulation, &c. of America. Unfit Place of Residence. Reflections concerning the American Loyalists of every Description.

THIS unhappy and unfortunate war having terminated in a manner so peculiarly unfavourable and inauspicious to the future prosperity of both countries, particularly to that of America, in a total separation of government, interest, and connections, as far as people proceeding from the same origin, habituated to the same manners and customs, speaking the same language, and professing the same religion, can possibly admit of; and what is still more extraordinary, and equally to be regretted, this fatal event is universally confessed to be absolutely against the known and acknowledged interest of both.

For

For these new formed United States of America, at the expence of real freedom and the greatest share of felicity that ever was or will be possessed by any people or community upon earth, at the expence of an increasing commerce and population, of opulence and perfect security in person, property, and laws, of a name, as British subjects, then held in the highest respect and veneration by all the powers in the known world; in short, at the expence of every blessing that could possibly be desired, possessed, and enjoyed, not only by the public at large, but by every individual thereof, have acquired what is absolutely nothing better than a shadow, " a momentary, delusive, " misconceived consequence in the estima- " tion of other powers;" which will vanish, like the phantom from whence it proceeds, upon a more intimate knowledge and experience of its deception and fallacy.

Nay, they have acquired what is worse than a shadow; they have shackled themselves

selves in fetters, which every future struggle to disengage themselves from, will only rivet more firmly and render more heavy and oppressive; and to the support of which every year's experience will evince them to be altogether inadequate.

For when the enormous load of their debt, contracted during this war, is considered, the interest of which alone is sufficient to bear them down, added to their necessary and unavoidable expences in supporting the dignity of thirteen different governments, with the naval, military, and civil establishments of the whole; besides the annual presents to the Indians, and the enormous expences of ambassadors, envoys, &c. at foreign courts, to watch over their skeleton commerce and interest, to keep up their shadow of dignity as free, independent, and sovereign states, and to procure them some small degree of respect among other powers: These vast and continued expenditures, compared with the resources from whence they all must necessarily be derived,

rived, viz. a country, instead of advancing in opulence and strength, actually immersed in poverty, and decreasing in population in a degree that might alarm the most powerful; a government unsettled, precarious, and doubtful, destitute of energy, vigour, and firmness, and actually incapable of enforcing their own decrees; a commerce fluctuating and unprofitable, with the balance of trade in every channel against them; two thirds of their subjects absolutely disaffected to their rule, which is certainly the case, notwithstanding all that has been alledged to the contrary, secretly wishing for the restoration of that government which has been so lately overturned; and the remainder running into riots, confusion, and every kind of culpable and criminal violence and excess, in open opposition to and defiance of all legal authority: Without artisans, without manufacturers; even common labour bearing an exorbitant price, and seldom to be procured at all: When all this is duly

duly attended to, what prospect is left of emancipation for this unfortunate country?

When their intoxication of having succeeded in obtaining their boasted fatal independence has worn off, and the unavoidable pressure of taxes begins to operate and become grievous, then will they look back with inexpressible concern and regret at the happy time when they enjoyed every felicity, security, and substantial benefit, under the auspices of the free and mild government of Great Britain. They will execrate the destructive measure, and most sincerely lament the fatal period of separation.

Nor will even hope itself, the great supporter in affliction, be left them for their comfort, to point out any method of extricating themselves from their difficulties.

For entangled in French politics, inthraled by ruinous obligations to, and an unnatural alliance with a nation totally different from themselves in habits, manners, and inclinations, in language and sentiments, in religion, in form of government, and, in short, in every thing; their rulers corrupted by French gold, captivated by the tinsel parade, grandeur, and affected amity of that artful, perfidious, gaudy people, and influenced by their promises and specious affability; unequal also to that subtle nation in policy, and infinitely inferior in opulence and power, what possibility is there of the American states disengaging themselves from their controul, or ever again becoming free?

From this representation, which is by no means exaggerated, every person with the least share of discernment, or even common understanding, must plainly see how undesirable, and indeed unfit, a place of residence the United States of America must be for any one whatsoever, either needy or affluent. For so far is it from being possible now to acquire a fortune in that country, that merely to retain what one already possesses without diminution nition is a matter of difficulty, and to procure a decent and comfortable subsistence by trade or labour must be next to impossible.

All the foregoing observations are evinced by the amazing depopulation of these provinces. A decrease, for the time, unexampled in history, and clearly proves every thing herein alledged.

For the reasons must be weighty indeed, that would induce men to abandon their native land, their friends, fortunes, and dearest connections, and leave the finest climate, country, and soil in the world, to settle where every thing is infinitely inferior, among strangers, or in an inclement barren wilderness, and in a region of frosts and fogs. Yet this is undoubtedly the case at present, and thus it will continue.

So that, instead of the numerous emigrations that formerly crouded to America, increasing her strength, population, and resources, with a rapidity beyond all example, the state of things is now reversed, and multitudes of the inhabitants

certainly

certainly are leaving the dominions of the American States as speedily as they possibly can.

This fluctuating state of the country, and their unsettled versatile government will likewise prevent a possibility of any exact account of the United States of America being given for many years to come, as during that time they will be perpetually liable to changes; so that what might have been a just representation in one year, may be found totally different in the next, the inevitable consequence of their present situation.

These observations naturally lead to a reflection on the situation of the American loyalists of every description. Among whom I include all who have been true to their sovereign in principle, whether they have publicly declared it or not, as well as those who have openly avowed their allegiance and taken up arms in favour of Great Britain and the old established government.

Of both these I consider the condition of such as have remained at their homes,

and

and are now subject to the domination of the Congress, as in reality the most deplorable.

The rest depend upon Great Britain for protection, and it would be an indelible stain upon her honour, policy, and her most sacred engagements, were she to abandon them.

But the other poor unfortunate men, whose hearts were as true as loyalty and virtue itself, and who have been constantly requested to remain in peace at their homes, and were always promised never to be given up or forsaken, and who, to my knowledge, would not have hesitated to shed the last drop of their blood, had they been called forth in support of their king and country, have now no power on earth to look up to for protection from the insults and barbarity of their illiberal, vindictive, implacable foes; even hope itself is withheld from them, and they must be reduced to absolute desperation.

Few have had such opportunities as I, of knowing and being witness to the ardent zeal, loyalty, and great desert, of these

these most unfortunate people, and my heart really bleeds for their distresses.

How hard has been the fate of all those truly meritorious but unhappy men, the the *American Loyalists* of every denomination! True to their king, faithful to their country, attached to the laws and constitution, they have continued firm and inflexible in the midst of persecutions, torments, and death. Many of them have abandoned their homes, their friends, their nearest and most tender connections, and encountered all the toils of war, want, and misery; solely actuated by motives the most disinterested and virtuous.

In short they have undergone trials and sufferings, with a determined resolution and fortitude, unparalleled in history; and have submitted even to death sooner than stain their integrity, honour, and principled loyalty with the odious guilt of rebellion against their king.

Yet these very men, whose virtues and and deserts are above estimation, have been publicly traduced, vilified, and defamed;

famed, with every species of obloquy and and opprobrious epithet applied to them and their conduct, by the partizans of a ruinous faction in this country, for which they have shed their blood, and sacrificed their all.

There cannot be a doubt but the more worthy and principled part of the nation reprobated such conduct, not only as illiberal, ungenerous, and unjust, but impolitic also in the highest degree; for such subjects, as the American Loyalists, were highly to be prized in any government, and were certainly entitled to every protection and encouragement that this could bestow.

For no compensation whatever can be adequate to the loss sustained by these deserving men, not only of their possessions, and the society of their friends and relations, but of that apparently established felicity and affluence, which they themselves, and their posterity after them, had the prospect of enjoying for ages to come.

FINIS.

ERRATA to VOL. II.

Page 5, lines 4 and 5, *read* six miles broad and running thirty miles north to the feveral. P. 10, l. 15, *dele* , P. 23, *for* Chap. III. *r.* LI. P. 33, l. 15, *dele* of. P. 94, l. 15, *r.* evince. P. 100, l. 8, *dele* dreary. P. 115, l. 3, *dele* , P. 116, l. 3, *r.* quantity. P. 138, l. 17, *dele* feparate. P. 160, l. 19, *r.* to the temporary command of the. l. 22, *r.* can be faid. P. 166, l. 10, *r.* manœuvres. P. 173, l. 10 and 11, *r.* hallooing. P. 179, l. 16, *for* is, *r.* enjoys. P. 181, l. 4, *r.* of St. Mary's. P. 206, l. 19, *dele* ; P. 221, l. 24, *r.* being alfo quite. P. 230, l. 1, *dele* of. P. 255, l. 6, *dele* , *dele* he, *r.* Hanfou and has. P. 256, l. 6, *for* it is an inland town, *r.* it is far inland. P. 258, l. 6, *for* ftand, *r.* ftands. P. 289, l. 20, *r.* againft me, was, P. 296, l. 25, *r.* fentry. P. 304, l. 11, *dele* Firft-ftreet. P. 309, l. 15 and 17, *for* are, *r.* is. P. 336, l. 16, *r.* with. P. 351, l. 9, *for* who, *r.* which. P. 353, l. 6, *dele* ; and. P. 368, l. 21, *for* two, *r.* twenty.

You may also be interested in these titles:

Townsends is please to make available a growing list of rare and valuable books from the 18th and early 19th centuries, including those listed below. Be sure to visit our website for a complete list of titles.

Cookbooks

The Art of Cookery by Hannah Glasse (1765)

The Domestick Coffee-Man by Humphrey Broadbent (1722) and *The New Art of Brewing Beer* by Thomas Tyron (1690)

The Complete Housewife by Eliza Smith (1730)

The Universal Cook by John Townshend (1773)

The Practice of Cookery by Mrs. Frazer (1791 & 1795)

The London Art of Cookery by John Farley (1787)

The Complete Confectioner by Hannah Glasse (1765)

A New and Easy Method of Cookery by Elizabeth Cleland (1755)

The English Art of Cookery by Richard Briggs (1788)

18th & Early 19th-Century Brewing by multiple authors

The Lady's Assistant by Charlotte Mason (1777)

The Experienced English Housekeeper by Elizabeth Raffald (1769)

The Professed Cook by B. Clermont (1769)

The Cook's and Confectioner's Dictionary by John Nott (1723)

The Modern Art of Cookery Improved by Ann Shackleford (1765)

The Country Housewife's Family Companion by William Ellis (1750)

A Collection of Above Three Hundred Receipts by Mary Kettelby (1714)

England's Newest Way in All Sorts of Cookery by Henry Howard (1726)

Biographies & Journals

The Hessians by multiple authors

Travels Through the Interior Parts of North-America in the Years 1766, 1767, and 1768 by Jonathan Carver (1778)

The Women of the American Revolution, Volumes 1, 2, & 3 by Elizabeth Ellet (1848)

The Backwoods of Canada by Catharine Parr Traill (1836)

Travels into North America by Peter Kalm (1760)

New Travels in the United States of America. Performed in 1788 and *The Commerce of America and Europe* by J.P. Brissot De Warville (1792 & 1795)

The Journal of Nicholas Cresswell, 1774–1777 by Nicholas Cresswell (1924)

An Account of the Life of the Late Reverend Mr. David Brainerd by Jonathan Edwards (1765 & 1824)

Travels for Four Years and a Half in the United States of America During 1798, 1799, 1800, 1801, and 1802 by John Davis (1909)

Travels through North and South Carolina, Georgia, East and West Florida by William Bartram (1792)

A Tour in the United States of America, Volumes 1 & 2 by John F. Smyth Stuart (1784)

Townsends

www.townsends.us

www.ingramcontent.com/pod-product-compliance
Lightning Source LLC
Chambersburg PA
CBHW070525090426
42735CB00013B/2863